Conversions and Visions
in the Writings of
African-American Women

Kimberly Rae Connor

The University of Tennessee Press • Knoxville

Library of Congress Cataloging in Publication Data

Connor, Kimberly Rae, 1957–
    Conversions and visions in the writings of African-American women / Kimberly Rae Connor.—1st ed.
        p.   cm.
    Includes bibliographical references (p.   ) and index.
        ISBN 0-87049-818-5 (cloth: alk. paper)
    1. American literature—Afro-American authors—History and criticism. 2. American literature—Women authors—History and criticism. 3. Women and literature—United States. 4. Afro-American women in literature. 5. Conversion in literature. 6. Religion and literature. 7. Visions in Literature. I. Title.
        PS 153. N5C64 1994
        810. 9'9287'08996—dc20
                                          93-14499
                                          CIP

Contents

Preface

For consider your call, people; not many of you were wise
according to worldly standards, not many were powerful, not
many were of noble birth; but God chose what is foolish
in the world to shame the wise, God chose what is weak in
the world to shame the strong, God chose what is low and
despised in the world, even things that are not, to bring
to nothing things that are, so that no human being might
boast in the presence of God.
—I Corinthians 1:26-29

In undertaking this cultural study of the ways in which religion and literature have collaborated in history to promote self-affirmation among black American women, I have strived to be sensitive to the kinds of issues bell hooks raised when I heard her speak at the University of Virginia in 1989. She warned her audience of how efforts by white intellectuals to study African-American culture carry the tendency to reinscribe paradigms of authority without fully negotiating issues of difference. A certain vantage point remains inaccessible to me as a white woman, and I cannot carry the authority to speak about black women from the perspective of experience. But I believe that, although I cannot write from such a perspective, my interest in the topic can be informed by sincerity and conscientious scholarship and my research can contribute to an understanding of certain dimensions of black culture. I do so reminded of something Sherley Anne Williams said, at another lecture delivered at the university, when she cautioned her audience that any effort by white scholars to study African-American culture cannot be undertaken with the expectation of approval or validation. Each scholar, in whatever field, must find affirmation on her own terms and pursue a line of inquiry for reasons other than seeking validation from those who are under no imperative to grant it.

African-American studies, as Cornel West emphasizes in *Breaking Bread*, "was never meant to be solely for Afro-Americans. It was meant to try to redefine what it means to be human, what it means to be modern, what it means to be American" (33). Part of this process of redefinition, I believe, must include an examination of the religious dimensions of black culture, an effort that West acknowledges has largely been ignored by the academy even though religious scholarship itself may mediate some of the aforementioned concerns. My work is based on the premise that religion is one of the most universal forms of human expression and that the capacity for change and transcendence that I characterize with reference to black women writers is a quality shared among the human community. The visions these women seek and the conversions they experience not only identify characteristics and qualities of black female imagination and spirituality but in their distinctiveness point to the great variety and creativity of religious imaginations in general. Every age and culture displays various degrees of continuity and discontinuity in religious expression with respect to certain historical trends, and any examination into religious modes of being must accept these particularities in order to gain an understanding of the universal forms and feelings that underlie them. Once one becomes aware of the forces of oppression that operate both within and without to deny people full humanity and recovers a sense of the sacrality of each life, one begins to realize that the movement of the human agenda is inclusive and that all spiritual seekers are the same in the eyes of God. I hope that my work is fully respectful of the unique perspective shared by some black women, and that in my attempts to honor it I have not done it a disservice. I also hope that in some way my scholarship contributes to what West identifies as a "politics of conversion" and stands in witness to the radical changes in consciousness he implores we all undergo.

Having become aware of the deep respect for ancestral influence that is expressed by so many black women writers, it seems appropriate at this point of prelude to honor my own intellectual and spiritual "ancestors" and thank them for their contributions. Among them are Joseph A. Brown, S.J., for being "right on time"; Nathan A. Scott, Jr., for his presence; Samuel T. Lloyd III for his constancy; Charles H. Rowell for the opportunity; and Deborah E. McDowell for her example. John Coulson, my tutor at the University of Bristol, England, by welcoming and encouraging me as a foreign student, showed me ways in which scholarship can help one break down cultural boundaries. The staff of Alderman Library at the University of Virginia provided invaluable service on countless occasions. Jean McMahon Humez, Jean Fagan Yellin, and Geraldine Duclos each reacted with enthusiasm, patience, and collegial support to my unsolicited pleas for help. My students at James Madison University responded to my call with "word" and brought to my intellectual discussions an important dimension of experience. Carol Wallace Orr, formerly of the University of Tennessee Press, first solicited this manuscript and gave me the confidence to try to publish it. Despite her departure, I am grateful to the press for staying with me.

Albert Murray, my self-proclaimed "literary briar-patch uncle," taught me how to slay a dragon. Encouragement and advice also came from Margaret Saunders, who read this manuscript at a critical stage of its development. Tom Hewitt assisted me in my research and never ceased to believe in my abilities, even when I did. Ewa Stajkowska-Setaro taught me that change is the nature of life and our hope. Mary Lyons was a generous friend and colleague without whom I would never have had the courage or the sanity to complete this project. Helen Benet-Goodman and her daughter Theresa shared my enthusiasm and provided a constant source of affection. Helen also assisted me with proofreading and preparing the index. Carolyn Jones has been with me since the beginning and perhaps understands better than anyone what this accomplishment *signifies.*

My family provided me not only examples of a deep and abiding faith that inspired my interest in religious studies but also actual demonstrations of the quality of unconditional love that trusts and encourages without expectations. My husband, Ed, is one of those remarkable men who delights in women's accomplishments, and because of his love and support (and computer wizardry) this book is as much his as mine. Our creatures, Bristol and Ella, served to bring me back to reality when my work threatened to carry me away.

This book is dedicated to the memory of Norman E. Richardson of Gettysburg College. He was one of those rare teachers who was not unwilling to accept the perilous and demanding role of mentor. He was unconcerned of where his influence would lead me because he trusted me to be thoughtful and to care, to realize that our scholarship says something not just about what we do but also about who we are. With the right proportions of "heat and light," he reminded me, I could say something meaningful, and with an attention to the source of my gifts and my responsibility, he showed me, I could give something back. He prompted many of my conversions, and although he crossed over before this last metamorphosis, his spirit sustained me in the blooming of a gardenia and other small miracles. The presence of all these people in my life—and many others unnamed—was nothing less than grace.

1

Conversions

I think that wherever your journey takes you, there are new gods
waiting there, with divine patience and laughter.
—Susan Watkins

At the conclusion of Zora Neale Hurston's novel *Their Eyes Were Watching God*, the protagonist, Janie, is sitting on her porch, meditating on her life. Having described her experiences and journeys to her friend Pheoby, she sums up her life's learning in the following way: "Two things everybody's got tuh do fuh theyselves. They got tuh go tuh God, and they got tuh find out about living fuh theyselves" (285). This statement by Janie reflects the wisdom of a convert, a woman who is "full of that oldest human longing, self-revelation" (18). Having sought and found her own vision of a meaningful life, Janie underscores the belief that going to God and living for one's self define the parameters of the human quest for identity.

The writings of black women comprise a broad and diverse literary tradition, but often what is presented is a narrative of personal growth and development directed toward creating a whole self. As Deborah McDowell has claimed, "imagining the black woman as a 'whole' character or 'self' has been a consistent preoccupation of black female novelists throughout their literary history" ("'Changing Same,'" 283). Although the concept of an identifiable black women's literary tradition is also today "contested terrain," according to P. Gabrielle Foreman a "strategic essentialism" is still appropriate, indeed necessary, to fight erasure of black women's writings. Black women writers still "share (if not as lived experience then as awareness of the 'race's' positioning) a cultural, religious fabric and/or socio-political positionality" (650). One can see, therefore, a human quest like Janie's rendered in powerful terms because there is a recurrent pattern of emphasis on and concern with identity formation. Borne of the particular experience these women share by virtue of being black women in America, the attempt at self-definition recurrently involves a confrontation with a sense of alienation, to become aware not only of what W. E. B. DuBois called the "double consciousness" of being black in America but also of what it means to be a black woman in America. In such a confrontation, all aspects of one's being and relationship to reality are called into question: race, gender, social status, intellectual and cultural background, and finally spiritual orientation. Engaged in this kind of existential confrontation, a black woman, as Toni Morrison has written, "may very well have invented herself" ("What the Black Woman Thinks," 63).

Self-invention, however, does not occur in a vacuum but in the cultural and historical continuum the poet Jay Wright calls "cumulative communities" that collectively form an "enhanced world" (Rowell, 12). As inheritors of this "enhanced world," contemporary black women writers are attempting to unravel the historical and cultural threads that make up their inheritance and to reinterpret the past from the perspective of what their own needs suggest. Each writer, therefore, can be seen as "An aching prodigal, / who would make miracles / to understand the simple given" (Wright, "Beginning Again," 15). By retaining a historical memory of what was "given," the "miracles" these women make are themselves and the personages they create— women who have found a locus for their identity and achieved a depth of self-acceptance largely through an awareness of their cultural identities and an appreciation of the religious faith that was so strongly expressed by black women throughout their history in America.

Moreover, this faith often requires definition with reference to an experience of conversion, although the types or manifestations of this conversion have not always been traditional in character. Religion is inextricably bound to the African-American woman's literary tradition, a fact that is better understood now that we have greater access to the narratives of nineteenth-century black women. There are cultural and religious dimensions to the writings of these women that affirm a religious sensibility by communicating and preserving religious ideas. In her essay "Conversions and Visions," Zora Neale Hurston describes the experience of conversion as an important aspect of Negro religion (SC, 85–87). In this concept of conversion, particularly as it functioned in the cultural and religious life of nineteenth-century African Americans, there is an enlightening and heretofore unexplored way that we may read certain twentieth-century African-American women's writings.

The confrontation of issues of identity and culture by which a black character claims a distinct sense of self, Marilyn Richardson has said, "is one of the classic recurring scenes in all early black writing" (Washington, *Invented Lives,* 11). When this confrontation in nineteenth- and twentieth-century texts is read as a "conversion" experience, new light is shed on the writing strategies of black women writers, demonstrating that the quest for identity is not simply the concern of contemporary women, nor are the qualities they aspire to exclusively secular values. The writings of these women can be read as dramas of conversion into selfhood in which the writers draw on available religious categories that may not be sanctioned by existing theological categories but nonetheless are influenced by broader cultural categories that include a religious dimension.

Realizing this, one becomes aware of the fact that the forms of collective tradition and the patterns of individual revision in African-American women's writings can be remarkably complex. Missy Dehn Kubitschek, in her study of African-American women novelists and history, reminds us that "changes wrought in the individual must take place within that individual, but the individual is always situated within a wider, constructing context" (*Claiming the Heritage,* 12). Deborah McDowell underscores this point in her essay "New Directions for Black Feminist Criticism," where she calls for a contextual approach to African-American women's writing, an approach grounded in African-American history and culture that "exposes the conditions under which literature is produced, published and reviewed" (156).

From the earliest published work until the present day, African-American women writers have been engaged in a developmental process that can be characterized by the traditional religious experience of conversion. Moreover, these women represent a unique form of conversion; for rather than turning away from sin, they have been moving beyond roles that are products of certain social expectations to a more stable and conscious level of identity. Although there is some cultural expression of the need to cast off their "original sin," more often than not these women personally seek to reclaim their "original blessing." Through conversion they have sought not only spiritual empowerment through redemption by God but self-empowerment by affirming qualities of selfhood and womanhood and claiming them as sacred. Conversion signaled a connection to God and a connection to self—it was an imaginative act of transforming themselves by way of adopting a new image of themselves and of God based on characteristics they chose and knew to be real.

In their effort to reclaim the sacred qualities of their own identities, these women reflect a sentiment of black religious experience that expresses, as Vincent Harding has said, "self-love as a religious calling" (hooks and West, 93). These women are engaged in a process the theologian Hans Mol has called a "sacralization of identity." Self-realization, Mol argues, is a sacred ideal, and to achieve selfhood one turns not to the chaos of the world but to one's self and to a transcendent order symbolized in stories and religious traditions. The kind of whole-soul recovery of a sense of self indicated by conversion is incomplete if it does not include some integration into a history, a community, or a tradition. As Baird Tipson has demonstrated, despite the unique and individual character of each convert's experience, the vast majority of converts understood or made sense of their experience along the lines of the traditional categories at their disposal. Moreover, this experience more often than not indicated a use of the faculties of both will and intellect, or, as he phrases it, "the Holy Spirit respected human integrity in conversion" (697).

The literature produced by black women amply demonstrates that it is precisely the search for this sacralization of identity, a search that commands all their will and intellect and talent, that has frequently constituted their deepest commitment. African-American women recognize themselves not solely in isolation but in relationship to other women, to culture, and to creation. They develop individual identities by embracing the collective religious consciousness of black culture. For what is found in most cultures (African-American culture being one of many formidable examples) is that it is by way of the religious life that one is best able to discern human modes of being.

Even as religious consciousness has evolved and cultural conditions have influenced personal needs and choices, there remains, as William James, Mircea Eliade, and other historians of religion have suggested, a historical and psychological universality to the experience of conversion. Although the writings of African-American women have, indeed, tended to reflect certain predominant cultural concerns, an experience of conversion has also tended constantly to focus their basic sense of their identity. Cultural continuities and discontinuities point out both the desire for conversion and the difficulty of its attainability. Contemporary black women do not easily capitulate to the transcendent kind of God who "gave" Rebecca Jackson the ability to read and who "spoke" to Sojourner Truth. But in their search for identity, black women amplify questions pertaining to personal development in two important ways: by paying honor to the tradition of their African-American culture and its essential religious dimension and by creatively inventing new strategies for describing this traditional response as it is felt and spoken by modern black women characters seeking some definition of self.

In the nineteenth century, cultural conditions contributed to black women's motives for conversion, creating an example of what Hurston calls a "voluntary conversion," the cultural pattern of the person seeking a vision, a process that involves both internal and external struggles

(SC, 85). This process was an attempt to render their lives meaningful by participating in the culture African Americans had created—a culture with values, characteristics, and identities apart from those to which the dominant society assented. In other words, black women converts conformed to shared structures of religious experience and tapped the potency of the God that was so available to them through their culture. *The Narrative of Sojourner Truth,* the writings of Rebecca Jackson, and *Incidents in the Life of a Slave Girl* by Harriet Jacobs (Linda Brent) all demonstrate and give expression to the religious dimensions of the drama represented by a black woman's quest for personal fulfillment. Each woman, by trying to absorb and respond to the challenges presented in her own life, voluntarily assented to and became a witness to her inherited faith. It was not the wrath of an angry God that impelled their piety, but their internal struggle to appreciate that they were empowered by God because of his great affection for them. Yet despite their natural assent to a culture that defined reality in religious terms, these women also maintained a critical stance and struggled with those external forces that sought to limit the terms of their identity. They challenged received theological notions about the role of women and laid foundations for future feminist speculation.

In the twentieth century, African-American culture has diversified, and religion no longer assumes the all-encompassing influence it once had. Personality determinants that were once seen as predominantly religious now assume broader cultural forms. Writers like Toni Morrison, Paule Marshall, and Alice Walker (again in Hurston's terminology) present in their writings women who could be termed "involuntary converts," who have received "a call to preach" (SC, 86–87). The vision that sought them is their foremothers' stories—the cultural and religious qualities of the past—that they rehearse and in which they find meaning in order to create identities for the personages in their dramas. They have found that "the presence of the female ancestor allows self-assertion, which creates and affirms the self" (Kubitschek, *Claiming the Heritage,* 1). Although these writers do not always employ the religious rhetoric found in nineteenth-century African-American women's writings, their stories of black women asserting personal worth and dignity resonate with earlier writings because they demonstrate that spirituality is still an intrinsic dimension not only of human consciousness but of cultural consciousness as well. Their protagonists claim an authority and sense of power not dissimilar to that which their predecessors claimed, and express it in ways that are appropriate to the historical episode they occupy. In other words, these writers attempt a recovery of African-American culture that necessarily involves a recovery of the religious feeling that so dominated its early development. By recovering a religious ethos through culture, these women also open up possibilities for a recovery of the more personal qualities of religious faith. For "in defining their individual selves, which are also simultaneously selves-in-community," they explore "the interplay of history and developing female identities, enlivened by individual improvisation" (Kubitschek, *Claiming the Heritage,* 7). Their conversions are not literal but literary.

In between these writers Zora Neale Hurston occupies a pivotal position in the development of African-American women's writings. Her most prominent legacy is one of resurrecting African-American culture from its diluted state and proudly characterizing its most vital components. In this process of cultural affirmation, Hurston singles out religion as a primary aspect of her cultural heritage, but in emphasizing its cultural significance she does not always promote the intense, personal nature of religious feeling so strongly conveyed by nineteenth-century African-American women. Moreover, because issues pertaining to women's liberation were still unresolved in her time, some of the very qualities of her culture that she attempts to preserve are themselves complicit in maintaining a sexist status quo.

Nonetheless, Hurston becomes an authority for the "old stories," and ensures that they will be passed down from ancestors to heirs, who themselves can affirm the culture she so vigorously seeks to preserve yet within a context of a more liberated view of women. In her autobiographical works she continues and improvises on the nineteenth-century spiritual narrative tradition by assigning the origin of her personality to her culture and its religious traditions. Moreover, she draws attention to a sense of continuous process that is essential to black culture. One aspect of an African-American female model of conversion that Hurston recognizes is that conversion is a lifelong commitment that demands a continuous modification of individual and communal identities. Although her emphasis on the lifelong nature of identity formation causes problems for scholars who try to fix her life in certain categories, Hurston was telling us what Cornel West continues to remind us—that "if we are serious about acknowledging and affirming other people's humanity, then we are committed to trusting and believing that they are forever in process" (hooks and West, 12). Her anthropological studies establish a theoretical, methodological, and historical basis for interpreting this culture and identify what she perceives as the uniquely creative and spiritual qualities of the "Negro imagination." Finally, in *Their Eyes Were Watching God,* through the development of the character Janie, Hurston anticipates and creates the tone and the style by which twentieth-century black women writers will come to tell their stories, a manner that revitalizes the spiritual and emotional concerns of the women who wrote before them. Or, as Alice Walker has written, Hurston preserves a "sense of black people as complete, complex, *undiminished* human beings," and in her writing "gave them back all the stories they had forgotten or of which they had grown ashamed (told to us years ago by our parents and grandparents—not one of whom could *not* tell a story to make us weep, or laugh) and showed us how marvelous, and indeed, priceless, they are. . . . they could not hold back the smiles, the laughter, the *joy* over who she was showing them to be: descendants of an inventive, joyous, courageous, and outrageous people" (Hemenway, xii).

The historical and psychological universality of the conversion experience implies a reciprocal universality of religious feeling. For all except the most recent phase of the history of a minority of the world's peoples, religion has been embedded in the core of human life, material as well as spiritual (Genovese, 162). This is because in history, religion and its environing culture have always developed in a dialectical fashion of adaptation and invention. Literature as one expression of culture is integrally related to religion as it (consciously or unconsciously) encodes and expresses religious ideas. Moreover, one of the most important and conspicuous features of literature's relation to religion is one of affirmation, in the sense that literature functions to preserve and communicate religious ideas and actions. Inasmuch as the study of religion frequently involves the study of narrative texts (and oral traditions), one is constantly engaged in the process of expanding the notion of what constitutes a religious text, seeking in literature of all genres themes and issues that convey a religious dimension.[1] Many contemporary black women writers have turned to the stories of their ancestors and looked upon them as sacred stories that relate directly to their own lives.[2] Sacred stories, as Stephen Crites explains, are "stories that orient the life of people through time, their life-time, their individual and corporate experience . . . to the great powers that establish the reality of their world" (295).[3] Moreover, these stories may carry the authority of scripture for the people who understand their own stories in relation to them. "Consciousness is molded by the sacred story to which it awakens and in turn finds expression in the mundane stories that articulate its sense of reality" (297). Every sacred story is a creation story that creates a world of consciousness and the self that is oriented to it.

In the nineteenth century, women such as Sojourner Truth, Harriet Jacobs, and Rebecca Jackson, by formulating narratives of how black women had reckoned with the American scene, gave to African-American women "sacred stories"—paradigmatic forms wherewith they could comprehend their own reality and experience. Part of this strategy involved an emphasis on witnessing or telling the story of their experience so that it would not be forgotten. This kind of testimony, as James Cone has written, "is an integral part of the Black religious tradition. It is the occasion where the believer stands before the community of faith in order to give account of the hope that is in him or her. Although testimony is unquestionably personal and thus primarily an individual story, it is also a story accessible to others in the community of faith. Indeed the purpose of testimony is not only to strengthen an individual's faith but also to build a faith of the community" (hooks and West, 1).

The perspective from which these women testified was a depiction of their lives as representative of a process of cultural, political, and personal development. Released from the need to authenticate and to comply with narrative conventions and blessed with a greater sense of personal freedom, twentieth-century African-American women writers are able to re-create the lives of their foremothers and sacramentalize them at the same time. As Toni Morrison has written in her essay "The Site of Memory," despite her familiarity with the writings of nineteenth-century women, she detected in these writings no mention of an interior life because the writers had to "drop a veil" over the details of their daily existence.[4] She sees her work as a fiction writer, therefore, as a way to gain access to that interior life because it contains the truth about her past that she needs in order to write. Morrison believes she can get it only by imagining it and therefore uses fiction to conjure up what was real. Confronting the past, in all its pain and glory, is "a fundamental necessity for the construction of a tenable black female identity" (Kubitschek, *Claiming the Heritage,* 5).

This enterprise, which Morrison describes as a "kind of literary archaeology," demonstrates that the texts we are dealing with are almost mythic in character. These myths, however, are "not the distorted history of a dead past but a living embodiment of lasting forces" (Kubitschek, *Claiming the Heritage,* 16). They describe things that insist on imaginative acts and spiritual modes of interpretation to be understood because they pervade levels of consciousness not accessible by usual discursive methods.[5] The African-American woman's assertion of self in relation to the world and to God is dramatized in nineteenth-century spiritual and slave narratives as a struggle for freedom and continues in the twentieth century, where black women begin their own self-definition with reference to the sacred story—"the sanctified record and the directing text" (Andrews, *To Tell a Free Story,*

14)—of their ancestors. Contemporary black women have inherited a cultural tradition where all forms of human activity are invested with sacred qualities. Their religious experiences, however, are brought to articulate awareness in stages of personal growth—through a multi-faceted process of change associated with both personal and communal metamorphosis, through the ongoing process of conversion.

African-American culture in the United States possesses a rich heritage of religious sensibilities, in part because, as Charles Long has said: "Religious categories must always form part of any psychological analysis of the experience of oppressed peoples, for in many respects so many of the power valences, the concealments, and the dynamics of oppression are correlates of the social political situation. The oppressed person or community must deal with this and at the same time adjudicate the issue of ultimacy in existence, given the valences of oppressive power on societal levels" (130). Moreover, because "the truth of religion comes from its symbolic rendering of man's moral experience; it proceeds intuitively and imaginatively" (Genovese, 162), the adjudication of the issue of ultimacy in existence leads naturally into creative forms of expression.[6] African-American culture has produced a tradition of literature that powerfully conveys these religious sensibilities, translating religious categories into cultural forms. For, as Sabrina Sojourner has written, there is an inseparable spiritual aspect to black art, theater, music, and literature so that now, "even though raised outside the Church, there is rarely a Black individual who does not understand the Church's significance to the Black culture and community. Black theology and folk religion, like traditional African religions, seek the power or the spirit of God (Divine Energy) in all times and places and things; without that power, one is helpless. Because the Church has succeeded in providing for its community a 'heaven on earth'—a sense of joy in the face of adversity—it has maintained its central position" (61).

In the writings of African-American women we see this religious attempt articulated in the creation of identities through conversion. This coming into self can be seen as an act of will, a gift of grace, or both. Bearing qualities of both transcendence and immanence, the goal of conversion is to create: where there was absence to create presence; where there was no self a self emerges; where God was a transcendent listener on high, there is an immanent God participating in the lives of black women.

In order to demonstrate how this principle of conversion operates in African-American women's writing, it is necessary to examine the general origins and qualities of the African-American religious sensibility and also to examine closely the notion of conversion and how it has been used in analytical discourse. The concept of conversion has been variously understood and interpreted in a vast body of scholarly literature. Although it can be categorized as a psychological, sociological, theological, or historical phenomenon, the experience of conversion bears aspects of all these qualities. That is because conversion is not just an isolated event in an individual life but also a pervasive cultural phenomenon born of experience in a particular time and place. One could say that conversion parallels identity formation just as religion parallels culture. In all culture there are religious dimensions and in all personal growth and development there are changes that could be called conversions.

The religious quality of conversion, however, need not take on traditional forms of expression. In fact, in early African-American culture one finds more often than not a creative invention and improvisation on traditional religious forms of expression, as the rich life of spiritual imagination offered blacks an alternative to their lives in oppression and a form of creative response. For example, in slave communities, although the oppressors tried to shape the religious lives of blacks, African Americans overtly, covertly, and intuitively fought to shape it themselves, thereby creating a unique "black" religion.

C. Eric Lincoln explains black religion in the following way: "The Black Church evolved, not as a formal black 'denomination' with a structured doctrine, but as an attitude, a movement. It represents the desire of Blacks to be self-conscious about the meaning of their blackness and to search for spiritual fulfillment in terms of their understanding of themselves and their experience of history. There is no single doctrine, no official dogma except the presupposition that a relevant religion begins with the people who espouse it" (3). This church, moreover, "has held in common unity more black people than any other institution, and it has had more influence in molding the thoughts and the lives of black people in America than has any other agency" (Lincoln, 42). The religion of African Americans, like all religion, grew as a way of ordering the world and of providing a vantage point from which to judge it. Like all religion it laid down a basis for moral conduct and an explanation for the existence of evil and injustice. Yet, "while the Christian faith and church are not to be excluded," Charles Long reminds us, we need to "expand the meaning of religion in America in general and among African-Americans in particular" (131). Christianity was the faith blacks fell heir to, but they transformed it into something of their own by realizing what Major A. Jones calls the "revolutionary potential of Christian ideas in relation to the black experience" (13). In their own way, African Americans demonstrated that whatever the full truth or falsity of Christianity, it spoke for all humanity when it proclaimed the freedom and the inviolability of the human soul (Genovese, 176).

Moreover, the uniqueness of the African-American woman's spiritual orientation is a definitive position from which new modes of thinking are called for that may not be able to be included within the structure of religion as we normally perceive it.[7] The experiences of black women have not been a part of the structure and substance of traditional theology, yet they have an experience of faith in God that has been articulated and needs to be understood. The issue, as the writings of these women demonstrate, is not just a change of style but a change of content. For African Americans conversion is an experience founded on a religion of spiritual resistance where women and men ask not for God's forgiveness but for God's recognition. In confrontation with a dominant culture that not only devalues but oftentimes erases their identity, black women find in their own stories and the stories of other African Americans an agency of power within themselves that they can command, possessed of an authority based on their own experience. Conversion for these women yields to creation—creation of a self and of a story—and categories of identity (like gender, race, sexuality) are collapsed into a whole spiritual being, just as categories of writing (autobiography, anthropology, fiction) are collapsed into a myth of the rite of passage into selfhood.[8] From a religious perspective, the claims for what is essential to individual experience and what is socially constructed are also transformed by the presence of God in human development. Finally, the notions of "text" and "author" are broken down and new categories are created. It does not matter, for example, that Sojourner Truth did not actually *write* her narrative; although she was not the scribe, she was the author. The fact that Rebecca Jackson did not transcribe her visions in order to publish them as a unified composition does not mean that her writings are not texts worthy of analysis.

The first creation, however, before any story is told or written, is the creation of self. For both the self and the story, authenticity comes from experience and the communal assent that these experiences are true. The hardships are as true as the vision these women hold, a vision of a self that is not simply liberated from false assumptions but generous enough to allow for complexity and diversity. For all that is shared among these women, there is no static identity they all come to assume, no homogeneous idea of what a black woman is. Part of the experience of conversion involves an appreciation of difference, for the uniqueness of each created being. As no two lives are the same, no two conversions are the same. Some conversions are sudden; others develop through collective experience that upon reflection assume a miraculous character—not one event but many leading in a single direction.

Although all involve a strategy for survival (both literal and metaphorical), there are imaginative patterns that grant insight into the particular gifts and visions and improvisations of each imaginative approach to living, of creating a self and a story. This creation also involves an effect on the reader or culture in which boundaries of indifference are broken down, and these lives are understood with passion and concern, not simply as historical record. It could be said that these texts provide a basis for a liberation theology whereby a reader's (or a culture's) assent to their truth dictates a conversion to the principles of freedom and self-expression, with an adjoining imperative to make them a reality. As Joycelyn K. Moody has written, "through the participatory act of reading, contemporary readers become part of the protagonist's community, bound by each text to a collective duty to nurture and preserve the integrity of the black American woman" (646). Indeed, the relevance of such a perspective has been emphasized by Cornel West in his recent writings, where he calls for us to adopt a form of spirituality—"you used to call it conversion"—that offers "a chance for people to believe that there is hope for the future and a meaning to struggle" (hooks and West, 14). Citing the loss of hope as a pervasive contemporary disease of the soul, West insists that only a "politics of conversion" can conquer this disease, only a "turning of one's soul. This turning is done by one's own affirmation of one's worth—an affirmation fueled by the concern of others" (West, 54–55). Conversions serve as a personal way to bring into focus the communal vision of what is sacred in life. In the direct experience of spiritual power articulated by black women as a conversion, the vision is transmitted and transformed so that traditional elements give way to and participate in a perpetual turning of the soul to what is sacred.

African-American Religion

My mother, religious-negro, proud of
having waded through a storm, is very obviously,
a sturdy Black Bridge that I
crossed over, on.
—Carolyn Rodgers

Although C. Eric Lincoln states that "neither scholars nor practitioners are in precise agreement over what 'black religion' is or, for that matter, whether it in fact exists" (1), the term "Negro Church" has been the generally accepted rubric for the collective religious activities of black Americans as it functioned to structure and influence the social, economic, and political life of blacks (Daniel Collins, 210).[9] The Negro church initially functioned in such a way because, as Carter G. Woodson stated, "The first real educators to take up the work of enlightening American Negroes were clergymen interested in propagation of the gospel among the heathen in the New World" (Daniel Collins, 210). The content of these teachings provided a new orientation toward life for displaced Africans and laid the base for a common culture for the uprooted and tribally intermixed slaves.[10] The transmission of the Gospels, however, did not furnish a formal theology; rather, it provided a common religious experience and rudimentary forms for behavior by providing the means for enduring an unbearable life and granting an outlet for manifestations of qualities familiar to African religion and culture.

African Americans appropriated Christianity in order that it would express their own unique experience of divine presence in their lives and so that it would be descriptive of what they deemed sacred in the world and in themselves. For, as Lincoln points out: "The Protestant ethic which provided the political and economic thrust which founded America and shaped its development was not a salient feature of African or African-American ideological experience. The prevailing values which illustrated the practice of American religion and defined the American culture are precisely the values which created for the African diaspora a peculiar, involuntary experience which black religion attempts to view and interpret in meaningful perspective" (1–2). Because of their spiritual priorities, African Americans developed a religion within a religion in a nation within a nation as part of a conscious effort to find spiritual and ethical value in history. Moreover, because the spiritual emancipation of the individual was an important constituent of black religion, the personal experience of conversion led to the creation of a self within a self. By adapting a profound religious awakening to God to be descriptive also of an awakening to self, conversion became yet a further example of the ways in which African Americans turned to religious strategies for survival and growth. The profound religious awareness of African Americans emerged out of the experience of slavery, where, as Charles Long states: "the slaves had to come to terms with the opaqueness of their condition and at the same time oppose it. They had to experience the truth of their nega-tivity and at the same time transform it and create *an-other* reality. Given the limitations imposed upon them, they created on the level of the religious consciousness. Not only did this transformation pro-duce new cultural forms, but its significance must be understood from the point of view of the creativity of the transforming process itself" (177). That is to say that, in African-American culture, one cannot separate the religious from the aesthetic, or the sacred from the pro-fane.

God functioned in the early American black community as a trans-former of individual consciousness and became the basis for a resource that enabled blacks to maintain a human image without completely acquiescing to the norms of the majority population. God did not, in other words, sustain the status quo or confirm the reality of their be-ing within the structure of slave America. This was possible because from the beginning of their life in America, the sacred was not some-thing blacks thought was antithetical to the secular world. For African Americans recognition of the sacred signified not a rejection of the present world but a way to describe the process of incorporating within the world all the elements of the divine (Levine, 31). Mircea Eliade describes religion in *The Sacred and the Profane* as a means of extending the world spatially upward so that communication with the other world becomes ritually possible, and extending temporally backward so that the paradigmatic acts of the gods and ancestors can be continually reen-acted and indefinitely recoverable. By creating sacred time and space, one can perpetually live in the presence of one's gods, can hold on to the certainty that within one's own lifetime "rebirth" is continually pos-sible, and can impose order on the chaos of the universe.

Through visions and by the rituals of daily life and contact with the natural world, African Americans were able to read sacred meaning into their mundane existence. They created a world apart that they could control. The Christianity that was "given" to the slaves by their oppressors had within in it a mechanism of control that in turn made it necessary for them to submit it to certain transformations, in order that it might become truly theirs. As Eugene Genovese has said, "no matter how obedient—how Uncle Tomish—Christianity made a slave, it also drove deep into his soul an awareness of the moral limits of submission, for it placed a master above his own master and thereby dissolved the moral and ideological ground on which the very principle of human lordship must rest" (165). Or, as Alice Walker has said of African-American religion, although it was given to pacify the slaves, they "transformed [it] into an antidote against bitterness, making it at once simple and noble" (MG, 16). How religion functioned in the black community can be seen as a metaphor for the personal experience of conversion and the way it changed individual lives. In other words, what religion did for the African-American community, conversion did for the individual soul. African Americans not only adapted forms of Christian religion to become expressive of their African origins and their existential situation, they also adapted the notion of God and themselves as created in the image of this God.[11] They achieved this adaptation because they never lost the African sense of the past's persistence in the present nor the importance of the ongoing need for self-definition regarding their contemporary situation. They took individual responsibility for establishing connections to the past and to God because, as bell hooks points out, "slaves brought to new world Christianity a sense of personal relationship with God. Not a collective relationship to God that brings about enlightenment and transformation, rather our personal relationship to God" (hooks and West, 81–82).

Hence, the spiritual legacy of black life in America is one of creating a sacred world in the midst of a world that denied meaningful forms of personal integration, thereby providing the opportunity for the attainment of a status, a self. This sacred world was not confined to Christianity; it went beyond the literal beliefs to which the slaves were converted and incorporated aspects of their own folk culture. As Josiah Young points out, elements of African religions, combined with specific liberation motifs from the Old Testament, imbued African-American religion with revolutionary potential (9). In ways indirect, distorted, ambiguous, and even confused, the spiritual experience of African Americans took shape as part of a tradition emanating from Africa (Genovese, 210). Africa, as a place, retained powerful symbolic meaning as a Zion from which blacks were forced to separate. Turning to this appropriated religion was like turning home.

God came to them in America not because of but in spite of their conditions. There was a this-worldly dimension to the otherworldly pronouncements of the faith. Religion did not take African Americans out of the human condition but immersed them in it. Life was seen not as random or haphazard but as meaningful, since one could read in the naturalistic order a sacred order. Transcending the narrow confines in which they were forced to live, African Americans internally created an expanded universe and willed within themselves the desire to be reborn in their new image, in this new world. It is important to recognize that the eschatology within this religion had a worldly dimension, or, as Young says, that "in the black religious experience, talk about heaven . . . has a double meaning" (43) because divine freedom enabled them to endure oppression and gave them the strength to participate with the divine in the destruction of oppression here on earth. Heaven existed for African Americans as otherworldly, yet so, too, did it exist as a this-worldly idea of freedom and community. It was not held out simply as an ideal realm in order to reconcile them to their lot of slavery. Heaven was an idea that transmitted the notion of a place where there was equality before God, thereby inducing a sense of self-worth and reducing the status of worldly masters. African Americans believed that God had acted, was acting, and would continue to act within human history and within their own particular history. The actions of God and the sentiment expressed in the spiritual that "He promised never to leave me alone" cannot, as bell hooks reminds us, be heard as "an affirmation of passivity. It does not mean we can sit around and wait for God to take care of business" (hooks and West, 17). Conversion created a sense of individual value and personal vocation that contradicted the dehumanizing forces of slavery and helped blacks to assert and maintain a sense of personal value, of ultimate worth, and often inspired them to challenge the system of slavery itself.

The Bible provided African Americans with an inexhaustible source of good advice for a proper life but not an unchanging body of doctrine. In his development of a theology of liberation, James Cone claims that the *norm* of black theology is to relate the condition of black people to that of the biblical tradition. History, including biblical history, was a source for theological interpretation of God's work in the world. As part of their translation of their political position into religious terms, African Americans viewed biblical figures as historical witnesses for application in their situation (Genovese, 242). For example, a particular emphasis for the black preacher was to base his message on the low earthly station of the Son of God. The image of Moses, the this-worldly leader of his people out of bondage, and Jesus, the otherworldly Redeemer, blended into a pervasive theme of deliverance. Or, as Julius Lester writes, blacks fashioned their own kind of Christianity, that they "turned to for strength in the constant times of need. In the Old Testament story of the enslavement of the Hebrews by the Egyptians they found their own story. In the figure of Jesus Christ, they found someone who had suffered as they suffered, someone who understood, someone who offered them rest from their suffering" (79). Moses became Jesus and Jesus became Moses, and with their union the two aspects of African Americans' religious quest— collective deliverance as a people and redemption from their terrible personal sufferings—became one through imaginative power. This assimilation, as Genovese points out, "solved the problem of how to achieve spiritual freedom, retain faith in earthly deliverance, instill a spirit of pride and love in each other, and make peace with a political reality within which revolutionary solutions no longer had much prospect" (255).

There was little tolerance for a doctrine of original sin because to blacks sin meant wrongdoing and they did not earn their suffering by wrongdoing. Enslavement or an oppressed existence might be shameful, but it could not produce guilt. In Southern slave communities, therefore, the life of worship was imaginatively designed to reinforce ideas of self-worth and autonomy. It was a lively, creative endeavor, full of innovation, that led to the development of an African-American idiom in terms of style and form. Community involvement in worship integrated various forms of human expression—song, dance, oratory—that were created by blacks to be descriptive of their own experience. The spirituals, for example, were devoid of any sense of depravity or unworthiness, and pervaded by a sense of change, transcendence, ultimate justice, and personal worth, emphasizing confidence, not despair, a sense of blacks as being chosen people of God, and God as an intimate, personal, and immediate redeemer (Levine, 39).

Worship was often led by black preachers. The example of and faith in black preachers gave personal expression to faith in God because for African Americans especially, faith in God meant faith in oneself, in one's own soul and worth. Moreover, the message of the black preachers limited the degree of degradation they would accept. Although society was structured to reinforce a sense of unworthiness and inferiority, worship gave blacks a ritual by which to objectify their experience of slavery, thereby placing them in a better position to cope without distancing them from its reality. It allowed them to exercise control over forces that would otherwise have overwhelmed them. Worship gave African Americans strength from direct communion with God and each other, and provided a sense of autonomy—of constituting not merely a community unto themselves but a community with leaders of their own choice.

Most important to remember is that in the African-American community of worship, as in African-American culture in general, there was no separation of sacred and secular activities. The church was the center of social, economic, and educational activity (Raboteau, 266).

It was the one institution blacks could control. The sacred and the secular coexisted in harmony, and religion sustained blacks throughout their history in America "with a gospel that has been interpreted without a dichotomy of social-religious, soul-body, or priestly-prophetic categories" (Lincoln, 5).

The process by which and the rate at which African Americans converted to Christianity remain unclear (Genovese, 183), yet there were vast numbers who converted, and religious sincerity played a role in their conversions because the protection they sought rested on a spiritual doctrine of equality before God. Blacks took the tradition of conversion and made it their own expression of freedom. For, as Paul Radin says: "The antebellum Negro was not converted to God. He converted God to himself. In the Christian God he found a fixed point and he needed a fixed point, for both within and outside of himself, he could see only vacillation and endless shifting. . . . there was no other safety for people faced on all sides by doubt and the threat of personal disintegration, by the thwarting of instincts and the annihilation of values" (Levine, 33). The conversion experience itself led to the establishment of a new set of values. Since blacks were deprived of the usual forms of development and the attainment of status, education was not a standard of judgment; rather, "a converted heart and a gifted tongue" were prized (Raboteau, 133). In the experience of conversion, all souls were leveled before God, and value judgments were based on a respect for spiritual power, wherever it originated. Moreover, emphasis on the inward experience of conversion tended to deemphasize the outward status of people so that all could feel personally that they were God's children.

What African Americans faced in conversion was a sense of their own humanity, but not a sense of humanity as circumscribed by race only, but humanity circumscribed by the divine nature of God who could not be reduced to or by any other categories. This confrontation with divine power, however identified with the sociological situation of minority oppression itself, was in fact a manner in which these human beings recognized their creatureliness and humanity before

God, and it is this essential humanity that is not given by the slave system or any master. This inner experience had a universal dimension that at the same time emphasized the uniqueness of each individual. In addition, the conversion experiences, which by their nature were intensely personal, inward events, were also occasions for creating a community solidarity—a community of believers with a positive bond of unification over and against the negative bond of oppression. In the process of conversion, religion was used by blacks to create a new sacred space of meaning, freedom, and transcendence; they created and shaped a religious sensibility upon which their own religious system could be built and their own identities could be created.

The African-American religious tradition presents a picture of people with confidence in religious strategies for survival. Black Americans realized, as Victor Turner has said, that when a person's "back is against the wall, he seizes roots, not straws" (Turner, 71). Through conversion they effected not just a readaptation of a preexisting Christian pattern but a wholly new individuation and inward reintegration. Conversion provided an ideal combination of a natural striving for a unified personality and for a fixed God as the center of the world who demanded one live a certain kind of life and become a certain kind of person. What is especially important here is the fact that for African Americans, God had to recognize them and to prove himself. The recollected experiences of many converts gathered in *God Struck Me Dead: Religious Conversion Experiences and Autobiographies of Ex-Slaves,* compiled by Clifton H. Johnson, indicate quite clearly that God had literally to struggle with the converts. God had to fight not to persuade them to give up their sins but to force them to be willing to express themselves, to fulfill their mission—in other words, to attain individuation. They looked to God to validate their own humanity. Through conversion African Americans gained the power to name not only themselves but their God. They personally identified with and named their own God and participated in an intimate relationship with him. Moreover, they could instruct themselves on the nature of God based on what they had absorbed in hearing and participating in their families' stories. In most of the conversion narratives, religious experience is woven in with ordinary events, maintaining a unity of the sacred and profane. Daily experience was a criterion of meaning, and practical images became symbolic vehicles (Cooper-Lewter and Mitchell, 7).

The religious legacy of African-American culture is one that encourages engagement in reality and attention to the contingencies of that reality. As Lawrence W. Levine says: "the unremitting system of slavery made its subjects not merely idealists who created a sacred universe which promised change and triumph, allowed them to reach back to relive the victories of the past, and drew them into the rich texture where justice and the goodness that had existed before would exist again; it also made them realists who understood the word as it operated in the present" (134). They also realized how it would operate in the future. Built into the African-American cultural system is an African ancestral belief that they are not only heirs to a legacy but debtors with a responsibility to those who came before them (Genovese, 213). As we will see in the writings of twentieth-century African-American women, a powerful respect for their ancestors underlies the ways in which these writers revitalize the history which expressed an irrepressible affirmation of life. Like their ancestors they attempt to recover and transform history, not to escape it.

The rich life of the religious imagination (that evolved for many of the women and men into literary imagination) was a balance to or a context for evaluating self and the world African Americans inhabited. Yet this imagination was not "free" in the way we usually attribute freedom to artists and writers because it was controlled and directed by a need for harmony and organized—however loosely—within the framework of Christian dogma and controlled, to a certain extent, by a need to express the abolitionist political agenda of the time. In addition, since many blacks were nonliterate, the religious concepts they believed in were not ideas distinct from behavior. J. D. Y. Peel, in the essay "Syncretism and Religious Change," demonstrates how literacy changes the ways in which beliefs are held. Sacred stories passed down through generations are diluted by cultural changes that do not reinforce their meaning and reality.

Although twentieth-century writers, in returning to the motifs and values of their ancestors' lives, display aesthetic literary freedom as we know it, they have to wrestle with the consequences of a worldview that has been diluted by the introduction of literacy that established a duality not understood in oral traditions. The sacred stories no longer sustain faith in the same ways. Black women writers, however, have taken advantage of this higher degree of acculturation to create a refined religious consciousness that draws much of its power from the roots of traditional African-American religion. This complex cultural process of shifting emphases and reaffirmations permits certain new traits to permeate but simultaneously emphasizes specific traditional loyalties and characteristics. Revitalizing the past in the context of new concerns and with new requirements for complexity is the challenge African-American women writers in the twentieth century have accepted. However they respond in belief, action, or writing, they are rehearsing the ultimate religious act of apprehending self in relation to whatever they consider divine.

In sum, we can see in the Negro church that

> Afro-Americans accepted Christianity's celebration of the individual soul and turned it into a weapon of personal and community survival. But their apparent indifference to sin, not to be confused with an indifference to injustice or wrongdoing, guaranteed retention of the collective, life-affirming quality of the African tradition and thus also became a weapon for personal and community survival. The slaves reshaped the Christianity they had embraced; they conquered the religion of those who had conquered them...[they] developed an Afro-American and Christian humanism that affirmed joy in life in the face of every trial. (Genovese, 212)

In the religious history of African Americans the conversion experience was an integral phase of growth for each individual personality, an event in the process of living and adapting to a changing environment, first as an internal creation of a world that could be lived in and understood, and then as a response to the external world in which they wished to participate. The quality of a conversion experience is by its very nature intrinsically individual, but it becomes meaningful when it is validated by community standards. Seen in the context of societal changes, there is a certain uniformity to the individual experience of conversion because it is a cultural mode of expression. This is not to say, however, that society is the agent of transformation because the inner resources of the individual are what provide a basis for a new consciousness through conversion.

Yet the culture developed by the early African-American community possessed its own norms and ideals and forms of expression that created an environment where the emphasis was placed on cooperation, respect, and individual fulfillment through conversion within the community. This culture, of which the religion was an essential part, defended African Americans against personal degradation, bolstered their self-esteem, gave them courage, confidence, and autonomy, and prepared them for conversion into selfhood (Blassingame, 147). The consciousness upon which African-American culture is based is a religious consciousness that became the basis for an aesthetic response— a narrative description of the meaning of one's own life, the history of one's culture, and one's relationship to God.

Conversion

So through God you are no longer a slave but a child,
and if a child then an heir.
—Galatians 4:7

Most scholarship on conversion—how it affects the individual and how it operates in a cultural context—examines the phenomenon as an investigation into theological and doctrinal expressions originating from a Christian tradition. The terms and characteristics of a conversion experience, however, are not solely the result of dogmatic Christian influences. This is especially important to consider when applying this concept to African-American religion and writing. The religious experiences and expressions of African Americans should not be equated with the theology of Christianity or any other religion, although there are ritual images and meanings behind the religious experience of African Americans that may be Christian.

The word *conversion* derives from the Latin *conversio,* which means a turning, and the Greek *metanoia,* which means transformation. Biblical writers used these terms metaphorically to describe encounters between humanity and God. Conversion as a turning occurred as a result of a conscious decision, and conversion as transformation occurred as an experience of divine grace. Within the context of the larger Judeo-Christian tradition, conversion has had a significant and varied history. General definitions of conversion point to it as a phenomenon associated with personal and communal metamorphosis. Change pervades religious history and experience since individuals and groups manifest various intensities and durations of transformation. Conversion is always, however, a dynamic, multifaceted process of change. In some cases this change will be abrupt and in others it will be gradual, because religious conversion is a natural phenomenon that may take as many forms as human need dictates. There is also generally a blending of intellectual, emotional and moral factors that manifest themselves in different ways and degrees in the varying experiences of different individuals.

Lewis Rambo distinguishes three dimensions in which conversion should be understood: tradition, transformation, and transcendence (73). Tradition encompasses the social and cultural matrix that includes symbols, myths, rituals, worldviews, and institutions. Tradition structures the present circumstances in which people live and ensures connection with the past. African-American culture reveals a tradition wherein beliefs and practices encourage, shape, and evaluate religious change. Tradition is generally the dimension examined by sociologists, historians, and anthropologists. Transformation is the dimension of conversion examined by psychologists wherein the process of change is understood through the alteration of people's thoughts, feelings, and action. Both objective and subjective, this is the level where aspects of the self, consciousness, and individual experience are explored. Finally, transcendence refers to the domain of the sacred—the encounter with the holy that, according to many religions, constitutes the source and goal of conversion. This is where God is affirmed as working within the human situation in order to bring people into relationship with the divine and provide a new sense of meaning and purpose. This is the domain theologians explore in assigning conversion as an integral aspect of the process of human transformation. I hope it is apparent from this schematic description of conversion that there is no simple approach to the subject. Conversion is a progressive, interactive process that has consequences in the community; it is not always or only a single event, but can be an evolving process that incorporates traditional, transformative, and transcendent qualities.

A basis for understanding the traditional aspects of conversion in African-American communities can be found in the work of Anthony F. C. Wallace, whose landmark essay, "Revitalization Movements," established how a phenomenon like conversion is an innovation on the part of a major cultural system to revitalize itself.[12] He defines a revitalization movement as "a deliberate, organized, conscious effort by members of a society to construct a more satisfying culture. Revitalization is thus, from a cultural standpoint, a special kind of culture change phenomena: the persons involved in the process of revitalization must perceive their culture, or some major areas of it, as a system (whether accurately or not); they must feel that this cultural system is unsatisfactory; and they must innovate not merely discrete items, but a new cultural system, specifying new relationships as well as, in some cases, new traits" (265). Wallace goes on to argue that conversion, unlike any other process of change, is a deliberate intent by members of a society to effect this kind of revitalization.[13] The conversion of African Americans to Christianity and the innovations they made in this faith illustrate a deliberate attempt to create for themselves a new cultural system they could control and with which they could identify. This attempt was necessary because of what Wallace terms "stress—a condition in which some part or the whole of the social organism is threatened with more or less serious damage" (265), such as the "stress" slavery inflicted on black communities and individual identities. What is required in this endeavor, Wallace points out, is not only an image or vision of self but also an image of the society or culture one needs to sustain self. He calls this image "the mazeway," a combination of nature, society, culture, personality, and body image (266), and believes that through conversion experiences one can manipulate self and others to create an environment where stress is minimized. In other words, a choice must be made whether or not to maintain the mazeway one is living in and tolerate the existing level of stress, or to change the mazeway in an attempt to reduce stress. To change this mazeway is to undergo conversion—a total gestalt of one's image of self, society, and culture, and nature and body and ways of action. The collaboration of a number of persons in such an effort is what makes it a revitalization movement.

These movements, Wallace notes, are not unusual phenomena but are recurrent features in human history that are of profound importance. Certainly, the creative adaptation and invention of a culture by African Americans is a brilliant example of this kind of change. It was through the acquisition of and improvisation on religious faith that blacks were able to reduce the "stress" the conditions of slavery or oppression placed upon them and create a new "mazeway"—a world for themselves that they controlled and that sustained for them a vision of who they were and what their world was. By way of an experience of conversion they made a passage from a dehumanizing to a humanizing experience. Conversion was a deliberate, conscious, organized effort to create a more meaningful culture based on the truth of religion as African Americans perceived it, fashioned around a vision of life that was benevolent and sustaining.[14]

William McLoughlin and Jerald Brauer have applied some of Wallace's ideas to their studies of American cultural life in the nineteenth century. McLoughlin particularly emphasizes the Tillichian notion of religion being the soul of culture and culture being the form of religion and sees the religious awakenings in America as fundamental to the development of an American identity as a chosen people. It is interesting to note that while white American Puritans were using the experience of conversion and the writing of conversion narratives as evidence for election into established religious communities, African Americans were undergoing conversions as a way to create their own religious community. Religious identities were being formed coincident to the establishment of national identities, one the enfranchised nation America, the other the disenfranchised "nation within a nation." Brauer, emphasizing the experiential nature of conversion, describes it as a profound, self-conscious, existential change and expands McLoughlin's idea even further by uniting the religious movements in America with universal human patterns in history in which conversion plays an essential role.

As one moves from the traditional dimension of conversion and an emphasis on the cultural role it plays, there is an exhaustive and complicated history to the scholarship on the psychological aspects of religious conversion and the role it plays in transforming the life of the individual. As James T. Richardson notes in his essay "Conversion Careers," it is much easier for psychologists to say what conversion is *not* rather than what it is. Most enduring and influential has been the work of William James, who in *Varieties of Religious Experience* established the terms and methodology by which this dimension is studied. He was the first to use life histories and narratives in examining conversion, when he identified religion as "the feelings, acts, and experiences of individual men in their solitude, so far as they apprehend themselves to stand in relation to whatever they may consider divine" (42). James was building on the work of Edmund Starbuck, who defined conversion by its cause—a struggling away from sin rather than a striving toward righteousness—and stressed the suddenness of the experience. James's most important contribution to the study of conversion could be his emphasis on the process as an individual rather than a social phenomenon. Unlike Freud, who saw conversion as a sign of neurosis related to a person's Oedipus complex (a regressive defense against repressed hostility toward authority), James believed that conversion is essentially a psychological process of unifying a divided self. James begins a chapter on conversion with the following classic definition: "To be converted, to be regenerated, to receive grace, to experience religion, to gain assurance, are so many phrases which denote the process, gradual or sudden, by which a self hitherto divided, and consciously wrong, inferior and unhappy, becomes consciously right, superior and happy, in consequence of its firmer hold upon religious realities. This is at least what conversion signifies in general terms, whether or not we believe that a direct divine operation is needed to bring such moral change about" (160).

He also had a great respect for the role the unconscious plays in conversion and the unification of self in the midst of stresses that divide individual consciousnesses. For James, conversion occurs when peripheral religious ideas take on a central place and effect a unification in an individual. He stresses that this is a quantifiable, experiential phenomenon that is defined by the nature of experiences and causes.[15] Much of what he says resonates with Wallace's claims, as James identifies on the level of the individual consciousness what Wallace sees on a cultural level. Both offer theories of unification: Wallace of a unified society, James of a unified self. James also distinguishes conversions as being either voluntary or involuntary—a characteristic clarified in terms of African-American religion by Zora Neale Hurston.

The important thing to consider about James's work, however, is that he asserted and made credible the notion that religious faith has an effect upon the health and wholesomeness of the individual, that yielding to and claiming an identity based on religious faith is an important constituent of human growth. James's notion of unifying a divided self had great impact on other psychological studies on conversion, and generally the field is distinguished by those who concentrate on the causes of religious conversion and those who study the effects of conversion on the life of the individual.

There seems to be general agreement among those who study the psychological dimensions of conversion that conversion is closely linked to, if not inseparable from, the process of identity formation. Walter Conn describes conversion as a process of self-transcendence that can be interpreted in terms of developmental psychology (there is a bias toward aligning conversion with an adolescent state). Joe Edward and Mary Anne Barnhart see it as something "naturalistic," a complex personal process that is part of ordinary living. James Bissett Pratt, in his psychological study *The Religious Consciousness,* emphasizes the moral dimension of conversion by insisting it is not just an emotional state and change in feeling but something much more objective and concrete. As he says, conversion is "won not necessarily by sudden insight or reformation but by a gradual process in which increased self-control, intellectual illumination, and an absolute unification of values play important and mutually helpful parts" (132). He also challenges the conventional notion of conversion as a struggling away from sin rather than a striving toward righteousness as an artificial form of experience, his point being that in conversion one does not give up trying but begins trying, begins creating.[16] Wayne D. Oates goes so far as to say that conversion is not a uniquely religious experience and that the kinds of change that can be described as conversion may be secular as well as sacred—a psychological experience with far-reaching social and interpersonal effects. In fact, he claims that many people have religious conversion experiences but do not identify them as such because they have been taught or have come to disbelieve religious language. Real conversions can occur without the assistance of anything specifically religious.[17]

This is important to remember when examining the texts of twentieth-century African-American women writers because the same qualities of religious experience that were available to their foremothers are not always available to them. American culture has become increasingly diverse, and ways of describing religious experience have multiplied. Part of their identity quest is bound up in reappropriating or redis- covering religious language and feeling.[18] This is demonstrated in their conscious choice of narrative strategies that take them back to the be- ginnings of black life in America, and the way they reveal a cognitive need to understand, on a religious level, those things that make their lives meaningful. As V. Bailey Gillespi points out in *Religious Conver- sion and Personal Identity: How and Why People Change,* if the subject struggling through an identity crisis should attach some subjective re- ligious quality to the experience, it could be construed to be a reli- gious conversion—a resolution of an identity crisis within a religious context. For one of the main characteristics of conversion as a spiri- tual turning is its dynamic interpretation of life as a pilgrimage of the spirit. It is a lifelong process and experience in which culture, as a transmitter of ideas and emotions coming into one's mind by ordi- nary channels, sinks into the subconscious religious ideas that there germinate and associate with emotional complexities and the tenden- cies to action—a gradual transformation. This is not to say conversion consists in the "burrowing and mining of subconscious ideas and the splitting and doubling of consciousness; it is, instead, merely the un- dramatic change of values which the most normal and common-place of us notes at work within himself in almost every epoch of life" (Pratt, 163). More often than not, however, conversion begins with a vision that one persistently follows in order to bring about a change in char- acter. For African-American women such a vision involves a recogni- tion of their sacred story—a radical look at the way they constitute self, others, and the world in relation to the particular values, powers, and stories of reality they take as ultimate.

Many theologians have discussed the transcendent dimension in conversion experiences, including some of the systematic theologians like Barth and Tillich. More often than not, their views of conversion are so oriented as to support their theological systems. Yet for these purposes, theological systems are not very helpful. The songs, stories, and rituals of black American faith form a body of witness or testimony rather than a theological system or set of dogma. The African-American religious sensibility was created and endured more in an improvisational manner that was not conventionally systematic but that sustained a concept of a transcendent reality.

In his study on religious change, now considered a classic, A. D. Nock uses conversion to indicate "the reorientation of the soul of an individual, his deliberate turning from indifference or from an earlier form of piety to another which implies a consciousness that a great change is involved, that the old was wrong and the new was right." He correctly establishes that conversion "seen at its fullest is the positive response of a man to the choice set before him by prophetic religions" (7). Prophetic religions create in people the need that they claim to fulfill by way of conversion. African-American religion, coming as it does out of a prophetic tradition, shares this characteristic of reorienting the soul of an individual from an earlier form of piety to another.

Donald Gelpi, in *Experiencing God: A Theology of Human Experience,* stresses how in conversion there is the assumption of personal responsibility for responding appropriately to the historical self-revelation of God, a phenomenon that was surely evidenced in the slaves' apprehension of God. Gelpi describes conversion as a natural process in which one assumes conscious, personal autonomy for oneself in a controllable area of personal growth (178). The motivation for this assumption of responsibility is what is transcendent—it is when one's attitudes and beliefs have been touched by a sense of ultimacy. The work of grace is what makes such a conversion religious, but essential to the acceptance of grace is a principle of human freedom whereby one chooses to exercise will as a spiritual faculty. Yet it is through conversion that one receives the guarantee of freedom, comes in possession of spiritual essence, and makes a decision "to assume conscious, personal responsibility for one's own future development, for the subsequent development of a distinguishable realm of experiential growth" (313). Gelpi goes on to describe that these realms of personal growth are physical, emotional, intellectual, and moral. He claims that the experience of conversion aspires to integrate growth in all these realms and cast it as personal growth before God in response to every authentic instance of divine self-revelation. Gelpi's theological understanding gives one a description of the kinds of changes experienced by African Americans in the process of establishing their identity through religious belief.

Perhaps the most illuminating theological perspective has been written by Hans Mol in *Identity and the Sacred,* in which he claims that religion serves in the "sacralization of identity" and describes conversion as the process by which this sacralization occurs. Much of what Mol argues is based on a theory of identity in a continuum between what is personal and what is social. Identity on a personal level is a "stable niche" one finds oneself in amid the chaos of the world. This stable niche must be defended. On a social level, identity is a stable aggregate of basic and commonly held beliefs, patterns, and values that maintains itself over and against the potential threat of cultural elements. Conversion occurs when one moves beyond clearly defined expectations and roles that are products of social expectations to a more stable and conscious level of identity.

Identity, in other words, is more enduring than the roles one plays during different phases of existence. Identity is selfhood, anchored in a transcendent order symbolized in concepts and myths—not unselfconscious but certainly taken for granted. It is "the most essential nucleus of man which becomes visible only after all his roles have been laid aside" (143–44). Identity defines what a person is and morality what a person does. Identity, therefore, is that which gives meaning to experience and that experience which interprets life itself. Identity is discovered and sacralized through conversion, because, as Mol says, the idea of self-realization is a sacred ideal. Conversion, therefore, is a sacralization pattern for the individual (as revitalization, it could be said, is a sacralization pattern for societies)—a mechanism for incorporating rather than annihilating change. It desacralizes an old identity and sacralizes a new identity. In so doing, conversion cooperates with parallel mechanisms not altogether religious (like the act of writing, art, play, sexuality) in an effort to protect identity, a system of meaning, or a definition of reality, and modifies and legitimates change and strengthens identity.

It could be said that conversion is a movement from profane to sacred, in which all things are invested with sacred values. Marginality—for example, the situation of blacks being denied access to all levels of American society—is an important aspect of this process of sacralization because it emphasizes the process of becoming or making sacred over and against a static notion of "being" sacred. Specific mechanisms of sacralization are objectification—summing up the variegated elements of mundane existence in a transcendental point of reference where they can appear more orderly, consistent, and timeless (and may even provide leverage for transformation); commitment—emotional attachment to a specific focus of identity, both personal and social, that anchors a system of meaning in one's emotions and can lead to visions and a state of awe; and ritual—which maximizes order and reinforces the place of the individual in society. Conversion incorporates change for personal identity and sacralizes the experience of marginality—of not belonging—by creating a new order and a place for the individual in that order.

In the twentieth century there is more competition for what is to become the focus of one's identity, especially as religion has come to assume a less than prominent face among competing secular forces. This is why it is helpful to go back into history and to see how religion functioned in ordering the lives of and creating identities for individuals. The richest and clearest demonstrations of the transcendent dimension of conversion are not necessarily found in theological writings but may appear in conversion autobiographies like those written by Saint Augustine, J. H. Newman, Thomas Merton, Simone Weil, and others. These narrative accounts describe the unique qualities of the transcendent forces at work in conversion, and they give significant representation to personal effort involved in conversion because they seek not only to conform to traditional theological norms, but to reveal the strivings of the individual soul within the context of a culture that either inhibits or encourages conversion. It is to this canon of conversion narratives that I would like to add the writings of several African-American women.

Many works by African-American men, of course, could be included in the general pattern of conversion I have been describing. Most notable and familiar among them is the *Narrative of the Life of Frederick Douglass,* which is essentially a spiritual autobiography in which religious conversion is closely linked with his acquisition of skills of literacy.[19] For Douglass the assurance of grace in conversion parallels the assurance of the word he discovers in the achievement of literacy—a traditional casting of the principle of Word as Logos—the revealed design of God. Although this provides a useful model for the study I am undertaking, what I want to do is distinguish those qualities in women's writing and their religious experiences that make their conversions different or unique.

Sheila Collins points out in *A Different Heaven and Earth: A Feminist Perspective on Religion* that theologies—the attempt to give shape and content to one's experience of the transcendent—arise out of a cultural context and are promulgated by means of culture. Theologies change by way of changes in cultural experience and cannot be separated from the communities they represent. The community of women, however, is not always represented in traditional theologies. There can be a conflict for women between the weight of religious authority and the meaning of their own religious experience and what their spiritual needs suggest. Recognizing this conflict, Collins sees two options for women: either to reform religion by way of a new hermeneutic of received tradition, or to revolutionize religion by bypassing authority and finding other sources of validity for one's religious experience (37).[20] Whether one is a reformer or a revolutionary, however, the first step toward developing a female perspective on religion begins with a discovery of women's history. This discovery acts as a form of revelation for women and opens up a new dimension of religious life.

Feminist theologians attempt to develop theories on women's

spirituality by placing *women's experience* at the methodological center of their thought. They reject kerygmatic theology that denies, by its prior assumption of a unique and changeless revelation, the realities of women's experience, and align themselves more with existentialist theologians who use human experience as a base from which to derive questions of meaning. Yet even still, existentialist categories of being and nonbeing, alienation and estrangement, are meaningless to women who are caught up in very concrete expressions of nonbeing and estrangement. Rather than building theologies (a systematized body of knowledge about God), feminist theologians see themselves as engaged in "theologizing"—a dialectical process of religious reflection grounded in praxis. Instead of the word *religion,* associated with historically established and institutionalized forms, feminists often choose the word *spirituality* to label their discovery and affirmation. Amanda Porterfield makes such a distinction in the following way: "Spirituality refers to personal attitudes toward life, attitudes that engage an individual's deepest feelings and most fundamental beliefs. It encompasses the religious attitudes and experiences of individuals and may often be used as a synonym for religiousness. But spirituality covers a larger domain than that staked out by religion because it does not require belief in God or commitment to institutional forms of worship" (6).

Porterfield also effectively develops a thesis based on the fact that historically women's spirituality has been formed by the lives of *women* in contrast to lives men lived. Many feminist theologians, therefore, assert that spiritual depth and its representation in deity can be found in women's selves. Carol Christ, for example, in *Diving Deep and Surfacing: Women Writers on Spiritual Quest,* encourages a faith in women's stories. The narratives of women's lives demonstrate women's ability to reach moral resolution through the telling and interpreting of their stories. Katie G. Cannon, in *Black Womanist Ethics,* has developed a system of ethics based on black women's writings. The literary tradition of black women, she asserts, is "the nexus between the real-lived texture of black life and the oral-aural cultural values implicitly passed on and received from one generation to the next" (5). Black women's writings, she asserts, are the best repository for understanding the ethical values black women have created and cultivated by participation in society. Writers function as continuing symbolic conveyers and transformers of the values acknowledged by the female members of the black community.

It is out of women's stories—real, imagined, historical, literary, and theoretical—that feminist theologians have begun to make sense of and validate their religious experience. One thing they all agree on is that the spiritual tradition of women that has persisted through vast changes in social and intellectual consciousness has always embraced and encouraged both self-expression and the self's capacity for transformation.[21] Moreover, as Carol Christ and others emphasize, the spiritual quest of women has a social dimension that is inseparable from the spiritual dimension and in fact calls attention to the need for spiritually transformed women to question conventional notions of being and power in the world.

A woman's awakening to great powers that ground her in a new sense of self and a new orientation to the world helps her to appreciate one aspect of the psychology of women discussed by Carol Gilligan in her book *In a Different Voice*. Gilligan shows how the moral development of women has been devalued and misrepresented and described in terms as vastly different from that of men. Gilligan attempts to show how women's characteristic "sin," unlike men's central sin of pride or egocentricity, is the different one of denial of development of the self. Whereas the moral voice of men stresses justice and rights, the voice of women stresses caring and responsibility. A woman is more inclined to define a moral problem as one of obligation in which she needs to exercise care and avoid hurt. A woman's identity is defined in the context of relationships and judged by a standard of responsibility and care to those with whom she is related. This, Gilligan argues, does not make women morally immature, just different. Moreover, this different voice does not belong naturally to women only but arises in a social context.

The theological implications for female psychology are clarified by Valerie Saiving in her ground-breaking essay, "The Human Situation: A Feminine View." Saiving clearly establishes that customary theological representations of human sin as self-assertion, self-centeredness, and pride are more descriptive of the experience of men than of women. Women's sin, she asserts, is better described as "underdevelopment or negation of the self" (37). In her book *Sex, Sin, and Grace: Women's Experience and the Theologies of Reinhold Niebuhr and Paul Tillich,* Judith Plaskow expands on Saiving's ideas to include a feminine representation of grace. Plaskow follows Saiving's argument that understanding pride or self-centeredness as the primary form of sin overlooks the fact that for women sin is primarily self-denial or avoidance of the necessity to become a self. She continues, however, by asserting that the grace that follows sin is not, therefore, the shattering of pride through obedience but a movement toward genuine self-love and acceptance of the responsibility for self and self-realization.[22]

Many contemporary black women theologians and literary theorists are now using the theories of Gilligan and other women-centered psychologists and theologians to reclaim caretaking by focusing on its empowering aspects.[23] The social context for African-American culture, in particular, has always demanded a different voice be spoken. Critics such as Mary Helen Washington see that African-American women do in fact assert a positive sense of self not only over and against what they were told to believe about themselves but also over and against what limitations their circumstances forced upon them precisely because of their cooperative sense of responsibility. As she writes, "selfhood is not defined negatively as separateness from others, nor is it defined narrowly by the individual dyad—the child and its mother—but on the larger scale as the ability to recognize one's continuity with the larger community" ("'I Sign My Mother's Name,'" 159). By claiming relational identity as a source of strength, black women are redefining moral categories. Much of what I will argue is that what enabled these women to assert self was a spiritual view of reality that was founded on a faith tradition created in order to sustain self, not deny self, and that recognizes also the communal dimensions of faith and identity.

In the twentieth century we have witnessed a growing expansion of the view of women's moral development. The feminist movement has drawn attention to the rights of women and helped them to transform their moral judgments. Women have learned that it is moral to care not only for others but for themselves as well, but that there is a necessary relational quality to the advancement of self. The philosopher Mary Midgley has drawn an analogy between women's commitment to the feminist movement and the process of religious conversion—life that had been meaningless suddenly takes on meaning as women move from self-abnegating isolation into self-affirming fellowship. Moreover, "that outgoing identification with others and self-giving for a cause which are characteristically religious lead past immediate enjoyment of society to the forwarding of the group ideal" (Midgley and Hughes, 19). In her book, *From Sin to Salvation: Stories of Women's Conversions, 1800 to the Present,* Virginia Lieson Brereton underscores Midgley's observation. Brereton compares the contemporary feminist experience of a "click! of recognition," first introduced by Jane O'Reilly in a 1973 *Ms.* article, to a traditional conversion experience of seeing the light (108). Brereton goes on to show how classical Protestant conversion narratives have shaped the ways contemporary women have told "out of church" or secular stories of radical personal transformation. Conversion to feminism, lesbianism, women's studies, and deliverance from addiction are some of the narratives Brereton relates. And for some black women, as the scholar, artist, and activist Bernice Johnson Reagon has pointed out, the civil rights movement represented a similar communal and cooperative vehicle for conversion (Anderson, 11).[24]

In addition to the claims of feminist and social movements and what they can offer women in terms of identity formation, however, there remains in the perspective of many African-American women an essential spiritual dimension that is necessary for a full sacralization of identity. Although the black church may have lost, to a degree, the all-encompassing function it served the community in its origin and development in America, it remains a vital source of inspiration, guidance, and moral leadership.[25] Many black women writers, therefore, are revitalizing the stories of their foremothers, whose conversion experiences bring together transcendent spiritual reality and immanent natural social reality in order to interpret life. They bring their own subjects and experiences to the faith of their ancestors and combine contemporary critical reflection with the power of symbolic imagination that was handed down to them. They transform literal conversions into literary conversions. Twentieth-century African-American women writers open themselves to a deeper self, a recognition of the role of paradox, images, and social symbols that make one who one is and assist in the rewriting of the past. Having enjoyed the freedoms that are their ancestors' legacy and having absorbed historical indignities, contemporary African-American women writers are reclaiming the mythic ideal their ancestors created—the values built into their own selves by virtue of participation in a particular social class, religious tradition, and ethnic group. Aware of the paradoxes of such a state, they are open to new depths of religious experience, spirituality, and revelation, and this is what their writing explores. They continue the African-American search for religious relevance and demonstrate that it is through cultural expression that religious ideas are sustained in ways not always direct, but affirmative nonetheless.

2

Voluntary Converts

Black women . . . do not deal with themselves as God, nor do
they remove Him from the human frame of reference.
—Toni Cade Bambara

When they were brought to this country, African Americans appropriated Christianity and made it descriptive of what they deemed sacred in the world and in themselves, expressive of their own experience of divine presence in their lives. This adaptation Valerie Smith
describes as "a way of recovering a lost ideal," because the Christian
faith suited a system of values and priorities conditioned by African
cultural practice (*Self-Discovery and Authority*, 19). An integral step
in recovering this lost ideal was the appropriation of the conversion
experience as an empowerment of the self. Conversion was not just
redemption by God and a deliverance from sin but a deliverance from
limitations by claiming and affirming aspects of identity as a vital spiritual achievement. For African Americans, conversion was an imaginative act of transforming self through the creation of a new image of
self and a new image of God.

The writings of nineteenth-century black women give voice to the
drama of conversion into selfhood by presenting a powerful vision of
women in the process of changing and developing their full human
potential. In three exemplary texts, *Incidents in the Life of a Slave Girl*
by Harriet Jacobs, *The Narrative of Sojourner Truth*, and *Gifts of Power*

by Rebecca Jackson, one can detect a pattern of conversion in these women's accounts of their lives. In showing how religious factors contributed to their personal development, each woman, in her own way, asserts the right and necessity for self-definition according to an understanding of God's intentions for her as an individual. Their decision to write about their experiences was an essential part of their assertion of this right and necessity.[1]

In asking how their narratives were written, how their conversions were remembered, one is also asking how conversion "re-members" the convert in the world as a converted person. Since it is the experience of conversion that provides the motive for articulating an account of it, an important issue is not so much what makes conversion possible as what conversion makes possible. A conversion experience and attempts to articulate it reorder and reveal a clarity and unity that one can find only through careful searching and recollection. As Brian Taylor has suggested, "knowledge about the experience of conversion is brought to life as description only because of ongoing acknowledgment of the *conversion of experience* logically consequent upon the *experience of conversion* itself" (321). Called to testify, the narratives black women wrote were retrospective endeavors that helped them to define, even create, their identities, because, as William Andrews has stated, the act of writing itself was self-liberating in "redefining freedom and assigning it to oneself" (*To Tell a Free Story,* xi).[2]

Harriet Jacobs, Sojourner Truth, and Rebecca Jackson demonstrate in their narratives such a conversion of experience as each reflects on her own personal encounter with a sense of being different and how that encounter established her claim to full humanity and irrevocably changed the course of her life.[3] Their conversions differ inasmuch as "what conversion means is relative to how one has defined what is wrong with humanity. The goal of conversion will be an ideal correction of this definition of what is wrong" (Reuther, *Womanguides,* 135). The kind of conversions each has varies considerably, and these texts were chosen with such diversity in mind.

Harriet Jacobs's text is the least overtly religious work inasmuch as her encounters with alienation are described especially with reference to her enslavement and her attempts to break free of various kinds of oppression. Her conversion comes by way of a critique of both the hypocritical "white" Christianity espoused by slaveholders and the accommodating "black" Christianity of slaves she perceived as resigned to their lot in life. This dual critique sets in motion a series of events in which she is increasingly empowered by the assertion of her own identity and self-worth. Her narrative demonstrates the profound, if at times subtle, influence religious principles had in the African-American community.

Rebecca Jackson's writings deal most specifically with the personal transformation entailed by an experience of conversion. A free Northern black woman, she is frustrated by her inability to read scripture and her reliance on others to give her access to the word of God. After Jackson's conversion occurs she is miraculously given the ability to read. From this moment on she takes control of her outer life and frees herself from conventional obligations, seeking and finding among the Shakers a religious community with which she is comfortable. With the Shakers she is able to concentrate on her inner life—a sequence of visions that she records in journal entries. Her visions are her "gifts of power," and they assist her in interpreting reality by conflating biblical texts with personal accounts of how God's grace infused her spirit and worked in her life to effect a transformation.

Finally, Sojourner Truth describes with great power her experience of conversion that she places in the context of her life in the African-American community. Her narrative is an account of her years spent in slavery and her later career as a preacher and an abolitionist. Her conversion is symbolized by her taking of the name Sojourner Truth, which, unlike her given slave name, describes who she would become.

In the process of their conversions these women all undertook one or another kind of reconstruction of their religious heritage, directly challenging patriarchal notions of what a woman is and who God is. The religious faith they embraced found its basis in a concept of divinity that includes feminine as well as masculine qualities, that deemphasizes the doctrine of original sin, that limits the authority of a traditional ordained clergy, and embraces other prophetic voices, thereby encouraging women to seek roles other than those of marriage and motherhood as acceptable ways to express their spirituality. Each writer realized that whatever she accepted of her patriarchal religious heritage, she still had to find a spirituality within herself; that despite her condition she could improve her position by discovering and calling upon the powers within herself. Harriet Jacobs, Sojourner Truth, and Rebecca Jackson all confront patriarchal presuppositions and in turn engage in a definition of themselves according to those "aspects of the self outside the margins of normal, acceptable, definable as conceived by the dominant culture" (Andrews, *To Tell a Free Story*, 1–2).

Yet despite the challenges they present to received religious traditions, as defenders of human dignity they grounded their arguments in appeals to religious sanctions. All three of these women were "voluntary" converts who, while developing and exercising formidable will and consciousness, were also responding in an appropriate way to the cultural conditions already established within the African-American community. In seeking a better life for themselves (and their families and communities), these women sought a vision and induced a greater understanding of their roles and talents through an awareness wrought by the religious faith expressed in their communities. Religion, in other words, cooperated in their efforts to authenticate themselves. Their narratives, unlike the better-known male narratives of the same period, do not focus on the heroic and political dimensions of their lives, although there are these aspects to their accounts. Rather, these women concentrate on the dynamic power of the spiritual dimensions of their lives. Their engagement with a spiritual life gives expanded meaning to their lived experiences and becomes the basis for the sacred story of black women—the quest, the human search for meaning by way of building multiple layers of spiritual evolution. For, as William Andrews maintains, narrators like these women are "models of the act and impact of biblical appropriation on the consciousness of the black narrator as bearer of the Word" (*To Tell a Free Story*, 64). Their personal history, therefore, is sacred history because the essence of the spirituality of African-American women is best captured by il-lustration—in their stories—not by conceptual definition.

Although contemporary critics tend to make a distinction between "slave" narratives and "spiritual" narratives (Jackson's text being the only one that would customarily fall into the category of spiritual nar-rative), it must be argued that such a distinction is unnecessary.[4] What Robert Stepto identified in slave narratives as a secular quest for free-dom and literacy (*From Behind the Veil: A Study of Afro-American Nar-rative*), or the terms "identity" and "veracity" that William Andrews uses as the two propositions to which African-American autobiographies addressed themselves (*To Tell a Free Story*), need not be excluded from what is identified in spiritual narratives as a quest for righteousness and a holy life. The goals of the political and the spiritual quest are essentially the same—the achievement of a worthwhile sense of self and a fundamentally positive identity. As has been stated earlier, in the cultural life of nineteenth-century African Americans, the sacred and the secular coexisted in harmony, each empowering the other. To separate these twin aspects of the culture diminishes the strength of both political and spiritual acts and their consequences. In certain texts there is the appearance of one motivation taking precedence over the other, yet the personal fulfillment each woman sought originated at a level of ultimacy and involved such a depth of being that no act—of living or of writing—can be seen as simply and only political or spiritual. These women who "claimed equal access to the love and forgiveness of a black-appropriated Christian God" (McKay, "Nine-teenth-Century Black Women's Spiritual Autobiographies," 140) re-alized that the fullness of their humanity rested on an achievement of both political and spiritual emancipation. They place great emphasis on the religious implications of their experiences and the clues they give them about their identities and the ultimate significance of their lives.[5] They show how religious beliefs, values, and commitments can shape a person's character and orient her toward an understanding of her own personal history. For, as William Andrews states, blacks trace freedom to an awakening of "their awareness of their fundamental identity with and rightful participation in logos, whether understood as reason and its expression in speech or as divine spirit. The climax of the quests of both kinds of autobiographer comes when they seize the opportunity to proclaim what are clearly complementary gospels of freedom" (*To Tell a Free Story*, 7).

Unlike their male counterparts, nineteenth-century black women sought autonomy in a world that was restrictive not only because of race but also because of caste and gender. The threats to their quest for a positive identity so compounded, black women maintained the balance between sacred and secular and derived power from both forms of expression as strategies for survival. Through religious faith they were able to achieve a vision of freedom and a degree of confidence in their own special abilities, and by believing in political principles of equality they were able to challenge male authority, becoming leaders and transformers of consciousness.[6] The goal of their autobiographies, as Sue E. Houchins states in her introduction to the Schomburg Library edition of *Spiritual Narratives*, involves a complex of motives that she identifies as a need to privately meditate on the meaning of a life of struggle, to create an objective reconstruction of the past and a public demonstration of the qualities of selfhood, and to "initiate a dialogue with those who doubted the very existence of the souls of blacks and their possibility for redemption" (xxx). Nineteenth-century black women, as Nellie McKay has written,

> express female identity through the religious faith that gave them direct access to God in the Self—the highest authority; this knowledge imbued them with pride, self-respect, and control over their intellectual lives. In the face of other inhumane circumstances, they believed that in the "democracy of saved souls" all "were on an equal spiritual standing with them before the Lord." In bypassing and defying the place that white people and black men allotted them by asserting their right to control their perceptions of themselves and their assumptions of full

selfhood, they declared an independence of spirit that made them out-spoken feminists of their time. In the words of Alice Walker, we need to receive them as gifts of power in themselves. ("Nineteenth-Century Black Women's Spiritual Autobiographies," 152)

Harriet Jacobs (1813–1897)

When the literature of our race is developed, it will of necessity
be different in all essential points of greatness, true heroism,
and real Christianity, from what we may at the present time
for convenience call American literature.
—Victoria Earle Matthews

In 1861 Harriet Jacobs, a former slave and activist in the abolitionist movement, published *Incidents in the Life of a Slave Girl: Written by Herself* and omitted her name as author. Although she asserts author-ship in the subtitle, "Written by Herself," she does not identify her-self in the text. Instead, she creates a first-person narrator who claims to be relating her own biography and calls herself Linda Brent. In the preface Jacobs claims her account is "no fiction," but that she has "concealed the names of places, and given persons fictitious names." She does so with "no motive for secrecy on my own account, but I deemed it kind and considerate towards others to pursue this course" (xii).

Despite the claims of its editor, Lydia Maria Child, and the wide appeal and acceptance in abolitionist circles it enjoyed when it was published, the authenticity of this text was held in doubt until as re-cently as 1981, when Jean Fagan Yellin proved definitively that the narrative was written by Harriet Jacobs and that the account she gives of her life and escape from slavery is indeed accurate. Since Yellin es-tablished the narrative's credibility, it has been anthologized and reis-sued in several editions and has become a widely discussed text. Schol-ars have welcomed the introduction of a woman's account of slavery, since so many of the available and frequently critiqued narratives were written by men. The acceptance of Jacobs's text opened wide the dialogue on slave narratives and introduced a whole new set of critical terms by which they could be read, providing what Houston A. Baker calls "striking modifications in the Afro-American discursive subtext" (50).

In and through the creation of the protagonist/narrator Linda Brent, Harriet Jacobs transforms herself into a literary subject. By doing such she is able to present her private history as a subject of public concern, projecting what Yellin calls "a new kind of female hero" (Introduction, xiv). Hazel Carby argues that self-protection also motivated Jacobs's need for a pseudonym, and that "the construction of the history of Linda Brent was the terrain through which Jacobs had to journey in order to construct the meaning of her own life as a woman and mother" (50).

The most widely accepted reading of *Incidents in the Life of a Slave Girl* is that it "achieve[s] a creation of self through subversive interplay with readers' expectations, as [Jacobs] draw[s] on and reshape[s] popular female genres—the seduction novel and the domestic novel—as well as an Afro-American genre, the slave narrative" (Doriani, 200). Valerie Smith, Hazel Carby, and others show how Jacobs took advantage of certain novelistic conventions by consciously and consistently exploiting the ironic potential inherent in traditional literary techniques.[7] She did so in order to win the identification of potential abolitionist women with her own plight.[8] For Northern women, Thomas Doherty notes, "the basic text, after the Bible, was the slave narrative" (82). Jacobs, by blending the high moral purpose of religious testimony with the entertainment appeal of women's fiction, attempted not only to appeal to "true believers" in the abolitionist cause but also to create converts.

Ironically, it was these very conventions that kept the narrative's authenticity in doubt for so many years.[9] *Incidents*, as Elizabeth Fox-Genovese points out, strains credulity at many points primarily because it is cast as a tale of virtue defended against overwhelming odds ("To Write the Wrongs of Slavery," 69). In recounting Linda Brent's protracted struggle with her master, Jacobs takes many opportunities to distinguish Linda Brent from most slave women. She had a free grandmother, her parents were light-skinned, and her father was a talented carpenter who "had more of the feelings of a freeman than is common among slaves" (7). She herself "was so fondly shielded that I never dreamed I was a piece of merchandise" (3). She does not even know she is a slave until age six when her mother dies and she learns "by the talk around me, that I was a slave" (5). In addition, Linda Brent's diction contrasts sharply with the dialect of the other slave women. The more implausible aspects of Jacobs's narrative, however, derive directly from the climate in which she knew herself to be writing.[10] In order to secure an audience, Jacobs had to present her protagonist in such a way that white and free women readers could identify with her. She even goes so far as to claim that "her descriptions fall short of the facts," in order to protect her readers from the hideous details of the "wrongs inflicted by slavery" (xii), and ends her preface by appealing to sentiments of faith with a humble prayer: "May the blessing of God rest on this imperfect effort in behalf of my persecuted people" (xvi).

She achieves the effect of appealing to a genteel sensibility exceedingly well, yet the subtext of her narrative reveals that while adopting current literary standards and conventions, Jacobs also performs many imaginative variations. However much Harriet Jacobs may have wanted her readers to identify with Linda Brent as a virtuous woman and a devoted mother, she did not identify her protagonist with her readers. She recognized the fallacy of their professed Christianity and their unwillingness to challenge the patriarchal order. This recognition came by way of an awareness that the law protected the womanhood of white women and the domestic relations between white women and men, but that she herself had no such protection. Her "protection" came from her own internal resources. Jacobs's narrative quite clearly indicates that Linda Brent's life is one of a gradual conversion to the sacred qualities inherent in her own identity as a black woman—her independence, self-reliance, and strength. Indeed, even the Reverend Francis H. Grimke, upon delivering Jacobs's eulogy, described as one of her strongest character traits her "great will power. She knew how to say no when it was necessary, and how to adhere to it. She was no reed shaken by the wind, vacillating, easily moved from a position. She did her own thinking; had opinions of her own, and held to them with great tenacity" (Smyth, 37). As Linda Brent said of her master, although he "had power and law on his side," she had "a determined will. There is might in each" (87).

Jacobs's narrative, which gives "considerable, albeit often indirect, insight into the religious life of its author," also "broadens our understanding of the diversity and complexity of the religious life of Afro-Americans under slavery" (Taves, 60). Her appropriation of Christianity was critical, and although baptized she worshipped only sporadically. Despite her ambivalent stance on institutionalized forms of the Christian faith, Jacobs is steeped in the faith by virtue of her culture and her personal relationships. The combination of her willful criticism and her devotion to her family and people create unique conditions for establishing the form her conversion will take. Jacobs's conversion comes by way of a series of actions and choices that gradually reveal her identity to herself. She confronts the issues of identity and culture to claim a distinct sense of self through her selection among life's possibilities. These choices reveal what she values of the world of her family and how she views the world of the larger society. With each choice she is increasingly empowered and confident in herself. She gradually undergoes a conversion in her experience of life as she comes to realize what is sacred in contrast to the profanity all around her. She discovers feelings, instincts, and sensitivities long repressed and also her capacity to shape her own identity. Or, in the words of Frances Smith Foster, she comes to "proclaim [her] validity" (13), and her "resolution to quit slavery is, in effect, a climax to a conversion experience" (85).

Harriet Jacobs's narrative is essentially an account of how Linda Brent preserved the sacred things that she discovered within herself, how they were revealed, and how she reordered dimensions of her experience to create clarity and unity. Her image of sacrality is deeply rooted in the world of her own experience. Initially Linda Brent acts as a woman protecting her virtue, but each event also serves to bolster her own self-esteem and place limits on the degree of degradation she will accept for herself, and later what she will permit her children to accept. Linda Brent's spirituality is expressed when, through her personal attitude toward life that engages her deepest feelings and most fundamental beliefs, she becomes aware of alternatives and of her potential for self-determination. As Sidonie Smith has stated, in a narrative like Jacobs's, the break away from the imprisoning community of slavery is a "re-enactment of the sacred quest for selfhood" (29). Harriet Jacobs's personal attitude encompasses religious attitudes and also experiences that may be seen as synonymous with religiousness. In other words, she expresses her relationship to a divine presence in language that reflects her dominant experience—that of being a black woman (and a mother) in slavery.[11]

Incidents in the Life of a Slave Girl presents a black woman confronting American culture at a particular point in history that inevitably influenced not only her development as a person but her career as a writer. Her conversion comes by way of her growing awareness of her situation as a slave. As seen above, Jacobs shows how at first Linda Brent had to realize she was a slave but even then, under the protection of a "kind mistress" who taught her to read and spell, she experienced only "happy days." Yet when Linda is twelve her mistress dies; transported to another situation, Linda begins to learn "that blight, which too surely waits on every human being born to be chattel" (5).[12] At this point in the narrative, where Linda is reflecting on her initial awareness of how the system of slavery affects her own life, Jacobs introduces the concept of spiritual equality by referring to slaves as "God-breathing machines" who, in the sight of their masters, are no more "than the cotton they plant, or the horses they tend" (6). What Harriet Jacobs establishes early in her narrative is a pattern of disillusionment immediately followed by spiritual growth, where Linda Brent learns the lessons of reality and translates them within a spiritual context.

From the first moment of her service with Dr. Flint, a physician, Linda's life begins a series of downward spirals. When her father dies, her heart "rebelled against God," who has taken away from her so many of the people important to her. Her grandmother, who in the narrative is the reassuring and stable spiritual guide in Linda's life, comforts her by saying, "Who knows the ways of God? Perhaps they have been kindly taken from the evil days to come" (8). She and her brother had been taught by their parents to feel that they were human beings, so Linda does not easily resign herself to anything less, and, in an unusual rejection of the solace that Christianity offers a slave a better life in death, she imagines other possibilities. When a slave woman and her illegitimate child (fathered by Dr. Flint) both die in childbirth, Linda criticizes the promises of the Christian afterlife from two perspectives. She exposes the false piety of her slave mistress, who denies that there is a heaven "for the like of her and her bastard," and also the faithful resignation of the slave woman, who "thanked God for taking her away from the great bitterness of life" (12).

These early experiences establish in Linda a resolve that she will maintain her virtue in the face of Dr. Flint's sexual advances and that she will not simply succumb to the reassurance of a simplistic faith. Encoded in the acceptable tale of a woman defending her virtue is a critique of the theological assumptions of that virtue—a critique of the patriarchy that supports it and the inadequate solace it affords. Although her grandmother tried to make her and her brother accept that their life "was the will of God: that He had seen fit to place us under such circumstances; and though it seemed hard, we ought to pray for contentment," Linda "reasoned that it was much more the will of God that we should be situated as she was" (15)—free. She admired the beautiful faith of her grandmother and judged it at the same time since it came from "a mother who could not call her children her own" (15).

Linda Brent soon begins a series of maneuvers to avoid the fate of the abused slave woman, outwitting her master at every turn.[13] She does so in full awareness of the dangerous implications of her attitude: "I had not lived fourteen years in slavery for nothing. I had felt, seen and heard enough, to read the characters and question the motives of those around me. The war of my life had begun; and though one of God's most powerless creatures, I resolved never to be conquered. Alas, for me!" (17). Linda is strengthened by a like attitude adopted by her uncle Benjamin, who, upon his first escape and recapture rejects his mother's urging to put his trust in God and refuses to humble himself before his master. As Linda says, "He that is *willing* to be a slave, let him be a slave" (25). Linda, like her uncle, is unwilling to be a slave.

Jacobs demonstrates through Linda's unwillingness to be subservient and in her ceaseless struggles with Dr. Flint that commonly accepted gifts from God, like beauty or grace or the desire to be virtuous, are a curse for a slave woman, inviting abuse and exploitation: "If God has bestowed beauty upon her it will prove to be her greatest curse. . . . that which commands admiration in the white woman only hastens the degradation of the female slave" (57). Lonely and frustrated, at this point in the narrative Jacobs has Linda interject a plea for sympathy from her readers and chastise them at the same time for being silent. Ever aware of her readership, Jacobs deftly constructs Linda's comments, taking care to praise those abolitionists who do speak out, asking God to bless them and give them strength and courage. When Linda exclaims, "God bless those, everywhere, who are laboring to advance the cause of humanity" (29), one knows that Harriet Jacobs, in a validation of her own efforts, is including herself in that blessing.

Jacobs returns to Linda Brent's story and details her many refusals of her master's sexual advances. All the while, Linda trusts that "some threads of joy would be woven into my dark destiny" (30). When she is sixteen, Linda falls in love with a man who is an "intelligent and religious man" (41), a freeborn carpenter, just as her father was. Dr. Flint refuses to allow Linda to court this man and even refuses to let him buy Linda. Although she can accept when God takes someone in death, Linda cannot accept when couples are forcibly separated, as happens to her and her lover. In retrospect she realizes she "indulged the hope that the dark clouds around me would turn out a bright lining" (36) and accepts that "the dream of my girlhood was over" (42). At the time, however, she contemplates running away. As Linda considers life in the North, Jacobs introduces her most bitter attack on Christianity but this time goes after not the false proclamations of white piety but the naive assumptions of Christian slaves who are afraid of a life of freedom: "It is difficult to persuade such that freedom could make them useful men, and enable them to protect their wives and children. If those heathens in our Christian land had as much teaching as some Hindoos, they would think otherwise. They would know that liberty is more valuable than life. They would begin to understand their own capabilities, and exert themselves to become men and women" (43). She follows up these remarks by characterizing slaves who do "protect wives and daughters from the insults of their masters" as "partially civilized and Christianized" (43). She implies that a true Christianity will not resign slaves to their circumstances but will make them understand their own "capabilities" and encourage them to exert themselves in the exercise of their will. This sentiment becomes explicit later on when she attacks white Christians who "satisfy their consciences with the doctrine that God created the Africans to be slaves. What a libel upon the heavenly Father, who 'made of one blood all nations of men!'" (45). At this point she digresses further from Linda's tale to recount others' experiences in slavery, giving more examples of the hideous crimes and false piety of slaveholders. She does this in part to gain more sympathy from her readers and to prepare them for the revelations in her own life that will soon follow. In telling of a slaveholder who mercilessly tortured slaves, Jacobs adds: "The master who did these things was highly educated, and styled a perfect gentleman. He also boasted the name and standing of a Christian, though Satan never had a truer follower"; but Jacobs follows this up with an example of a mistress whose religion "was not a garb put on for Sunday and laid aside till Sunday returned again" (50).[14]

What Jacobs clearly demonstrates is that at this point in her life Linda Brent is able to distinguish between a faith that ennobles and inspires and one that diminishes and defeats individuals. Moreover, she is able to place this understanding in a context that does not discriminate between black and white. Neither race as a whole embodies true faith since there are examples of both kinds found among black and white. This clarity of vision and wholeness of comprehension allow her to see that slavery is "a curse to the whites as well as the blacks" (53), a scourge that can corrupt even religious faith.

This understanding prepares Linda Brent for the trials she has yet to face. She does more than trust her knowledge, however: she takes action. When it seems she can no longer avoid Dr. Flint's advances, she exercises what she sees as her only option and takes a white lover. She does so with great reluctance, and Jacobs assures her readers that Linda "wanted to keep myself pure; and, under the most adverse circumstances, I tried hard to preserve my self-respect; but I was struggling alone in the powerful grasp of the demon Slavery; and the monster proved too strong for me" (54–55). Linda defends her decision by casting it in terms of exercising her own choice: "It seems less degrading to give one's self, than to submit to compulsion. There is something akin to freedom in having a lover who has no control over you, except that which he gains by kindness and attachment." She admits that although there "may be sophistry in all this," the "condition of a slave confuses all principles of morality, and, in fact, renders the practice of them impossible" (55). Upon reflection she asserts that a slave woman "ought not to be judged by the same standards as others" (56).

Linda admits to Dr. Flint that by her actions she has "sinned against God and myself" (59), but her trust in the forgiveness of God and in her own self-esteem assures her that this was an option she could live with because she maintained control. As Valerie Smith notes, this incident is but one example of Harriet Jacobs's inscribing a subversive plot of empowerment beneath an orthodox public plot of weakness and vulnerability (*Self-Discovery and Authority*, 30). Linda Brent has clearly moved into another level of conversion into selfhood with this choice, and the liberating potential it offers prepares her for her subsequent challenges.

Among the challenges Linda faces are her own internal feelings of shame that are complicated by the external judgment of others about whom she cares. When she confesses to her grandmother that she is pregnant from her affair with Mr. Sands, her grandmother exclaims: "O Linda! has it come to this? I had rather see you dead than to see you as you are now. You are a disgrace to your dead mother" (57). She takes back Linda's mother's wedding ring and silver thimble and throws Linda out of the house. This critical moment in Linda's life is read by some critics as a further demonstration of Jacobs's attempt to pacify her readers while inscribing an attack on white Christian morality, a critique that Jacobs also extended to passive blacks, including her own beloved grandmother. Laura E. Tanner, however, sees a dual problem in such a reading when she says, "Linda Brent's judgment of herself, whether viewed as a sign of the influence of narrow white Christian morality or as a concession to maintaining propriety in order not to offend her audience and jeopardize her cause, is equally injurious, for it calls into question the basic premise of the slave's right to freedom—the notion that the black man or woman is a human being with all rights and privileges that status affords" (418). Ann Taves goes even further to trace the lingering traces of shame that are evidenced not only in the narrative but in correspondence from throughout Jacobs's life. She identifies as a central conflict in Jacobs's life the "ongoing struggles with issues of autonomy and shame" (Taves, 63).

Yet it seems clear also that the facts of Jacobs's life—and the testimony of the Reverend Grimke—reveal that the lingering pain of shame may not have been as intense as suggested by Taves, nor her complicity with denying the humanity of blacks as damaging as Tanner claims. The language of sin and shame that Jacobs employs is culturally appropriate but perhaps not altogether theologically significant. When Dr. Flint joins the church to improve his position in society and urges Linda to do likewise, she responds that she would gladly join if she "could be allowed to live like a Christian" (77). Flint counters that by doing what he requires and by being faithful to him, she can be "as virtuous" as his wife. To this Linda responds: "the Bible didn't say so" (77). Clearly, Linda has a command of the liberating potential of scripture and an acute understanding of how Christian practice and pretensions deviate from Christian ethics. Moreover, never does Jacobs express an ambivalence toward her children being the product of a shameful liaison, and her insistence that "I must write just what I have lived and witnessed myself. You shall have truth" (Yellin, "Written by Herself," 485) undercuts any claims that she would be denying her own humanity.

Linda's love for and responsibility to her daughter inspire her to begin to claim a fuller sense of identity. Since he has lost a degree of power over Linda, it is her child on whom Dr. Flint focuses his revenge. Although Linda initially sees her child as a trial God has set before her, she also sees her as representative of a moral obligation to secure freedom. No longer can she think only about how the consequences of her actions affect her, she must think also of her child. She has a "new tie to life," and at this point in the narrative Jacobs digresses once more to discuss the insurrection of Nat Turner and follows up with a meditation on the church and slavery. This juxtaposition of motherhood, political acts, and religion is deliberate on Jacobs's part, as each represents a dimension of her experience as a slave that allows her to consider the possibilities of freedom and self-determination.

The insurrection of Nat Turner, Jacobs claims, encouraged slaveholders to give slaves enough religious instruction to keep them passive, but she gives testimony to support the fact that this notion failed their intentions. The slaves had no interest in a preacher who instructed them that to disobey an earthly master was to disobey the Heavenly master; but when a certain minister "addressed them as human beings" and gave "simple, understandable sermons" (73), the slaves responded. Although startled that they would ever hear such a thing, blacks could trust a clergyman who said, "Try to live according to the word of God, my friends. Your skin is darker than mine; but

God judges men by their hearts, not by the color of their skins" (74). Jacobs also shows how blacks worshipped in contexts other than those established by the slaveholders and gives examples of religious slaves and how their faith sustained them. In one particularly poignant example, she shows how Linda tries to teach one of the faithful how to read so that he might have access to the Bible himself. This launches her on an admonition of those who withhold learning from blacks and those who are unmoved by this depravity. She appeals this time from a religious perspective: "Tell them they are answerable to God for sealing up the Fountain of Life from souls that are thirsting for it" (76). She goes on to explain to her readers what she already has learned from experience: "There is a great difference between Christianity and religion in the South" (77).

By the time Linda Brent has her second child, a son, she backslides in her faith and claims to envision no release other than death, thereby only reinforcing her status as childlike, immature, and spiritually weak and dependent. Her children eventually serve as the vehicle for her spiritual maturity. Before having her children, Linda can only intellectualize her faith and her experiences, but after her son's birth she begins to translate that faith into personal reassurance. When she has her children baptized Linda feels quiet resolve: "When I entered the church, recollections of my mother came over me, and I felt subdued in spirit" (80). The moral rupture that might have occurred between Linda and her grandmother (and the memory of her mother) when she took a white lover, Linda resolves to heal by heeding her grandmother's advice to "stand by your children and suffer with them till death. Nobody respects a mother who forsakes her children; and if you leave them you will never have a happy moment" (93).[15] Up until now her actions have been informed by pride and bitterness, but in coming to terms with her role as a mother she begins the climax of her conversion—her escape from slavery. Rather than contemplating death, a final separation from her children, she sees escape as the only viable alternative to guarantee their safety. In reflecting on Dr. Flint's threats to sell her children, Linda asserts, "God being my helper, they should never pass into his hands" (81). It is her love for them that makes her aware of the moral imperative to obtain freedom and sets her off on her most dramatic demonstration of self-determination. As she casts her grandmother's wisdom in her own words she exclaims: "Every trial I endured, every sacrifice I made for their sakes, drew them closer to my heart, and gave me fresh courage to beat back the dark waves that rolled and rolled over me in a seemingly endless night of storms" (92).

Linda's grandmother, who continually preached faithful acceptance, begins to stand up to Dr. Flint, too, as when she admonishes him to "be saying your prayers. It will take 'em all, and more too, to wash the dirt off your soul" (84). Her actions help bolster Linda's own reconciliation of her faith with deeds so that, when spring comes, Linda takes hope in the season's renewal and plots her escape, hoping that in her absence the children's father would be able to secure their freedom.

In a symbolic demonstration of what faith provides, Linda's escape is planned to commence on the Sabbath. On that day she prays at the graves of her parents in the slave burial ground near the remains of an old slave church that was destroyed after Nat Turner's insurrection. In a climactic scene of reconciliation with the past, Linda honors her ancestors and finds the will to plot her own course and to endure what she must:

> The graveyard was in the woods, and twilight was coming on. Nothing broke the death-like stillness except the occasional twitter of a bird. My spirit was overawed by the solemnity of the scene. For more than ten years I had frequented this spot, but never had it seemed to me so sacred as now. A black stump, at the head of my mother's grave, was all that remained of a tree my father had planted. His grave was marked by a small wooden board, bearing his name, the letters of which were nearly obliterated. I knelt down and kissed them, and poured forth a prayer to God for guidance and support in the perilous step I was about to take. As I passed the wreck of the old meeting house, where, before Nat

Turner's time, the slaves had been allowed to meet for worship, I seemed
to hear my father's voice come from it, bidding me not to tarry till I
reached freedom or the grave. I rushed on with renovated hopes. My trust
in God had been strengthened by that prayer among the graves. (92–93)

In the place where slaves "hear not the voice of the oppressor"
Linda finds her own voice. A slave burial ground and church were the
two places where African Americans were allowed to express a measure of pride and dignity, so it is no coincidence that at this site that
represented black autonomy Linda associates her love of family and
God with self-determination. The black stump that marked her mother's
grave was a desecration of the spirit of her mother. According to Robert
Ferris Thompson, it was traditional to plant trees at grave sites as a
sign of the spirit; trees were identified with the dead person. A flourishing
tree meant all was well with the spirit of the departed (138–39). Linda's
response to this sacred place and the presence of spirits, her symbolic
awareness of the damage done by slavery not just to her family but to
the world, indicate how her faith went beyond the simple rudiments
of Christianity as presented by the slaveholders to encompass an African concept of God as an indwelling spirit.

This moment is the climax of Linda's conversion, where all she
has thought and expressed finally reaches the depth of her being and
gives her the confidence and the faith to begin her escape from slavery, her new life. As with any convert, from this moment on her life
is irrevocably changed. Although she has many trials yet to endure,
she knows she can do so because she is operating out of faith and self-
determination, not hopelessness and self-pity. As is typical in African-
American religion, God responds to her not when she abandons hope
but when she is willing to take on the challenge of creating a meaningful life. God affirms her not in her status as a slave but in her role
as a concerned mother and a self-determined woman.[16] Linda understands that she needs freedom to make a full commitment to God and
accepts the role her willful determination plays in creating opportunities for this relationship, and others, to flourish. In effect, she "trans-

forms the conditions of her oppression into the preconditions of her liberation and that of her loved ones" (Smith, Introduction, xxxiii).

Linda's escape is achieved not without the help of God, who "in his mercy raised up 'a friend in need'" (101), after which Linda begins a period of an incredible seven years spent hiding in a garret, a space so small she can neither sit nor stand comfortably. She refers to this place as her "loophole of retreat"; it is, as Valerie Smith points out, more than a place of confinement because even by exercising her will to choose her own mode of confinement, she renders herself "spiritually independent of her master" (Smith, *Self-Discovery and Authority*, 29).[17] From this vantage, however, she can observe the goings-on in the community, see her children, and is kept apprised of Dr. Flint's attempts to find her. She frustrates his every move and even outwits him by arranging for her lover, Mr. Sands, to covertly buy the children himself. In realizing that they are free, Linda feels vindicated: "I have not suffered for them in vain. Thank God!" (111).

In this cloistered life Linda survives and tries to be thankful for her "little cell" and "even to love it, as part of the price I had paid for the redemption of my children" (125). Yet by her own admission, she backslides: "Sometimes I thought God was a compassionate Father, who would forgive my sins for the sake of my sufferings. At other times, it seemed to me there was no justice or mercy in the divine government. I asked why the curse of slavery was permitted to exist, and why I had been so persecuted and wronged from youth upward. These things took the shape of mystery, which is to this day not so clear to my soul as I trust it will be hereafter" (125–26). What Jacobs is implying here, from her retrospective vantage point, is that although she may have been converted in her escape from slavery, the act of writing about it with the hopes of influencing others to take similar action is necessary for her ongoing understanding. As Rita Dove remarks in her reflections on the conversion of Saint Paul, such a change affects not just the individual but the world he inhabits, and things are no longer "compact and orderly" but "falling into a mystery." The mystery for Saint Paul and for Harriet Jacobs is "what initially fills the void when the old self is struck down and out? What rushes in before the light?" (168). Harriet Jacobs did not have time for an initial response. Her precarious position as a fugitive slave did not allow much opportunity for her to fill the gap. She finally unravels the mystery when her freedom is secure and she decides to write her narrative. It is interesting, too, that Linda is not the only one who continues to question "divine government." When Mr. Sands leaves Linda's son up North, her grieving grandmother needs reminding from a friend: "Don't murmur at de Lord's doings, but git down on your knees and thank him for his goodness" (137). Upon overhearing this Linda herself prays for forgiveness as she realizes that the life of her son is no more (as it is no less) important than that of any slave.

Only when both of her children have secured safety up North does Linda prepare for her inevitable escape from the garret. Now that her children are safe, she can take risks with her own life. Upon the eve of that escape, as before when she visited the graves of her parents, Linda begins with prayer and remarks of her grandmother's prayers, "On no other occasion has it ever been my lot to listen to so fervent a supplication for mercy and protection. It thrilled through my heart, and inspired me with trust in God" (160).

She experiences difficulties up North, confronting for the first time the fact that not only are most people unaware of the horrors of slavery, but that she is advised not to speak too openly about her experiences because it might give some people a pretext for treating her with contempt. As she relates: "That word contempt burned me like coals of fire. I replied, 'God alone knows how I have suffered, and He, I trust, will forgive me. If I am permitted to have my children, I intend to be a good mother, and to live in such a manner that people cannot treat me with contempt'" (166). In a strong declaration of her self-worth, Linda knows now that she wants to be judged by her life not as a slave but as a human being, as one converted to all the rights and privileges of freedom.

Having secured good employment with the Bruce family in New York, Linda finds herself traveling to England, where she has a "memorable event in my life, from the fact of my having there received strong religious impressions" (189). She contrasts the piety she finds there with the professed faith in the South and is inspired "with faith in the genuineness of Christian professions. Grace entered my heart, and I knelt at the communion table, I trust, in true humility of soul" (190).

Finally, after several years of freedom, Linda is reunited with her children and risks telling her daughter of Mr. Sands; she is reassured by the child (who already knew the circumstances of her parentage) that this does not change her love for her mother. Linda thanks God "that the knowledge I had so much dreaded to impart had not diminished the affection of my child. I had not the slightest idea she knew that portion of my history. If I had, I should have spoken to her long before; for my pent-up feelings had often longed to pour themselves out to some one I could trust" (193–94).

At this point, however, Linda is not free enough to pour out all her feelings because she is still technically a fugitive slave. When her whereabouts become suspected she despairs and grows bitter, too:

> There I sat, in that great city [New York], guiltless of crime, yet not daring to worship God in any of the churches. I heard the bells ringing for afternoon service, and with contemptuous sarcasm I said, "Will the preachers take for their text, 'Proclaim liberty to the captive, and the opening of prison doors to them that are bound'? or will they preach from the text, 'Do unto others as they should do unto you'?" Oppressed Poles and Hungarians could find a safe refuge in that city; John Mitchell was free to proclaim in the City Hall his desire for "a plantation well stocked with slaves;" but there I sat, an oppressed American, not daring to show my face. God forgive the black and bitter thoughts I indulged on that Sabbath day! The Scripture says, "Oppression makes even a wise man mad;" and I was not wise. (204)

Harriet Jacobs's narrative, like Linda Brent's admission to her daughter, is the result of long-pent-up feelings that she permits herself to express only at the encouragement of abolitionist friends like

Amy Post and Lydia Maria Child. Like other slave narrative authors, Jacobs found, in the words of Joycelyn K. Moody, that "garnering sufficient self-esteem to relate their past depends on the active support of an attentive audience" (634). She does so twenty years after her flight from slavery, and only after Dr. Flint dies and her employer Mrs. Bruce legally purchases her freedom from his heirs. Linda feels cheated at this outcome and wrestles with the guilt she feels at not being fully grateful for an act she deems morally unnecessary. Yet eventually she realizes that however unfair in the ultimate scheme of justice, she is lucky that "God raised me up a friend among strangers who had bestowed upon me the precious, long-desired boon. Friend . . . the word is sacred" (207). Upon realizing the significance of this friendship, Linda unites her will with that of God who "so orders my circumstances" (207) and remains in Mrs. Bruce's employment. Harriet Jacobs concludes Linda Brent's narrative in a decidedly nontraditional way: not with marriage but by remembering the great spiritual presence in her life, her grandmother. "For with those gloomy recollections come tender memories of my good old grandmother, like light, fleecy clouds floating over a dark and troubled sea" (208).

By ending with this memory of her grandmother, Harriet Jacobs acknowledges the contributions of others in her personal achievements. In relating *Incidents* to modern texts, Joycelyn K. Moody asserts that each "illustrates the interdependence of individuals within a marginalized society and the marginalized community to which they belong; unconditionally, the texts suggests, it must be 'one for all, and all for one' if either the individual member or the collective membership is to survive" (646). As Valerie Smith remarks, Jacobs's narrative is "not the classic story of the triumph of the individual will; rather it is more a story of triumphant self-in-relation" (*Self-Discovery and Authority,* 35). It is the story of a woman finding herself in relationship to her community, to her family, and to God, a characteristically feminine approach to development and growth. For, as Joanne Braxton phrases it, Jacobs "celebrates her liberation and her children's as the fruit of a collective, not individual, effort" (387). Houston Baker emphasizes this point also by claiming that Jacobs's work "gives a sense of collective rather than individualistic black identity" (55). Moreover, as Hazel Carby points out, Jacobs achieves this while at the same time adapting and transforming the dominant domestic ideologies of womanhood from which black women were excluded. She uses "the material circumstances of her life to critique conventional standards of female behavior and to question their relevance and applicability to the experience of black women" (47). What Jacobs does in telling her story this way is create a new category for describing the achievements of nineteenth-century black women.

Unlike the male slave narrators who mark their freedom as a coming to manhood, Jacobs invites the recognition that freedom and independence of thought are not male virtues. Moreover, she demonstrates that in a society controlled by white men, a black woman can develop the capacity for self-definition and self-respect, and do so "in a Christian spirit" (Yellin, Introduction, xii). Also, "by engaging [all] these issues and negotiating a course through them, she anticipates the literary and ideological position of subsequent generations of black women writers" (Smith, Introduction, xxvii). She does so by coming up with several innovations in the traditional slave/spiritual narrative form. By describing her book as the narrative not of a life but of *incidents* in a life, she introduces the notion of novelistic selection, and sets herself apart from most slave narrators, who tried to downplay their role in shaping their narratives (MacKethan, *Daughters of Time*, 28). Furthermore, by casting her story in terms of incidents, she is admitting that she is a convert, one who chooses to see her life as a process, a series of events that led to an eventual change in a specific direction. By creating the character of Linda Brent she achieves a transformation of herself into a literary subject, a sacred persona. Jacobs creates "Linda" in retrospect, and through the act of writing she expands the notion of freedom and takes her experience of conversion into a deeper level of meaning.

Through the creation of the character Linda Brent, Harriet Jacobs breaks down the "Jezebel" and "Mammy" stereotypes Deborah Gray

White identifies as having been assigned to slave women. White notes that although these are universal archetypes (correlative to the Eve–Virgin Mary dichotomy ascribed to women in general) to cast black women as either a wanton Jezebel or a righteous Mammy limited their developmental options. At the same time it excused miscegenation and sexual exploitation while endorsing service roles and offering up a character of moral steadfastness (61). Harriet Jacobs deconstructs both these roles by exercising her sexuality as a choice based on kindness and compassion, not lust, and by demonstrating the strength of her maternal love not through acquiescent service but by assuming the huge personal risk of escape.

Empowered by her determined will, wit, and intelligence, Jacobs demonstrates the aspect of an African trickster in this deconstruction. As Joanne Braxton points outs, all these qualities add up to "sass"— the habit of talking back. Sass (which bears a striking resemblance to the term "womanish" used by Alice Walker) was "an effective tool that allows 'Linda' to preserve her self-esteem and to increase the psychological distance between herself and the master . . . as a means of expressing resistance" (386). Yet when she composes her narrative, Jacobs is aware not only of the new kind of heroine she sets forth in her self-representation but also of the moral responsibility her actions entail. She even describes the narrative, while in the process of writing it, as in a "Chrysalis state" (Sterling, 81), a stage of metamorphosis. The book becomes for her literally symbolic of her own personal transformation and conversion, as well as representative of a public attempt to convert readers to a new understanding of black women. As she explains in a letter to Amy Post: "I have tried for the past two years to conquer [my stubborn pride] and I feel that God has helped me on. I never would consent to give my past life to any one without giving the whole truth. If it could help save another from my fate it would be selfish and unchristian in me to keep it back" (Sterling, 75).

As Anne Taves observes, "just as she decided to escape in order to save her daughter, so she decided to write to save others" (72). Her story is made meaningful not only by the particulars of her life and her innovative and resourceful writing, but because as a convert she feels the need to create order and meaning out of the chaos of her experience and because she needs to share her story for evangelical purposes. The narrative, as Sidonie Smith states, is an achievement of "spiritual transcendence over the brutalizing experience of slavery" (10). As she "moves back and forth between public debate and private confession, between the political and the personal" (Moody, 635), Harriet Jacobs both transmits and transforms sacred truths. She deconstructs metaphors of general human experience and then reconstructs them with individual experience, thereby reconciling her life with the public good and, finally, allowing a marginal voice to be heard.

Jacobs entered into the writing of her narrative in classic Christian sacrificial terms. Not only did she have to face the agonies of remembering, the actual composition itself was not easy for her. It took five years of writing in secret (since the husband of her employer was proslavery). All the while she was assuming a staggering load of chores in her job. She carefully crafted her ideas in a series of letters to abolitionist newspapers and then searched three years for a publisher, only to discover the narrative would not be published without Lydia Maria Child's testimony to its veracity.[18] To paraphrase Rita Dove, composing her narrative was Jacobs's way of filling the void left after conversion. It was hard work. She had to learn to forgive herself and to understand that "grace is a state of being, not an assault; and enlightenment, unlike epiphany, is neither brief nor particularly felicitous. . . . anyone who feels the need to connect the outside world with an interior presence must absorb the mysterious into the tangle of contradictions and longings that form each one of us. That's hard, ongoing work, and it never ends" (Dove, 174).

In 1867 Harriet Jacobs was finally able to take possession of her grandmother's home; upon returning she wrote to her friend Edna Dow Cheny of what it felt like to sit "under the old roof twelve feet from the spot where I suffered all the crushing weight of slavery" (MacKethan, *Daughters of Time*, 36). She found an attachment based on memories of people whom she had loved and from whom she had received so much help. Although "the change is so great I can hardly take it all in," she recognizes nevertheless the new identity she wrote into being and the completed self that now returns to "my old home."[19]

As the prodigal returned home, Jacobs's personal story takes on mythic proportions, describing a classic convert's journey to selfhood. Elizabeth Fox-Genovese demonstrates the mythic qualities of Jacobs's story in the following description: "Jacobs' narrative of her successful flight from slavery can be read as a journey or progress from her initial state of innocence; through the mires of her struggle against her social condition; to a prolonged period of ritual or mythic concealment; on to the flight itself; and finally to the state of knowledge that accompanies her ultimate acquisition of freedom" ("My Statue, My Self," 77). Harriet Jacobs continued an active life after writing the narrative, aiding in the abolitionist and later the Union cause because she was, as the Reverend Grimke remarked at her funeral, "the very soul of generosity" (Smyth, 37). Harriet Jacobs's life is circumscribed by symbolic symmetry. As her new life began on the Sabbath when she escaped from Auburn plantation, so too did it end on a Sunday morning in 1897. She was buried in Mount Auburn cemetery. When her life ended, "The very Spirit of the Lord was upon her," and she was remembered as "a woman of real, genuine piety, of deep heart-felt spirituality. Hers was no mere profession: she lived the life of a Christian" (Smyth, 38). Harriet Jacobs was eulogized in the same terms by which she was converted and converted others, in recognition of faith as a life lived, not a doctrine espoused. The inscription on her tombstone describes the qualities that empowered her being: "Patient in Tribulation / Fervent in Spirit / Serving the Lord."[20] Linda Brent represents a new voice with an ancient tone and through her Harriet Jacobs offers an example for black women and extends a challenge to white women when she invokes the words of Isaiah 32:9: "Rise up, ye women that are at ease! Hear my voice, ye careless daughters! Give Ear unto my speech."

Sojourner Truth (1797–1883)

What if I am a woman; is not the God of ancient times the God
of these modern days: Did he not raise up Deborah to be a
mother and a judge in Israel? Did not queen Esther save the
lives of the Jews? And Mary Magdalene first declared the
resurrection of Christ from the dead?

—Maria W. Stewart

The Narrative of Sojourner Truth, a Northern Slave, was first published
in Boston in 1850 and went through several printings before 1875,
when it was reissued with an addition from Sojourner Truth's "Book
of Life." This "Book of Life" was something Sojourner Truth actually
carried with her wherever she went, and it contained "the autographs
of many distinguished personages," as well as correspondence and
newspaper clippings pertaining to her life.[21] For a woman who was
unable to read or write, her devoted possession of such a book speaks
loudly of her understanding of the power of the word and the value
she placed on it. Yet Sojourner Truth was also astute enough to realize that the book of her life—her words—was only as important as
she proclaimed it to be. The book was little without her presence behind it and her promotion of it in the service of the causes about which
she cared. She decided to dictate her life story and have it printed as a
means to support her efforts as an activist and preacher. She would
offer the narrative for sale along with *carte-de-visite* portraits that proclaimed her motto: "I sell the shadow to support the substance."[22]
Unlike Harriet Jacobs, who creates the protagonist Linda Brent and
tells her story in the context of a traditional form, Sojourner Truth
declares herself as the subject and collaborates with an editor to as-
semble the facts of her life along with a collection of related materials,
and lets it all speak for itself.

Sojourner Truth's narrative is composed as many genres in one;
autobiography, biography, history, sermon, speech, and journalism are
all woven into a single discourse. The first part resembles a traditional
slave narrative, chronicling Sojourner Truth's experiences up to 1849,

when she cites her former master's repentance. The "Book of Life" chronicles her later activities as a preacher, abolitionist, and advocate for human rights through newspaper accounts, personal letters, and testimonies. The narrative does not follow a strictly chronological sequence but relates anecdotes of Sojourner Truth's life in order to emphasize specific points of her character or her beliefs and in this form resembles the approach of novelistic selection Harriet Jacobs employed when she cast her narrative in terms of "incidents."

Since the kind of verification Jean Fagan Yellin provided for Harriet Jacobs's text is not available for Sojourner Truth's narrative, some question will always remain as to how much editorial license was taken by her scribe, Olive Gilbert, and later by Frances Titus, the wife of a Battle Creek, Michigan, miller, who brought out later editions supplemented with the "Book of Life," correspondence, and memorial tributes.[23] Gilbert is known to history only for her collaboration with Sojourner Truth, whereas Frances Titus was a respected abolitionist and lifelong friend of Sojourner Truth. Titus managed Sojourner Truth's affairs in her later years and after her death continued the sale of the narrative to promote Truth's legend and to raise funds for a memorial in her honor. Carleton Mabee claims that both Gilbert and Titus were "gullible partisans" who were not careful in handling documents pertaining to Sojourner Truth (56). Mabee's frustration over the difficulty in authenticating the narrative is shared by many scholars. In her study of the rhetoric of Sojourner Truth and Frances E. W. Harper, Janey Weinhold Montgomery was able to verify the text of only four of the speeches found in the narrative by comparing them with eyewitness accounts and other historical sources.[24] But Lillian O'Connor, in her book *Pioneer Women Orators*, supports Montgomery's modest claims and more by asserting: "There is little reason to doubt the authenticity of texts. On the contrary, the prevailing public opinion against women speaking in public is almost certain evidence that all of the addresses were given by the individuals as named" (131).

The narrative section is written in the third person and reads like a biography, but it contains an abundance of direct quotations that, one assumes, given her own unique gift of language, must have been spoken by Sojourner Truth herself.[25] Also, the narrator makes an effort to cite times such as when Sojourner Truth "shudders . . . as she goes back in memory," or interjects a comment like "And now she says," indicating that what she is taking down is dictated directly by Sojourner Truth. Gilbert even poses questions directly to her in an effort to create authenticity. Much of what constitutes the narrative is iterated in the "Book of Life," as quotations from newspaper accounts of Sojourner Truth's lectures or interviews. The effect is of one listening in as Sojourner Truth reminisces on her life. The reader is powerfully drawn in to the story as it unfolds. Moreover, the arrangement of the details of her life, and the comments she chooses to interject, emphasize those things that were widely known by all to be central values in Sojourner Truth's life—her faith and her works in the service of abolition and human rights.

Still, problems attending the narrative's composition remain that may never be resolved. Although Sojourner Truth seems to be a popular figure for the writers of children's biographies, these works merely retrace the material given in the narrative. No scholarly biography on Sojourner Truth exists. According to Nell Irvin Painter, this is due to the fact that few autobiographical documents remain of this non-literate woman. Painter believes the narrative was "stylized and sanitized" and that the 128-page section of slave narrative represents stories Sojourner Truth told countless times on the lecture circuit "out of which by 1850 she had distilled nuance and affect" (13). Moreover, Painter continues, since Sojourner Truth was influenced by "divine rather than institutional realities" (13), and excluded from organizational loops of antislavery and feminist circles, she generated few documents and is rarely cited by others in their accounts or letters. Her remarks were often omitted from newspaper summaries or mentioned only briefly, as though her message were already well known. Because of this Painter refers to Sojourner Truth as a "phantom of the abolitionist movement" (13). All of these problems cause Painter to speculate on the potentially countless other women who may have been left out of traditional histories of the era due to lack of source materials and issues a call for a new approach to constructing biographies of nineteenth-century black women.

This new approach, however, must consider another issue that Sojourner Truth's narrative raises. In addition to the problems relating to the authentication or lack of source materials, there is a problem with the secondary sources relating to Sojourner Truth. More than one scholar has referred to the "myth" of Sojourner Truth and how this interferes with an actual reconstruction of her life and work. Carleton Mabee expresses the issue in the following way: "Much of the writing about her, in her time and ours, has been bent more toward making her into a myth for inspiration rather than toward documenting the reality of her life; and Sojourner herself sometimes contributed to the myth-making" (55). Bernice Lowe describes accounts of Sojourner Truth's life as an "intermingling of fact and fiction" (127), and Painter describes her as "famous for being famous" (3). Painter explores the difference between the historical figure and the legend of Sojourner Truth by examining in particular the article Harriet Beecher Stowe wrote for the *Atlantic Monthly* in 1863. This now-famous essay, "Sojourner Truth, The Libyan Sybil," was reprinted in the "Book of Life." Based on Stowe's memory of a meeting with Truth and cursory research (Stowe even claimed that Sojourner Truth had already died), this essay is seen by Painter as representative of how Truth was seen by her audience rather than as a source of information about her life. As such it reflects Truth as a mid-nineteenth-century persona, a black woman who appears "first and foremost as an exotic" (9). Stowe sees Truth primarily as a charismatic figure, an African native, and a character who embodies the "fervor of Ethiopia, wild, savage, hunted of all nations, but burning after God in her tropic heart" (161). What is significant to Painter is the way in which Stowe reduces Sojourner Truth to a type, to the status of a primitive. She notes that apart from Sojourner Truth, Harriet Tubman, who was also an untutored ex-slave, is the only black woman to have shared the notoriety that Truth enjoyed. Other educated black women like Frances E. W. Harper or Maria

Stewart, who were less resilient to being molded as exotic, were virtually unknown.

Because of the ways in which the Sojourner Truth legend was promulgated and distorted to serve the ideologies of white nineteenth-century Americans, her status declined among the black population at the turn of the century, and she was perceived, like Stowe's Uncle Tom, as an embarrassment to forward thinking Negroes. Sojourner Truth assumed a decidedly ambivalent status until the 1960s, when, as Painter claims: "her genius no longer complicated by a presentation that played into the hands of romantic racists, Sojourner Truth today symbolizes a self-made woman of extraordinary perception. She serves the interests of African Americans and feminists by demanding that feminist thought—so long the preserve of middle and upper class northern whites—include black women and poor women who have worked for other people all their days. Today Sojourner Truth is the embodiment of the need to reconstruct an American history that is sensitive simultaneously to race, class, and gender" (13).[26] Despite the problems that attend a characterization of Sojourner Truth, I think that her narrative can serve as an important document for describing the paradigm of conversion I am attempting to relate. Just as Harriet Jacobs's figure of Linda Brent can now be seen to have effectively deconstructed the images of "Jezebel" and "Mammy," so, too, can Sojourner Truth's life now be seen as deconstructing the image of an "exotic." Each character offers up a more benevolent image of nineteenth-century black women. Their lives underscore how their religious faith promoted their development into women who represent a more honest and authentic rendering of the sacred qualities inherent in black women.

Born into slavery in Ulster County, New York, Sojourner Truth cites her age with reference to the act of 1827 that freed all slaves in New York state who were twenty-eight years old and upward. More than six feet tall by adulthood, Sojourner Truth was the ninth child born into a slave family who spoke Dutch. When she was eleven her family was broken up, and by age thirteen she had been sold three times. Initially she believed slavery was "right and honorable" (33), but eventually she came to realize the "false position" both master and slave were in—each far too easily accepting the conditions of the status quo. She makes it clear, from her early recollections of life in slavery, that she does not attribute the cruelty inflicted upon slaves to any innate sin on the part of individuals but rather on the corporate sin of the slave system, described by Gilbert in the narrative as "that gigantic inconsistency, that inherited habit among slaveholders, of expecting a willing and intelligent obedience from the slave, because he is a MAN—at the same time every thing belonging to the soul-harrowing system does its best to crush the last vestige of a man within him; and when it *is* crushed, and often before, he is denied the comforts of life, on the plea that he knows neither the want nor the use of them and because he is considered to be little more or little less than a beast" (15). Early in her narrative Sojourner Truth establishes her belief in the redemption of humanity (including herself) and intimates by what witness her life will be shaped. Given the wisdom and the opportunity, a white man might elect not to be a slaveholder, and a slave will be able to retain the human image he or she loses during slavery.

As in Harriet Jacobs's story of Linda Brent, Sojourner Truth's narrative cites examples of early religious instruction, as when her mother, knowing she would soon be separated from her children, tells Isabella (Sojourner Truth's given name) and her brother of "the only Being that could effectually aid or protect them." "My children," she is quoted as saying, "there is a God who hears and sees you . . . and when you are beaten, or cruelly treated, or fall into any trouble, you must ask help of him and he will always hear and help you" (17).

She follows this by reassuring her children that wherever they are, the same stars and moon look down upon all of them, thereby strengthening the ties of family. These instructions were "held sacred by Isabella" and formed not only the core of her faith but also her narrative stance. As she comments: "And now . . . though it seems *curious,* I do not remember ever asking for anything but what I got. And I always received it as an answer to my prayers. When I got beaten I never knew it long enough before hand to pray; and I always thought if I only had *had* time to pray to God for help, I should have escaped the beating" (27). Sojourner Truth remembers her life from her perspective as a convert. Yet she admits to Gilbert that at one point in her life she also "looked upon her master as a *God;* and believed that he knew of and could see her at all times, even as God himself" (33).

Sojourner Truth's ability to discern the true nature of God (and herself) is not apparent in her early life, and all criticisms of the professed piety and "religious duty" of slaveholders are interjected by the narrator Gilbert, just as from time to time Harriet Jacobs would intrude into the narrative of Linda Brent in order to draw more general conclusions for the reader. For example, the occasion of Isabella's marriage is an opportunity for the narrator to comment on the practice of separating slave husbands and wives and to ask: "If there *can* be anything more diametrically opposed to the religion of Jesus, than the working of this soul-killing system—which is as truly sanctioned by the religion of America as are her ministers and churches—we wish to be shown where it can be found" (36). Also like Harriet Jacobs's work, Sojourner Truth's narrative repeatedly states that she cannot give all the details of her life in slavery, that her "long series of trials" must be passed over "in silence; some from motives of delicacy and others, because the relation of them might inflict undeserved pain on some now living" (30).[27]

Prior to her marriage to a slave named Thomas, Isabella had fallen in love with a slave named Robert. Because he was from another plantation, Robert's owner wished him to marry a slave woman on his plantation, thereby to increase his "property" through the procreation of children. Robert's master beat him severely for visiting Isabella, and she, like Linda Brent, was denied the opportunity to marry the man she had chosen. She subsequently agreed to an arranged match with Thomas.

Sojourner Truth had five children with Thomas and at the time "rejoiced in being permitted to be the instrument of increasing the property of her oppressors" (37). As with her professed belief that her master was like God and the system of slavery was honorable and noble, the narrator is attempting to shock the reader by presenting a mother who would gladly sacrifice her children to slavery. The point being emphasized is that Sojourner Truth, at the time in her life when she was being denied full humanity, does not act as a mother or a woman but responds as a "thing." Her personality, like her faith, is totally undeveloped, and the *real* Sojourner Truth appears in the narrative as a complete person only when she is converted.

Sojourner Truth's escape in 1826 comes before her conversion. Her master continually denied giving her her freedom, even though she was legally free by statute. He manipulated her loyalty to him and devised many rationalizations in order to make her stay, until finally "she concluded to take her freedom into her own hands, and seek her fortune in some other place" (41). Her plan to quit was grace from God, whom she credits for giving her the idea to leave early one morning before people were awake. "'Yes,' said she, fervently, 'that's a good thought! Thank you, God, for *that* thought!' So, receiving it as coming direct from God, she acted upon it" (41) and left at dawn with her infant daughter and prayed to God for help. As always for Sojourner Truth, her prayers lead directly to answers and she finds safe haven with a family of Quakers. The Van Wageners were devout Christians who abhorred slavery. When Isabella's master, Dumont, came looking for her, they agreed to purchase her from him and immediately emancipated her. Mr. Van Wagener told Isabella: "There is but *one* master, and He who is *your* master is *my* master" (43).

Up to this point in the narrative, Sojourner Truth's life had followed a pattern of need followed by prayer followed by blessing. The narrator, in establishing this pattern, is laying the groundwork for a discussion of Isabella's conversion. Even after her escape she is still Isabella and not Sojourner Truth. To become Sojourner she needed an experience of conversion, a radical alteration of her theology of "ask and it will be given." She needs to go beyond her own needs and realize that her deliverance from slavery was not enough, that her faith demanded more of her and that she was responsible to the God who answered her prayers with blessings. As Esther Terry points out, the experiences of being treated as an equal in God's sight by her Quaker friends, the Van Wageners, increased Isabella's feelings of self-worth and prepared her for her religious conversion (434).

Under the heading "Isabella's Religious Experience," the narrator informs the reader that she is turning from "the outward and temporal to the inward and spiritual life of our subject" (58). Sojourner Truth is credited with a "naturally powerful mind" that, left "almost entirely to its own workings, and the chance influences it met on its way," awakens to "that divine light" (59). The narrator is attempting to iterate the same point made early on that "truth and error [are] strangely commingled," that slavery can either defeat both black and white or serve as a catalyst for redemption. What effects the choice is faith and an understanding of the true nature of God. As demonstrated before, the faith Sojourner Truth received from her mother was honest but innocent and did not account for all the complexities a life in slavery inflicted on one's soul. Sojourner reflexively prayed as she was taught and clung to naive notions such as God's recording all her actions in a great book (just as her master kept a record) and his being able to hear her only if she uttered her prayers aloud.

She recalls how she would retreat to a "rural sanctuary" in order that she could present her petitions, speaking very loudly in order to be more easily heard. Here, as Gilbert explains, she "talked to God as familiarly as if he had been a creature like herself, and demanded with little expenditure of reverence or fear, a supply of all her more pressing wants, and at times her demands approached very near to commands. She felt as if God was under obligation to her, much more than she was to him. He seemed to her benighted vision in some manner bound to do her bidding" (61). As Corrine Brown Galvin notes, Sojourner Truth's early contact with God was based on a perception of him as a "great man" located "high in the sky" with whom she had informal chats, constantly punctuated with inquiring phrases such as "Think I wouldn't God?" or "Do you think that's right, God?" Although she related her troubles to God she also commanded his assistance and "bargained in terms of serving Him if He granted her wishes, and assumed that He was more obligated to her than she was to Him" (8).

Initially one sees Sojourner Truth demanding recognition from God, trying to strike deals with him by promising that if he did certain things for her, she would be good. She equated goodness with reward and became frustrated when she could not keep up her part of the contract. "She now began to excuse herself, by telling God she could not be good in her present circumstances; but if he would give her a new place, and a good master and mistress, she could and would be good" (61–62). Yet when she receives these things, when she could exclaim, "everything there was so pleasant, and kind, and good, and all so comfortable; enough of everything; indeed, it was beautiful!" then "God was entirely forgotten" (62). She recalls how she thought she did not need God because she had no troubles, and her theology instructed her that God was known to her only "as a help in trouble."

Sojourner Truth becomes so confused, she remembers her life with her former master ("looked back into Egypt," as she phrases it) as pleasant and decides to return for a holiday, seeking some excitement to contrast with her currently peaceful life. Yet just as she is to enter the carriage with her former master, she recalls, "God revealed himself to her, with all the suddenness of a flash of lightning, showing her, 'in the twinkling of an eye, that he was all over' . . . and that there was no place where God was not" (65). She then becomes conscious of having forgotten God and is overwhelmed with thoughts of her unfulfilled promises to God, and she "[shrinks] back aghast from the 'awful look' of Him whom she had formerly talked to, as if he had been a being like herself" (65). While she is in this state her former master leaves without her; Sojourner Truth contemplates how she can ever speak to God again, when "a space seemed opening between her and God, and she felt that if some one, who was worthy in the sight of heaven, would but plead for her in their own name, and not let God know it came from *her*, who was so unworthy" (66), then God might grant her petitions.

Sojourner Truth's unworthiness stemmed from the "sin" charac-teristic of oppressed people, one of not exercising their full humanity. Her disregard of God in happiness was but another example of the same attitude that before allowed her to rejoice in children for the profit they would bring her master. She was wholly unable to discrimi-nate between divine power and human power, and thus was unable to locate the original source of blessings in God or of sufferings in the system of slavery.

She achieves her understanding of her own humanity and of God's divinity in the traditional theological form of incarnation: when she identifies Jesus as her friend who intervenes between her and God and allows her to reestablish that relationship. Previously, as she admits, she had heard of Jesus but thought of him as an eminent man, "like a Washington or a Lafayette" (67), but through this personal experi-ence of conversion she sees Jesus as the link between her humanity and God's divinity, thereby diminishing the "terror" an all-powerful God represented to her. In equating her master with God it is no won-der that she perceived him as something fearful, and also not worthy of full respect; but with her understanding of the presence of Jesus in her life—godliness in human form—she is able to personalize God, to reconcile herself to him and in the process to acknowledge her full hu-manity. She does so by developing her own theology based on her expe-rience of Jesus as "a friend, standing between me and God, through whom love flowed as a fountain" (69), who represented the Creator upon his return to earth and with whom a personal union provided the only possibility of distinguishing human from animal. Until she recognized God in flesh she could not perceive the sacred qualities inherent in her own identity. But her religious conversion "triggered a profound psychological reorientation" and initiated "the growth of authentic, individually authorized selfhood" (Andrews, *Sisters of the Spirit*, 16).

Following this account of her conversion the narrative veers off in many directions, giving accounts of the lives of Sojourner Truth's chil-dren and several acquaintances, telling of the various places in which she lived and worshipped. It is not until forty pages into the narrative, when the story of Sojourner Truth's attempt to retrieve her son Peter is related, that the narrator demonstrates for the first time the tenacity and strength commonly associated with the character of Sojourner Truth. She takes on legal courts and bureaucratic systems and enlists the help of sympathetic acquaintances in order to void the illegal sale of her son. But she also fears that others wearied of her pleas for help and that "God wearied also" (50). She turns to Jesus as an intercessor, thinking that if "Jesus could but be induced to plead for her in the present trial, God would listen to *him,* though he wearied of her" (50). Her prayer for help sent up through Jesus is answered, and her son is returned to her. Sojourner Truth was one of the first black women to win a lawsuit in the United States.

She moves with Peter to New York City, hoping to earn more wages and find some training for Peter to secure good employment for him. Here she encounters segregated churches when she looks for somewhere to worship and refuses to attend them, selecting to worship instead at the all-black Zion Africa Church where she first begins testifying in public. While in New York she also undertakes charity work, volunteering at Magdalene Asylum, a shelter for homeless women, where she teaches the clients domestic skills that will enable them to gain employment.

The narrative returns, however, to further clarify Sojourner Truth's faith, such as when she derides Pentecostals and doubts "much whether God had anything to do with such worship" (87). It also explores her passing infatuation with the preachings of Robert Matthews (or Matthias, as he was called), as she believes for a time that "God had sent him to set up the kingdom" (91). Under his influence Sojourner Truth begins periods of fasting in order to achieve an inward lightness of spirit but soon discerns that Matthias is a charlatan more interested in material than spiritual matters. Having given all her money to Matthias and his commune, Sojourner Truth is swindled out of her savings and the community collapses in scandal. Moreover, newspaper accounts of the incident cite her as a witch, and she enlists the help of a reporter named Gilbert Vale to set the record straight. Vale published

"The Narrative of Isabella or Fanaticism: Its Source and Influence," which partially vindicated her. But Sojourner Truth persisted by filing a lawsuit against the papers that had slandered her and won an award for damages.

Following this experience she begins to rely more on her own spiritual intuitions and instincts. She develops a revulsion toward money and property and receives a call to preach. Collecting but a few possessions, she sets off for travels in the East because "the Spirit calls me there and I must go" (110). It is at this point that she ceases to be Isabella when she takes a new name—a "name with a handle"—and becomes Sojourner Truth, a complete woman dedicated to lecturing and "testifying of the hope that was in her" (101). Now authorized by God, Sojourner Truth is empowered and increasingly listens to and acts upon her own intuitions. Sojourner Truth comes to see herself in the tradition of the biblical prophets and sustains herself by traveling and preaching for room and board.

She refines her own personal theology even more in ecumenical terms that judged "no preference for one sect more than another" (105), as long as they evidenced faith in God, but admitted that she "never could find out that the rich had any religion" (103). She undertakes to learn the Scriptures better (insisting that she hear them without comment, quickly realizing that children were better prepared for this task than adults) and muses on the book of Genesis, wondering why God needed the nights to rest, stopping herself before she becomes blasphemous by recognizing that God created rest for man, not for himself. The teachings of the Bible were of interest to her as a source of comparison so that she might evaluate them in terms corresponding to the "witness within," seeking what James Cone identified in black religion as an ongoing attempt to relate biblical truths to reality. As Gilbert describes it, Sojourner Truth came to the conclusion that "the spirit of truth spoke in those records but that the recorders of those truths had intermingled with them ideas and suppositions of their own" (109). Sojourner Truth establishes her independence of character and her ability to find meaning in religion not as it is traditionally cast but as it bears significance on the facts of her own experience. Her experience of conversion—in which she confronted the weakness of her own identity—brought her back to an African-American sensibility that did not distinguish sacred from profane and taught her that God "was to be worshipped at all times and in all places; and one portion of time never seemed to her more holy than another" (107–8).

The remaining parts of the narrative contain references to Sojourner Truth's sermons and speeches, chronicling in a rather haphazard way her travels and the ways in which she confronts the issues of her time. With each speech her theology becomes more explicit and her tone more assertive, such as when she insists that she will not escape the fires of this world because Jesus will "walk with me. . . . Do you tell me that God's children *can't stand fire?* . . . It is *absurd* to think so!" (112). The narrator emphasizes how Sojourner Truth became a popular speaker who was prepared for any confrontation, so confident was she in her message and her belief that "perfect love casteth out fear" (122). The narrative concludes with Sojourner Truth citing the redemption of her master who "turned to a brother" and the hope that "all slaveholders may partake of his spirit" (125).

What follows the narrative is her "Book of Life." It has a certain narrative sequence provided by a geographical arrangement of Sojourner Truth's career as a lecturer. It features memorable moments and people she encounters in her work in various states and includes correspondence and newspaper accounts that relate particulars of each event. Among the chosen events are her trip to Washington, D.C., to speak to Congress and her speech before the Women's Rights Convention in Akron, Ohio. Having established a reputation in abolitionist circles in Northampton, Massachusetts, where she lectured for William Lloyd Garrison's American Anti-Slavery Society, Sojourner Truth began taking on other issues, including those of women's rights and later the Union cause and the needs and rights of free blacks. These episodes describe the development of Sojourner Truth's identity as she refines her faith through her mission and the needs she determines she must address. It is through these speeches that one encounters the Sojourner Truth that is best known—the convert—and reading them one has no indication that she was once a passive slave who blindly accepted the system into which she was born. Yet set in the context of her life they represent a woman who, even once she was converted, did not maintain a static spiritual identity but continued to challenge and develop her faith in God, humanity, and herself. Sojourner Truth's struggle with God during her conversion, William Andrews points out, is a typical trope in African-American spiritual narratives (*Sisters of the Spirit*, viii). The struggle is what strengthened African-American women and convinced them they were able to defend themselves against hostility and censure.

The most memorable speech, of course, is Sojourner Truth's famous "Ain't I a Woman" speech, addressed in 1851 to the Women's Rights Convention in Akron, Ohio. In it she recasts the traditional Christian faith to which she has been converted into explicitly feminist terms, appealing to biblical and historical precedents. Sojourner Truth was almost denied the opportunity to speak at the convention until Frances Gage intervened. Unlike anyone before her, Sojourner Truth linked the struggle over racism with gender liberation. Her comments are motivated by a minister's claim that men have superior rights and privileges because of superior intellect and because of the manhood of Christ. Sojourner displays a particularly feminine superior intellect when she challenges that patriarchal claim on several counts, citing as authority not only her own experience but her theological understanding of Scripture. To the charge that women need men to help them into carriages and over ditches, Sojourner responds with a litany of contradictions. Each time she challenges the traditional role of woman by citing her own experience as one who was never helped into carriages, has plowed and planted and harvested as well as any man, has endured beatings and borne children, ending every example with the rhetorical question: "Ain't I a woman?"

To the charge that women are intellectually inferior to men, Sojourner responds, "What's that got to do with women's rights or niggers' rights? If my cup won't hold but a pint and yours holds a quart, wouldn't you be mean not to let me have my little half-measure full?" (134). By asserting that human rights are every person's birthright regardless of their intellect or station in life, Sojourner Truth is expressing her belief in the democracy of souls before God. Although in this speech she may not challenge directly the assumption that women and blacks possess inferior minds, she does not need to because her very performance as a black woman stands as evidence of the falsehood of this assumption. Finally, to the charge that women cannot have rights as a man because Christ was not a woman, Sojourner exclaims, "Where did your Christ come from? From God and a woman. Man had nothing to do with him" (134–35). She follows up this feminist deconstruction of patriarchal theology by taking up the defense of Eve, asserting that "if the first woman God ever made was strong enough to turn the world upside down, all alone, these together ought to be able to turn it back and get it right side up again, and now they is asking to do it, the men better let them" (135).

As Karlyn Kohrs Campbell demonstrates, this entire speech is framed to refute stereotypes and misconceptions. Her responses "illustrate the power of enactment, the force of metaphor, and the use of theology to respond to biblical justifications for women's inferior position" (435). For Sojourner Truth it was not enough to speak, one had also to act, and the purpose of her lectures was to inspire right action, whatever it took. Once, as a letter relates, Sojourner Truth was accused by a man attending her lecture of being a man because her voice was so low and her manner so forthright. In vindication of herself, she bared a breast that had "suckled many a white babe," immediately defusing those who sought to undermine her message with a personal affront. As Mary Burgher points out, in the very act of describing the realities of her own life, Sojourner Truth establishes new standards for women: they can command great authority and still be compassionate; they can agitate and yet be gentle. Sojourner Truth, as Burgher continues, "creates vivid images of herself as a woman who views physical strength and native intelligence as life-sustaining forces and resilience and moral courage as invaluable tools of progress and freedom, however unfeminine they might make one appear to others" (109).

Nothing, it seemed, was beyond her ken. Despite her limited formal education, Sojourner Truth familiarized herself with everything that was crucial to her cause, and in her lectures and interviews she represented the African-American sensibility that does not distinguish politics from religion. In one brilliant display of this sensibility she recounts a conversation she had with God in a wheat pasture. That year the weevil had destroyed thousands of acres of wheat, and ruminating on this she asks God: "What is the matter with this wheat? and he says to me, 'Sojourner, there is a little weasel in it.' Now I hear talking about the Constitution and the rights of man. I come up and I take hold of this Constitution. It looks *mighty big*, and I feel for *my* rights, but there ain't any there. Then I say, God, what *ails* this Constitution? He says to me, 'Sojourner, there is a little weasel in it'" (147).

In the course of her lecturing career, Sojourner Truth is introduced to many famous people whom she treats no differently from anyone else, always confident in who she is and what her witness is. Indeed, Esther Terry remarks on how rarely scholars deal with "the very personality of the woman herself—defying as she does all attempts at refinement and containment" (425). Aware of her limitations, Sojourner Truth relies on what she knows best, her own experience. When the esteemed Reverend Beecher inquires about the text of her sermons she replies that she cannot read the Bible but that does not matter because she has "just one text to preach from and I always preach from this one. *My* text is 'When I FOUND Jesus!'" (154). After conversion, Sojourner Truth's life is always oriented around this experience, and she recounts it to anyone who will listen, each time tailoring her story to suit her audience or the particular point she wants to make, be it to a politician who needs instruction on human rights or a preacher who needs clarification as to the workings of God. Her mission is reflected in her name: "I wasn't going to keep nothing of Egypt on me, and so I went to the Lord and asked him to give me a new name. And the Lord gave me Sojourner, because I was to travel up and down the land, showing the people their sins, an' being a sign unto them. Afterward I told the Lord I wanted another name, because everybody else had two names; and the Lord gave me Truth, because I was to declare the truth to the people" (164). A new naming of herself is a symbolic expression of her conversion, articulating the new orientation to herself and to the world that she achieved through experiencing the powers of being, God's being and her own. The high value she placed on her own inner experience maintained her individuality. Carleton Mabee suggests also that her reliance on her own personal religious experience that reinforced her inwardness may have lent itself to fostering in her a bit of contempt for "intellectual learning and refinement" and interfered with any attempt on her part to gain skills of literacy (76).

Mabee goes on to demonstrate how Sojourner Truth's illiteracy may even have functioned to set her apart from other orators through her claims to a knowledge that they could not acquire. When she told her audiences, "I tell you I can't read a book but I can read the people," or "You read books, God Himself talks to me," Sojourner Truth set herself "up into a high pulpit," and in effect diffused any potential criticism that might be leveled against her for her lack of education (71).

I choose to think that Sojourner Truth's lack of literacy skills was, if not a form of piety, a kind of testimony to how she perceived her role and where she should concentrate her efforts. More than once the narrative mentions the difficulty she had in learning English, and other sources make references to futile attempts on her part to learn to read and write. As occupied and committed as she was to the advancement of her causes and the propagation of the gospel, it is likely Sojourner Truth simply chose not to devote the time to learning literacy skills and that in doing such she betrayed no lack of confidence or insecurity about her abilities but simply chose to exercise her talents in other forms she valued and in which she excelled. Her authority came from a source that did not depend on her being able to read or write, and her development out of an oral culture prepared her for her career as an orator. Even her preference for selling photographs of herself indicated a kind of figural imagination she found expressive. Finally, in response to Mabee's observation that even as she advanced in age and association with people Sojourner Truth "did not usually seem to choose to use more correct English. If anything, she seemed to make her speech less grammatical, more folksy, more in black dialect" (72), I would speculate that Sojourner Truth's use of dialect was a conscious attempt on her part to identify with black culture and to use her stature to grant black folk speech and images a measure of validity they might otherwise not have received, a strategy Zora Neale Hurston later employed in her speaking and writing.

For Sojourner Truth was a pioneer in her actions as much as in her words. She knew that words *do* things and that actions also *say* things. Whereas Harriet Jacobs established new standards of judgment for black women through her writing techniques, Sojourner Truth did so by her presence. She legitimized the causes for which she stood. Yet she never stopped taking risks, either. In one memorable scene she acted as a precursor to Rosa Parks by insisting that she be allowed to ride on a segregated streetcar, later suing the conductor for assault and battery and successfully having him removed from his job (184–85). All her works, however, were credited to divine revelation and her belief that she was an inheritor of the kingdom of God and therefore responsible to do God's work. She defined herself as an instrument of God's purpose and attributed her presence in the public sphere not to egotism or ambition but to Providence. Sojourner Truth, as Marilyn Richardson points out, may have been famous, but women like her were not atypical. She was but the most celebrated example of many women who saw themselves as inheritors of a black female tradition of activism founded on a commitment to religious faith, human rights, and women's struggles (Andrews, *Sisters of the Spirit*, viii).

Sojourner Truth contributed her talents to an astonishing array of activities and remained active well into her seventies. She worked for the Union war effort at the Freedman's Bureau and as a nurse for wounded soldiers; she lobbied tirelessly for the rights of freed blacks after the Civil War and attempted to persuade Congress to set aside part of the western territories for black settlement. She preached, always and anywhere, turning her public and civic duties into an expression of her duty as a Christian.

At a public meeting in Boston, Sojourner Truth joined a crowd gathered to hear Frederick Douglass, who went on at length about the irredeemability of white people, calling blacks to arms to redeem themselves because they could depend on help from no other source. Although in her narrative she claims, "I am a self-made woman" (v), she was also a woman who felt she owed her very sense of entitlement and self-worth to God. Douglass's notion that God had no place in the abolitionist struggle—her struggle—she took as a personal confrontation. So, after Douglass finished, Sojourner Truth stood and loudly inquired, "Frederick, *is God Dead?*" (168). These words are also engraved on Sojourner Truth's headstone, erected years after her death by devoted friends in Battle Creek, Michigan, on the edge of the western territory she sought to claim for her people. The inscription stands as testimony for the life of a woman who, once converted to her own power through God, believed nothing was impossible. As bell hooks observes, Sojourner Truth's "emancipatory politics emerged from her religious faith"; therefore, her name is "rooted in her religious faith, that the truth she saw herself seeking was the truth and Oneness with God and her sense that, by choosing God she was choosing to serve in the emancipation struggle of black people" (hooks and West, 51). Sojourner Truth sacralized her identity and found an especially bold form of self-authorization when she accepted a call to preach from God.

Rebecca Cox Jackson (1795-1871)

i found god in myself
& i loved her
i loved her fiercely
—Ntozake Shange

Unlike Harriet Jacobs and Sojourner Truth, who were born into slavery, Rebecca Cox Jackson was born a free Northern black woman. Her conversion did not involve an escape from the institution of slavery but did effect for her a subtler form of escape from the settled and traditional roles of marriage and motherhood that were assigned to women in the nineteenth century. Her religious experience led her away from her husband and family and set her off on what was to become a forty-year public career, first as a preacher and later as the founder of a black Shaker community where she lived the Shaker belief that "the basis and beginning of all knowledge is a consciousness of our being" (F. W. Evans, v).

Her autobiographical writings do not form a narrative story but are selections from a private journal she kept from 1830 to 1864. Written in phonetic spelling, unpunctuated and unparagraphed, the autobiography contains few references to external events or historical episodes. Unlike the works of Harriet Jacobs and Sojourner Truth, who specifically related their life stories in the service of an abolitionist agenda and whose works were read in their lifetimes, Rebecca Jackson's writings appeared in print for the first time in 1981 when Jean McMahon Humez meticulously collected, edited, and annotated all extant variants of Jackson's writings in a volume called *Gifts of Power*. Although still not widely read or discussed in scholarly literature, Jackson's writings deserve a place alongside the writings of female mystics such as Juliana of Norwich and Saint Teresa of Avila. Obviously, her Shaker friends believed them to be extraordinary because upon her death her writings were saved and carefully edited by Shaker elder Alonzo G. Hollister, who later included long passages from Rebecca Jackson's autobiography in his own (Sasson, 86).

An interesting feature of Jackson's autobiography (which is the only known black Shaker narrative), discussed by Diane Sasson in her book on Shaker narratives, is the multiple strains of influence that determine its unique style. Sasson notes that "because she portrays her personal experience both in the language of early nineteenth-century black Protestantism and mid-nineteenth-century Shakerism, the sources of Rebecca Jackson's religious idiom are complex" (158). Shaker narratives, in one sense, resemble the pattern of call and response found in African-American literature because although Shakers left an abundance of documents preserving their personal experience, they reinterpret them throughout the nineteenth century and present "modifications and innovations in response to the changing concerns of the community of believers" (Sasson, x). Yet there are dimensions to Jackson's autobiography that exceed anything found in Shaker documents of the same period. Shakers looked within their own culture for narrative precedents, while Jackson maintained a distinct black voice, despite her obvious attempts to present her entire life as consistent with Shaker theology. She was exceptionally gifted in her creative imagination and could synthesize material from Shaker doctrine and other religious traditions.

Yet she reveals an almost modern consciousness in her experience of tension between two sets of values—those of the outer, ordinary world and those of the inner, spiritual world. As Sasson remarks, "Jackson's narrative expresses an ongoing conflict between God's will, expressed in direct revelation, and the will of men, including men and women of the Shaker community" (215). Jackson's inner world of vision does not always coincide with its embodiment in the Shaker community. Her writings share a quality common to the narratives of both Sojourner Truth and Harriet Jacobs because they are "centrally concerned with how religious vision and ecstatic experience functioned for her and other women of her time as a source of personal power, enabling them to make radical change in the outward circumstances of their lives" (Humez, 1). Thus, as James H. Evans, Jr., explains, "Jackson's text is the progeny of the slave conversion narrative and the Shaker search for self-knowledge" (*Spiritual Empowerment*, 58).

Jackson's visions and her private, interior experiences form the bulk of her writings. She barely mentions her life prior to conversion; it is difficult to reconstruct a biographical sketch of her life from the autobiography alone. Unlike Sojourner Truth and Harriet Jacobs, in whose very lives and actions the sacralization of identity is expressed, Jackson's actual life was almost incidental to her visions. It is her "gifts of power," her visionary capacity, that sacralize her identity. Jackson's ambition to transcribe the details of her spiritual life rested on a profound conviction that she was a chosen instrument for revealing the will of God. Her writings, she believed, would express divine purpose because she saw herself as "only a pen in His hand" (107). As Humez points out, "in an apparent paradox familiar in religious thought, Jackson's denial of the importance of her individual self enabled her to make the strongest possible assertion of the power and reality of her inner sources of strength and knowledge" (Humez, 2). Through her visions Jackson had access to a unique source of knowledge that she used for her own edification and personal development. Although she was not a slave like Sojourner Truth and Harriet Jacobs, as a black woman Jackson was denied usual forms of attaining status, such as schooling or wealth, and her religious life offered her another kind of freedom. Her conversion signaled her break from the restricting definitions of womanhood even her own religious sect assigned her and made clear to her "the world of the Spirit, of holiness, and of freedom" (Eliade, *The Two and the One,* 77).

Her conversion, therefore, "set up a direct relation to God's authority that allowed [her] to denigrate or bypass man's authority—to defy man—for God" (Cott, "Young Women," 21). Her visions are so vivid and so overtake her writings that she virtually excludes all other things in her life. Her commitment to a life of vision was no less intense than Sojourner Truth's commitment to a life of activism. Yet however satisfying and sustaining her private life of vision, she did seek community. She had an intimate woman friend, Rebecca Perot, with whom she shared her life, and she made many efforts to find a spiritual family—to find holiness embodied in communal relationships and institutions.

Jackson claims to have been wholly illiterate but to have prayed for and received the "gift" of literacy in her search for autonomy after her conversion. This was a special blessing since it enabled her to read the Bible for herself and freed her from what Humez calls the "editorial tyranny of her more privileged" brother (Humez, 19). Just as Sojourner Truth found adults unreliable people to read the Bible to her (she preferred children, who would refrain from editorializing), Jackson relates how her brother would rewrite her letters. He also chastised her for complaining about his efforts. This hurt her deeply until "these words were spoken in my heart, 'Be faithful, and the time shall come when you can write'" (107). Subsequently, God put a thought in her head (as he had often done with Sojourner Truth) and she wondered, "Who learned the first man on earth? Why, God." At this point she picks up her Bible, opens it up, and prays to God that, if it is his will, she might be able to read: "And when I looked on the word, I began to read. And when I found I was reading, I was frightened— then I could not read one word. I closed my eyes again in prayer and then opened my eyes and began to read. So I done, until I read the chapter" (108).

Her brother wounds her again by disbelieving her ability to read until she proves it. She concludes her memory of receiving this ability by exclaiming, "Oh, how thankful I feel for this unspeakable gift of Almighty God to me! Oh, may I make good use of it all the days of my life!" (108). Literacy gave her independent access to past revelations that appeared in Scripture, enabling her to be an interpreter in her own right and to defend her own ideas and doctrines against attacks by hostile clergy. Jackson, like her contemporary black ex-slave writers, gives prominent place in her text to her own literacy training, which, although divinely inspired, aligns her with a tradition of representing the word with power.

The skill of literacy, combined with her visionary capacities, set up for Jackson a life in which "God was daily and hourly showing me things which I never before was nor heard, and I thought I would keep them to myself. But before I was aware, I would be speaking it or mentioning it in prayer, in praising God for His goodness and entreating them never to stop until they gained these heavenly things" (88). As important as the actual gift of literacy was for her, James

Evans emphasizes that "the quest for literacy in Jackson's narrative is determined by the kind of ignorance which she faces" (Evans, *Spiritual Empowerment,* 64), spiritual illiteracy always being her foremost concern because she believed the ultimate literacy and fount of knowledge was spiritual in origin and books were secondary. Rebecca Jackson, as Alice Walker says, "was taught to read and write by the spirit within her" (MG, 73), a process in which she affirmed not only the sacrality of her own being but the ultimate source of her sacrality. As for Sojourner Truth, her inner knowledge was always the dominant source of her authority.

At the time her autobiography opens, in 1830, Jackson is a married seamstress living with her husband in Philadelphia at the home of her brother, Joseph Cox, an A.M.E. preacher. Philadelphia was the site of the emergence of the black church in the North. In 1789 Richard Allen and Absalom Jones left St. George's Methodist Episcopal Church in response to the racist policies of that congregation, and Allen later founded the African Methodist Episcopal church. Because Joseph was a widower, Rebecca had the responsibilities for caring for the house and her brother's children. Joseph was an important influence in Rebecca's life, as was the church to which he belonged. Although she eventually left the A.M.E. church for the Shaker faith, "the religious sensibility which resided in that church provided a fund for her literary imagination as well as a foil for her emergent self" (Evans, *Spiritual Empowerment,* 58). As Humez points out in her introduction, there was a good deal of racial unrest in Philadelphia at this time, but Jackson's own life seemed relatively safe and comfortable. On the first page of her journal Rebecca recounts how in 1830, during a severe thunderstorm, she (who had previously feared thunder and lightning) experienced conversion. As she tells it:

> I heard it said to me "This day thy soul is required of thee," and all my
> sins from my childhood rushed into my mind like an over swelling tide,
> and I expected every clap of thunder to launch my soul at the bar of
> God with all my sins that I had ever done. . . . My sins like a mountain

reached to the skies, black as sack cloth of hair and the heavens was as brass against my prayers and everything above my head was of one solid blackness. Then, the old gave way to the new; . . . the cloud bursted, the heavens was clear, and the mountain was gone. My spirit was light, my heart was filled with love for God and all mankind. And the lightning, which was a moment ago the messenger of death, was now the messenger of peace, joy, and consolation. (71–72)

These images of storms, thunder, and lightning recur throughout Jackson's narrative, recalling Old Testament biblical imagery where God manifests power through nature. Moreover, as Diane Sasson notes, the storm serves as a metaphor for Jackson's internal condition and her need for salvation. Tracing these images throughout the autobiography, Sasson sees thunder as representing God's judgment and lightning his grace. Jackson never feared storms after this experience but found them to be reminders of her covenant with God and the necessity to obey her inner voice (Sasson, 163–65).[28]

Jackson's conversion experience transformed her from a self-abnegating woman who feels only the terror of a punishing God into an increasingly assertive woman whose obedience to the guidance of her inner spirit gave her permission to defy the authority of her upbringing and her society. At this moment of divine judgment Rebecca remarks that she had "no language to describe my feeling" (72), just as she describes her being given the ability to read as "unspeakable." The immediate effect of her encounter with the inner voice results, therefore, in a kind of illiteracy. She intimates why she relied on experiences of visions to instruct her. Her thought processes and her language operate symbolically, not discursively, for the primary literacy she seeks is spiritual. Her visions "are always stories of her personal empowerment and growth toward autonomy against the restrictions of her society" (Reuther, *Womanguides,* 141).

During a revival the following year, Rebecca received the gift of sanctification—the blessing of perfect love that some sects believed must follow conversion to assure higher experiences of divine grace—

and began preaching in the homes of fellow believers. During her sanctification experience she had a revelation that made her see "for the first time what the sin of the fall of man was," and she wondered "how to return home to my husband again" (76–77). She began practicing celibacy even before she was aware of the Shaker doctrine on the subject. Her practice and advocacy of celibacy was yet another example of her attempt to gain autonomy and control over her own self, and to preserve the sacred qualities within herself so that she might be a better instrument to receive spiritual instruction. As her account of "The Dream in the Garden" shows, when Jackson becomes aware of her sinful nature, she also becomes aware of the power of God and how her reception of that power gives her individual power: "Faith and prayer are my weapons of war. . . . This garden was my fallen nature. These berries was the fruit on which my carnal propensities subsisted. My person was my soul. My picking was my soul taking an active part in all its pleasures" (94). She eventually emerges from the garden unscathed, indicating not only that she has overcome her carnal nature but that she is reconciled to her spiritual nature—the source of all her self-empowerment.

She continued to practice celibacy and other ascetic rituals (such as fasting) for a year while living with her husband and brother, and eventually realized that her conversion had so radically changed her that she could not remain with them. "I had started to go to the promised land, and I wanted husband, brother, and all the world to go with me, but my mind was made up to stop for none" (87). She acquired a "gift of foresight" that enabled her to know what her husband was going to do, allowing her the opportunity to protect herself from his rage, for "if I had not had the gift of foresight given to me at the beginning, I must have fell in death by his hands" (145). Her conversion, therefore, enabled her to win a crucial form of independence from her husband as well as from her brother. Her gift of foresight, her visions, and her "secret and continual prayer" were her "wall of defense" (82) against the demands of a patriarchal society.

At this point Jackson, released from her "bondage" to her husband, has a vision of a mystical marriage to Christ (148–49) and in a theme Sasson finds rare in Shaker literature, expresses an "unassailable conviction that God prepared her for an extraordinary mission" (Sasson, 169). She began making extensive preaching tours, often offending male clergy who thought that she was acting improperly and that her actions were destructive to the mission of established churches. They were particularly resistant to her preaching celibacy and her insistence that humans could attain salvation through grace and deliberate resistance. Most church members believed they could be saved only by "the merits of Christ" and not by their deeds. But Jackson, in an unusual display of self-assertion for a nineteenth-century black woman, "disputed this as an evasion of personal responsibility to struggle for individual righteousness" (McKay, "Nineteenth-Century Black Women's Spiritual Autobiographies," 149). Her reading of the book of James convinced her of the futility of faith without works. In 1837 she was accused of heresy, whereupon she demanded a formal, interdenominational trial at which she alone would defend herself: "I wish nobody to speak in my behalf. If I am wrong, let me be righted by the Spirit and by the Scriptures" (151). She was refused the trial, and this led to an irrevocable break between Rebecca and her brother and the A.M.E. faith of her upbringing, separating her "further from the professed Christian world," even as she came "closer to the Lord" (87). For even though "religious laws and bureaucracies can dictate that only men shall be priests . . . the gods choose whom they will" (Falk and Gross, 39).

Her visionary experiences provided her the vindication she needed, and she confidently progressed without the support of church, husband, brother, or any other customary authority. Moreover, she soon found within herself another source of authority—a kindly, fatherly, instructor figure who appeared to Jackson in a dream. The instructor showed her three books covering "the beginning of creation to the end of time" and promised to instruct her in them (146). This man was still visible when she awoke, and he supported her during the long process of self-education she had begun upon learning how to read. As

Humez points out, a recurrent message in the spiritual instruction that Jackson received "was that self-control brought power" (Humez, 22), still a central redemptive message for oppressed people everywhere.

Yet upon separation from her family, Rebecca was lonely and frustrated in her attempts to create a life that provided a spiritual community without interfering with her intense desire for autonomy and control over her own life. It was not until she joined a white, female Shaker community at Watervliet, New York, that she was able to partially realize her ideals. Indeed, it is a vision that sets her out to find God's true people when she dreams: "my spiritual eyes was opened and I saw in the distance flocks of kids, white as snow, on beautiful green grass" (137). The Shaker faith, a female-founded sect, linked the perfection of humanity with the feminine as the higher element representing divine wisdom and love. As Mary Farrell Bednarowski writes, the Shaker faith was characterized by "(1) a perception of the divine that de-emphasizes the masculine, (2) a tempering or denial of the doctrine of the Fall, (3) a denial of the need for a traditional ordained clergy, and (4) a view of marriage which does not hold that marriage and motherhood are the only acceptable roles for women" (Yates, 67). The esteem attached to women is best represented by Ann Lee, the founder, who was seen as sharing incarnational status with Jesus. Shakers also asserted a commitment to "processual theology," a theology not only open to change but committed to it on principle (Procter-Smith, xiv). The Shaker faith, therefore, provided her a feminist theology which clarified and confirmed her own ongoing conversion. It inspired her to found and lead her own black Shaker sisterhood in Philadelphia. As she describes in a memory of the first time she saw Shakers, her inner divine voice said of them, "These are my people" (139), whereupon she had an ecstatic reaction and "the power of God came upon me like the waves of the sea, and caused me to move back and forth under the mighty waters. It was as much as I could do to keep my seat. . . . They all seemed to look as if they were looking into the spiritual world . . . as if they were living to live forever" (139).

For their part the Shakers were strongly impressed with Rebecca's spiritual powers and seem to have regarded her as an authentic prophet and integrated her fully into their community. Race was not a factor in the Shaker faith, for they had strong abolitionist sympathies. Shakers held to a belief in the equality of sexes and races. Despite all the support and encouragement she found at the Watervliet community, Jackson had problems in submitting to their requirements, as her inner voice was always taking precedence over what the community required. As she writes, "Being always led by an invisible lead, I would not submit to anything outward that was contrary to the inward" (250). She had clashes with authority figures that, combined with an increasing concern on her part about the "spiritual and temporal bondage" (282) of slaves and free blacks, caused her to leave Watervliet and return to Philadelphia in order to reach out to blacks.

After she returns to Philadelphia Jackson writes little, the last entries appearing some seven years before her death in 1871. Although she continued to have an active visionary and intellectual life, perhaps because she became more involved in evangelical outreach to the black community, Rebecca did not write much. Her experiences with the Shaker community made her aware that the white-led community could not satisfy the needs of blacks for a community of spiritual relations. Yet the Shaker faith that reinforced her belief in scriptural revelation and the workings of the divine in history was part of what led her to active service in the black community. The feature of Shaker theology that defended a doctrine of a four-in-one Godhead (the traditional Father and Son balanced with a Mother and Daughter deity) gave her confidence as a woman to assume a role of spiritual leadership. As she describes it: "I throwed myself on the Lord. I saw that night, for the first time, a Mother in the Deity. This indeed was a new scene, a new doctrine to me. But I knowed when I got it, and I was obedient to the heavenly vision—as I *see* all that I hold forth, that is, with my spirit eye. And was I not glad when I found that I had a Mother! And that night she gave me a tongue to tell it!" (153–54). In this vision the "Christ-Spirit, and therefore religious authority, is liberated from an exclusive manifestation in the male paradigm" (Evans,

Spiritual Empowerment, 83). Accordingly, her internal instructor undergoes a transformation, assuming qualities less masculine, and becomes more and more an image of herself and her own inner resources of wisdom and power: "This woman entered into me, who I had followed as my heavenly leader for three years. And as she entered me, the heavenly influence of her divine spirit overcame my soul and body and I can't tell the heavenly feeling I had" (133).

This transformation proves, once again, that conversion implies a continual need to change, to improve, and to grow in a positive view of oneself. This Jackson achieves by claiming her power as a woman who is aware of her own vast spiritual resources, whose perceptions of the possibilities of God expand even to include experiences of God's female faces. It is not surprising, therefore, that Jackson's last entry refers to the initial vision with her instructor and his three books. In a truly Christian manner, she ends where she begins—with the Word. Finally their identity and meaning are made known to her. The first book is the Bible, open in the middle to reveal both Old and New Testaments. The other two books were Shaker doctrine, the *Sacred Roll* and the *Divine Book of Holy Wisdom*—neither of which had been written when she received her first vision of them. Combined, these texts reveal to her "that I should have the spiritual meaning of the letter revealed in my soul by the manifestation of God," and contain "the mystery of God to the children of men, in time and in eternity" (290–91).

Although Jackson's public career was important to her as an example of the truly redeemed, her main priority, as Nellie Y. McKay asserts, was "the continual searching out and verification of the sacred force which guided her actions, which she was determined to obey in all things" ("Nineteenth-Century Black Women's Spiritual Autobiographies," 149). Her gifts of power and vision were maintained by work, the "spirit of labor" (115), that was redemptive. The writing of her narrative itself was a product of the spirit of labor. In fact, she was literally instructed to write in one of her visions, "The Vision of the Bride and Groom" (169–71). In this vision of matrimonial symbolism, a bride and groom appear before her. The groom is mute and smiling, but the bride speaks and commands her to write: "and I was told at the beginning to write the things which I seen and heard, and write them *as* I seen and heard them" (170). As James Evans emphasizes, this vision demonstrates clearly that Jackson "embraces the female paradigm for herself as a writer" (Evans, *Spiritual Empowerment*, 82).

As her writings reveal, Jackson was deeply engaged in contemplating, describing, interpreting, and reinterpreting familiar scriptural texts with images and sequences of events from her inner world. These descriptions, even upon relation, remain mysterious in character. Her method is scriptural, for like the parables of Christ, Jackson incorporates mundane analogies—images from female domestic labors like cooking, cleaning, and sewing—and makes the visions accessible. Also like the parables, which use simple language and metaphors, the visionary quality that underlies the texts illustrates the final inexplicability of the message in words other than those used by the writer. They can never be fully paraphrased or explained, and much of their spiritual authority rests on this mystery. In one example, "The Dream of the Cakes" (99), she feeds a hungry multitude by cakes that she bakes. Her skills as a cook symbolize and prophesy her ministry that nurtures both her and the masses. In "The Gold Box and the Laurels" (119), the sweeping brooms with which she gathers the dust in her house she interprets as an effort to bring about her own moral cleansing. In "A Dream of Washing Quilts" (100), the cleansing of her spiritual nature is symbolized by the washing of quilts. In her life, as in Harriet Jacobs's and Sojourner Truth's, there is no need for heightened prose or exaggeration—the natural drama of their own extraordinary lives was sufficient to convey the workings of the divine in themselves and in the world.

Jackson's use of so many images from female domestic labors presents a feminist revision of the workings of the spirit in the mundane world. Her religious personality takes on a unique, female authority through her worldview in which dreams and visions are interwoven into the fabric of daily life. Shaker theology, of course, dictated perfect equality of rights and dual leadership of men and women in their communities to represent their concept of a dual Godhead. Their social structures and theological beliefs rested in this reciprocal relationship. Yet the division of labor, as Marjorie Procter-Smith notes in her feminist analysis of Shaker communities, was traditional. Women did the sewing, the cleaning, and the cooking, and were generally viewed as residing in a separate sphere of work and nature. Still, the authority of Jackson's visions dignifies these labors, and her choice of embracing the Shaker faith, which recognized a female deity, was an essential part of her social and religious emancipation as a woman. Since Shakers believed it was a woman—Ann Lee—who saved women from the stain of original sin, Jackson's own community believed in the power of women to save women.

Another dimension of Jackson's emancipatory strategies can be found in the very concrete use to which she put her visionary life. Three areas of her life and consciousness are directed by her visions, and each has a special relevance for the experience of a nineteenth-century black woman: her body, her emotions, and her work. In controlling her own body Jackson began with practicing forms of asceticism such as fasting after her sanctification and a vision "of the savior on the cross in childhood" (85). She also changed her manner of dress due to the instructions of a female "holy leader" who appeared in a vision. The dress she adopts is "light drab" (93) Shaker style. She ultimately chose, perhaps to prevent the kinds of abuse women such as Harriet Jacobs endured, to become celibate. Although this choice may not seem a particularly liberating strategy from a contemporary perspective, it did win for Jackson a critical dimension of self-control. The choice, however, was made for her by her inner voice and a vision that told her that sex "of all things it seemed the most filthy in the sight of God—both in the married and the unmarried" (88). Finally, her gift of foresight prevented what she perceived as her husband's intention to abuse her and gives her another dimension of bodily control. Jackson equated sex with slavery, and men in general appear as tempters, enslavers, and even murderers. The fear of the violence of men—emotional and physical—is repeated in many of Jackson's visions throughout her autobiography and the threat of unpredictable violence, and the need to escape and find protection is a dominant theme (Sasson, 171). Among the visions of violence is a particularly graphic "Dream of Slaughter" (94) in which she is skinned by a robber. Although she gleans from this vision the lesson that "thy life is hid in Christ" (95), it displays motifs found in many of her visions, including the violence of men against women, the fear of imprisonment, the need for escape, and a recurrent fascination with avenues to freedom, such as doors, rivers, gates, windows, and roads (Sasson, 94). This dream is immediately followed by a discussion of a male Methodist preacher who she asserts "persecuted me in as cruel a manner as he treated my body in the dream" (95). In many ways Jackson draws attention to the basic levels at which women, in order to sacralize their identities, had to assert a measure of physical control.

A final aspect of Jackson's attempts to assert physical and mental control extends to the forces of nature. She cites several occasions in which she exercises control over the weather, such as when she stops the rain so she can attend a religious meeting she was instructed to attend (96–97). As Humez points out, "the power was allowed her in order to teach her a metaphorical lesson about self-control as a means to moral transformation" (23). She realizes, "if thou can climb to the heaven and take hold of the clouds, which are above thy reach, and have power over them, then thou can have power over thy light and trifling nature and over thy own body also" (98). Her visions help her emotionally and physically to do in her daily life what otherwise she would have found impossible, and at one crucial time enable her to heal a rift with an eldress at the Watervliet community (268–70).

Her emotional and physical control are both made possible by her visionary power and are exercised in the service of her calling. Indeed, her conflict with the eldress, Sister Paulina, seems to have emerged due to Jackson's desire to follow the instruction of her inner voice to "go forth and labor with the people" (277). Despite her affinity with a white Christian sect, Jackson appears to have retained a deep sense of her racial identity. Her desire to establish a community to serve the black population in Philadelphia is a bold break from her visionary life in Zion, as she describes Watervliet. The spirit world, however, instructs her that "I had yet a greater work to do in the world and I must return to the world" (249). Indeed, she expresses concern for African Americans nearly two years before she finally leaves for Philadelphia, and it was her being "brought into deep tribulation of soul about my people, and their present condition, seeing the awful event that is at hand" (213) that caused her to consult her inner voice for direction on how to help. For even though Jackson was born a free black woman, as Elizabeth Fox-Genovese remarks, "The very name 'free black' belies those communities freedom from the heavy hand of slavery as a social system and indexes their ties to the South" ("Myth and History," 222). Evidence of how Jackson's racial identity is bound with her spiritual identity is perhaps best revealed in an entry dated September 1862, when for the first and only time she makes specific reference to a historical event: "My cries to Almighty God, both day and night, were a continual prayer for the deliverance of my people from both spiritual and temporal bondage. I have now lived to hear the Proclamation of President Abraham Lincoln, framed in September of the Year of Our Lord 1862, that on the first of January, 1863, all the slaves in the United States shall be set at liberty, and I say, 'May God Almighty grant a prosperous issue'" (282).

Rebecca Jackson's narrative is unique in the way it weaves allusions to biblical images, motifs from Shaker literature, and the language and style of black Protestantism in a very personal narrative. Yet like Harriet Jacobs and Sojourner Truth, Jackson employs a roughly chronological framework within which some events are grouped together by thematic associations. The telling of one story suddenly touches off the memory of another. Themes are related through presence of the same characters and through her attempts to illustrate the same point in many ways. The method for all three women is a convert's natural way of generating meaningful links between past events in the process of reflecting upon them as a "new" person. As James Evans points out, this method reveals writing strategies more fictive than autobiographical. This tendency, Evans states, "is related to the concern of each writer with the issue of power" (Evans, *Spiritual Empowerment,* 54).

In the examples of these women, the power that animates their writings is spiritual. This power tends to subvert the autobiographical impulse. For these works are stories of the creation of a new person rather than the redemption of a former self—as Rebecca Jackson's inner voice tells her, "Thy make must be unmade and remade, and thou must be made a new creature" (98). Thus, "the surrender of the autobiographical impulse to the fictive act is symbolized by the surrender of the self before divine power" (Evans, *Spiritual Empowerment,* 68), self-denial being the key to self-empowerment. One of Jackson's most potent images of being remade comes in a vision she titles "The Resurrection" (189–90). In it God speaks to her at great length, revealing the difference between the physical and the spiritual life. Jackson develops this dichotomy between physical and spiritual by deconstructing each of six senses: hearing, seeing, smelling, tasting, understanding, and speaking. In doing such, she offers a way to maintain a harmony between things sacred and secular by indicating the proper spiritual use to which physical abilities must be applied. Beginning "pray to die to thy hearing. Then thou will rise in the hearing of thy Savior and then thou will hear his voice, and know it from all others. And you will be able to always obey" (189), it continues that instead of seeing with her physical eyes she must see God's will with her spiritual eye. Instead of smelling the stench of this world, she must smell the scent of God's kingdom. Instead of carnal tasting, she must be satisfied with obedience. Instead of following her own understanding, she must submit to God's understanding. Instead of speaking with her own voice, she must speak for God. These things Jackson must do not just to nurture others but to feed her own soul.

Jackson's narrative ends with an entry dated June 4, 1864, seven years before her death. The Philadelphia community she established lasted for perhaps another forty years after her death. A death certificate on file in Philadelphia records Jackson's death in 1871 and lists her place of burial as "Lebanon." Geraldine Duclos speculates that this probably referred to Lebanon cemetery, a private black cemetery of some five acres tended by beneficent societies. This cemetery no longer exists, as the graves were dismantled and moved sometime in the early part of the century. It was, however, consecrated ground, and in keeping with Shaker tradition individual graves were unmarked and a single stone identified those of the Shaker faith.[29] Jackson's death, like her life, is shadowed in mystery, and her identity subsumed before the presence of God.

Writing for God, Rebecca Jackson, Sojourner Truth, and Harriet Jacobs recreate reality as well as themselves and through this recreation urge a reader into a specific interpretive position of suspending disbelief, of changing the way one usually reads or hears a story. Written when they were, these nineteenth-century narratives serve as models for future black women, demonstrating how religious faith can give one the self-assurance needed to achieve a sense of autonomy—a sacralized identity—that otherwise would have been impossible. In the words of one of their contemporaries, Frances E. W. Harper: "If the fifteenth century discovered America to the Old World, the nineteenth century is discovering woman to herself" (Lowenberg and Bogin, 2).

In general, the nineteenth century witnessed a relocation of religion and a new definition of women in relation to it. Religion became an infinitely variable instrument for enlarging women's sphere beyond traditional roles. These narratives would not have been written, therefore, had these women not been converted. For them religious faith meant a self-empowerment so literal that they were able to tell their own stories. For "in their hands, the spiritual narrative turned the genre of autobiography into a forceful weapon to express and record another chapter in the history of black women's liberation" (McKay, "Nineteenth-Century Black Women's Spiritual Autobiographies," 150). Moreover, these women demonstrate how conversion operates in a concept of female development in relation to (or over and against) patriarchal religion and society, emphasizing the cooperation of sacred and secular motives in human development. For, as Bert James Lowenberg and

Ruth Bogin point out in their study of black women in nineteenth-century American life, "emancipation from restraints has to do with the shifting course of historical events and the shifting frontiers of human potentiality. Culture change and personality change evolve in continual interaction; each new convergence broadens the scope of the possible" (2).

Harriet Jacobs, Sojourner Truth, and Rebecca Jackson were converted by their culture and their individual attributes just as they also "converted" dimensions of their culture to be more inclusive of the sacred dimensions of black women's lives. Their lives reveal that resourcefulness, will, and courage need not be opposed to interdependence and sacrificial love. Their religious experience was, therefore, both a community heritage and a creative personal inspiration. At once secular and holy, religious feeling permeated black culture and generated a dynamic for action. For "if eternal kinship with the divine enabled them to keep on keeping on, eternal membership in the kingdom of God made secular ideals sacred. Both served as bases for social criticism and earthly hope" (Lowenberg and Bogin, 9).

Despite their spiritual empowerment and the confidence they received from it, however, each woman took an ambiguous stance toward her writings. Harriet Jacobs agreed to let her story become public only for the cause of abolition. She did not initially intend to write the narrative herself and in her correspondence betrays doubts about what she has undertaken. Sojourner Truth freely admits that her book was produced at a time when she was in ill health and in need of monetary support, and her illiteracy may betray a mistrust of the written word itself. Rebecca Jackson, for all the pleasure she took in reading and writing, wrote her autobiography as a private spiritual discipline; she read only the Bible and Shaker doctrine, believing that other books had little to offer her religious imagination compared with what her visions could provide. Yet their conversions—to freedom, to emerging feminism, to God, ultimately to the sacred within themselves—are what allowed them to write, despite their personal reservations. What Alice Walker says of Rebecca Jackson's "extraordinary document" is also true of the narratives of Harriet Jacobs and Sojourner Truth: "It tells us much about the spirituality of human beings, especially of the interior spiritual resources of our mothers, and, because of this, makes an invaluable contribution to what we know of ourselves" (MG, 78).

Harriet Jacobs, Sojourner Truth, and Rebecca Jackson, by giving us an understanding of their personal histories, allow us an imaginative comprehension of their historical identities. These historical identities, as subsequent chapters will demonstrate, provide a cultural record and a source of imaginative insight to which future black women writers will turn—either consciously or unconsciously—in shaping their fictions. For despite the social gains achieved for women and African Americans, the testimonies of Jacobs, Truth, and Jackson underscore a position of marginality that no change in any social system can alter. They understood that their fundamental neediness was not solely the result of societal structures but the very position of all humanity before God. Their particular genius and contribution to future generations of women was to recognize that autonomy and self-motivated action that has the potential to destroy a relationship with God can be transformed into a corporate act of expression—a collaboration with God. Every act of self-assertion becomes a moment of reestablishing their relationship to God and their ability to receive from God, thereby maintaining the experience of conversion as an ongoing event, a life process of sacralizing identities. Their conversions were not only momentary, individual events but part of a collective and progressive process. The continuous revelations about which they wrote say something new about the nature of humanity and of God. Moreover, they radically transformed the experience of domination by men or other authorities from a physical to a spiritual plane because "enforced obedience to a cruel earthly master meant emotional bondage" but "voluntary obedience to a beneficent heavenly master offered redemption" (Lowenberg and Bogin, 10). However circumscribed their lives were by the conventions of nineteenth-century American life, Harriet Jacobs, Sojourner Truth, and Rebecca Jackson each found the most radical form of freedom available to humanity.

3

Called to Preach

They stripped me of everything but my thoughts. But one day I
balled up my fists and held up both my arms. With my left arm I
held my freedom to think and my freedom to pray. With my
right arm I held on to my religion, my art, and my music.
—Phyllis Biggs

Phyllis Biggs was brought from the Congo in 1818 to be a slave in
America, eleven years after the slave trade from Africa was legally abol-
ished. She left no narrative account of her life, but a quilt she made
survives and was featured as part of the 1989 exhibition at the Mu-
seum of American Folk Art: "Stitched from the Soul: Slave Quilts
from the Ante-Bellum South." In the epigraph for this chapter, which
accompanied the display of her quilt, Biggs demonstrates how freedom is possible even in the shadow of oppression and that to achieve
it she had to step outside the dominant American value system and
assert her identity in terms that reflect prominent aspects of African-
American culture. She links her freedom not to a political order but
to a cultural order, to the ability to participate in African-American
cultural expression through religious faith and creativity. Phyllis Biggs
serves as a reminder that the culture from which African-American
women draw much of their inspiration and creativity is not always or
only narrative. Essential aspects of that culture have been preserved in
a variety of ways.

Preserving this culture in its various aspects and protecting it from corruption was perhaps the single greatest motivating force in the life of Zora Neale Hurston. Hurston's own life was modeled on the logic of a patchwork quilt, as she assembled from a variety of sources and inspirations a unique persona. A minister's daughter who grew up in the first incorporated all-black town of Eatonville, Florida, Hurston went on to lead a varied and ambitious life as a writer and anthropologist. She suffered, however, through critical and popular neglect—lived "in Sorrow's kitchen and licked out all the pots" (DT, 280)—and died in relative obscurity. Yet perhaps more than anyone of her time, Hurston realized that the kind of culture that sustained Phyllis Biggs (and the women mentioned in chapter 2) was at risk of being diluted and therefore lost to African Americans as a source of being and identity. Along with the aesthetic components of this culture, the religious qualities were also being separated from their cultural origins and lost in the desire for more "secular" political, economic, and intellectual opportunities. The unity of sacred and profane that had long characterized African-American culture was being challenged by the influence of the dominant American culture that expressed a clear dualism between sacred and profane aspects of life.[1]

Hurston, however, as Toni Cade Bambara asserts, had "a life-long concern with spirituality" (11)—she was "born with God in the house" (DT, 266). Hurston had a sensitivity to the ways in which religious attitudes and values were conditioned by and expressive of African-American culture, and in all her writing drew attention to the great cultural wealth of African-American religious traditions. As seen in chapter 2, nineteenth-century African-American women displayed a willingness to define their identities and roles in the world as having religious significance. With the emergence of Zora Neale Hurston and her analyses of African-American cultural forms of expression, one can detect a shift in emphasis. Rather than casting cultural identity in religious terms, she defines significant religious aspects of identity in general cultural terms. She sees them as connected to related cultural activities and values. Although she shifts her emphasis, Hurston maintains a concept of the unity of sacred and profane in African-American culture. As Karla Holloway suggests, "Hurston's point-of-reference was the nourishment of her culture" (*The Character of the Word*, 7).

Yet Hurston's culture also nourished her all the while she was sustaining it. This is due in great measure to her belief that "Negro folklore is not a thing of the past. It is still in the making" (SC, 56). As her culture evolved, so, too, did Hurston, who herself was a kind of continual convert. For her conversion was as much a state of mind, an attitude, as it was a dramatic moment. Although she dutifully records witnessing specific religious conversion experiences, she also notes that conversion "is an opportunity to reaffirm faith plus anything else the imagination might dictate" (DT, 257). Whereas she admits to having "achieved a certain peace within myself," she also adds that "the seeking after the inner heart of truth will never cease in me" (DT, 277). She viewed identity as a lifelong process of *becoming* and attributed the creation of her identity to an ongoing process of change rather than an episodic moment. As she says in her autobiography, "I know that nothing is destructible; things merely change forms. When the consciousness we know as life ceases, I know that I shall still be part and parcel of the world. I was a part before the sun rolled into shape and burst forth in the glory of change. I was, when the earth was hurled out from its fiery rim. I shall return with the earth to Father Sun, and still exist in substance when the sun has lost its fire, and disintegrated in infinity to perhaps become a part of the whirling rubble in space. Why fear? The stuff of my being is matter, ever changing, ever moving, but never lost" (DT, 279).[2]

Hurston's life is an example of conversion as a way to incorporate change for personal identity and to sacralize the experience of marginality by creating a new order and a place for herself in that order. This fluid view of life is borne out in the three forms in which she wrote and the ways each collaborates in inventing a dynamic sense of being, resisting any attempt at closure or definition. Not only a convert, Hurston was also one who was "called to preach"—to "take up the pen when you are told and write about what is commanded" (DT,

231)—to enlist other converts to her cause of preserving the unique aspects of African-American culture from which she drew so much of her identity. In her anthropological work Hurston continually uncovers her culture's historical legacy and background and can find no end to her delight in her community's folklore. She easily locates herself as a participant in her community's expression and shares its spiritual feelings. In her autobiographical work she composes not so much a life of herself but a spiritual record of a black woman confronting her culture at a specific point in history. In her novel *Their Eyes Were Watching God,* however, her narrative voice assumes such an intimacy of spiritual feeling and corresponds so closely with impressions and visions described in her autobiography that it reads more like an extended autobiography. In designating the spiritual motives at work in the protagonist Janie's self-development and self-fulfillment, Hurston provides a link not only to her own life but to the writings of nineteenth-century black women. Moreover, because the novel is full of cultural details, it reads as an accurately rendered anthropological document as well. In all her works Hurston "saves the text" of her foremothers and ensures its relevance.

Biographers are quick to point out the matriarchal influence in Hurston's life and to demonstrate that much of her inspiration seems to have derived from her mother. Hurston admits as much and cites a specific cultural pattern to explain this influence when she describes her awareness of "the universal female gospel that all good traits and leanings come from the mother's side" (DT, 20). It was her mother who encouraged her to "jump at de sun," although "we might not land on the sun, but at least we would get off the ground" (DT, 21). Although her mother encouraged Hurston to strive continually for individuality and self-expression, her father tried to get her to become more docile, more accommodating, because he believed white folks would not tolerate a black woman with too much spirit. Still, she credits her father as the source of one of her most vital characteristics, her wanderlust, and remarks that "some children are just bound to take after their fathers in spite of women's prayers" (DT, 32). When her mother died when Hurston was nine, she clung to her advice to jump at the sun, followed her father's habit of wandering and at age fifteen she left Eatonville. A series of odd jobs led to her enrollment in Morgan Academy and then Howard University, where she took courses intermittently until 1924. By 1925 she was off to New York City, with a recommendation from her mentor, Alain Locke, and made a public debut at the Urban League award dinner, where she received two prizes for literature.

During her years in New York, Hurston flourished because of the opportunities provided for artists and writers, "the New Negroes," as Alain Locke dubbed them, during the period known as the Harlem Renaissance. This movement had as one of its stated goals the reevaluation of African-American history and folk culture, but as Larry Neal points out, aside from Sterling Brown, Hurston "was the only important writer of the Harlem literary movement to undertake a systematic study of African-American folklore" (162).[3] She did so by winning a scholarship and enrolling at Barnard, where she became an apprentice of Franz Boas, the esteemed anthropologist. Her interest in anthropology as an academic discipline was a natural extension of both her literary talents and her deeply held cultural values. As she writes in her first anthropological work, *Mules and Men:* "From the earliest rocking of my cradle, I have known about the capers Brer Rabbit is apt to cut and what the Squinch Owl says from the house top. But it was fitting me like a tight chemise. I couldn't see it for wearing it. It was only when I was off in college, away from my native surroundings, that I could see myself like somebody else and stand off and look at my garment. Then I had to have the spy-glass of Anthropology to look at that" (MM, 3).

Hurston was famously flamboyant in expressing her personality, and this seems to have helped her in gathering the data she needed for her anthropological work in the city. Yet when she traveled south on her first collecting assignment, she was not successful because she postured in what she called "Barnardese," thereby alienating "the men and women who had whole treasuries of material seeping through their pores" (DT, 182–83). It was after this experience that Hurston, in the words of Katie Cannon, combined "the moral counsel which she learned from her family (especially from her mother) with the folk wisdom accentuated in the Black community," and "came to appreciate that surviving the continual struggle and the interplay of contradictory opposites was genuine virtue" (104). In other words, Hurston became aware of the fact that she would have to achieve a delicate balance of complexities. While taking advantage of the opportunities her era presented her, she also had to remember the essential qualities of her being that were instilled at an early age. In all her writing, Hurston concentrates on the psychic and spiritual pleasures experienced by African Americans rather than on the realities of their life in a harsh segregated society. Her concept of "uplifting the race" was to remind blacks of the wealth found in their cultural heritage rather than urging them to struggle to succeed by standards not borne of their own experience. She realized that it was necessary to establish new categories of perception and new ways of seeing culture in order to identify those things that had shaped it. In a sense she demythologized the status quo of the materialistic, dominant society and its standards of legitimacy and offered up in its place the new-old mythology of African-American folk culture.

In order to proceed with her mission of resurrecting or reinscribing black culture, Hurston was forced into uncomfortable relationships of patronage with wealthy white supporters. She received much criticism for being what was perceived by many as "living up to the whites' notion of what a darky should be" (Cannon, 105). [4] In addition to the criticism from her peers, her patrons often attempted to exert an influence over her work and to claim rights to it. Hurston was constantly having to balance the needs of her projects against such criticism and influences but chose to proceed with her work despite the personal degradation it caused her to suffer. Unable to make a living as a writer except by way of the tortured relationships of patronage with "Negrotarians," as she called them, Hurston put the work before herself because, in a sense, the work was herself. She knew the value of her cultural heritage and was aware of how black folklore and culture were generally misunderstood (even by some of the New Negroes) as inferior, comic, and primitive. She was also conscious of how she could be perceived as being complicit in the commercialization and exploitation of black culture. Yet her motives, although inspired by anthropological zeal and practical ambition, had a necessarily existential reality for her because her ongoing project of recording the resources of black culture not only served some greater good but was an essential component of her own growth and development as a woman and as a writer. Her continuing discovery of the wealth of her cultural heritage supplied the standards for her own self-fulfillment, continually fed her own ongoing conversion into selfhood, and gave her something about which she could preach. As she says in her autobiography: "Like the dead-seeming, cold rocks, I have memories within that came out of the material that went to make me. Time and place have had their say. So you will have to know something about the time and place where I came from, in order that you may interpret the incidents and directions of my life" (DT, 3).

Unlike many of her contemporaries, Hurston did not try to prove that intelligent blacks could assume the attitudes, behavior, and standards dictated by whites; nor would she implicate white antagonism as the cause of poverty and oppression. In an era of assimilation, Hurston proudly asserted cultural differences. As Robert Hemenway states, she "believed that an aesthetically oriented black subculture provided a striking contrast to the imaginative wasteland of white society" (162). She challenged both accommodationism and anger by collecting black classics in music, art, literature, and religion with the hopes of correcting dominant misconceptions about the quality of black life and asserting the accomplishments and abilities of African Americans. Anthropology proved to be a natural and legitimate way for Hurston to achieve this correction because by accurately rendering the existence and validity of African-American cultural forms she could also demonstrate how blacks established a pattern of living and a vision of reality. In all her writing she shows how African Americans could validate their own self-worth as human beings by embracing, not transcending, their culture. To Zora Neale Hurston, the woman and the writer, her folk heritage was "the boiled down juice of living"—the ontological source of her identity. To save this culture was to save herself.

Hurston ignored the assumption of so many of her contemporaries that the literary presentation of cultural traditions of the black rural South reinforced social stereotypes. As Cheryl Wall explains, "As a daughter of the region, she claimed these traditions by birthright. As an anthropologist, she reclaimed them through years of intense, often perilous, research. As a novelist, she summoned this legacy in her choice of setting, her delineation of character, and most devotedly in her distillation of language" ("Changing Her Own Words," 371).

The data Hurston gathers in her anthropological writings support the affirmative aspects of African-American religion and the experience of conversion. Her autobiography, *Dust Tracks on a Road,* reveals a spiritual motivation not dissimilar from that which inspired the lives and writings of nineteenth-century black women. She shows how such motivations collaborate in the establishment of identities. Finally, in *Their Eyes Were Watching God,* Hurston creates a bridge between the authenticity of folk life and the literary power of fiction, showing how the historical, spiritual, and cultural legacy of nineteenth-century African-American women finds further expression in a new form. This form provides creative opportunities for future black women writers to explore as it marks the transition between literal and literary conversions.

Anthropological Writings

It is singular that God never finds fault, never censures the
Negro. He sees faults but expects nothing different. He is
lacking in bitterness as is the Negro story-teller himself in
circumstances that ordinarily would call for pity.

—Zora Neale Hurston

Perhaps the single most important contribution of Hurston's anthropological works as they pertain to this study is the way in which they give evidence of the self-affirming qualities of black religion. This self-affirmation takes on many forms. Hurston did not systematize the qualities of black culture she recorded because her understanding of this culture—and of herself—was predicated on a holistic view of reality and nature: one could not simply categorize one aspect as sacred, another as profane. Storytelling sessions she recorded often alluded to biblical incidents, while accounts of conversions could indicate a career change from field hand to herb doctor. Many of the tales are moral lessons that show virtue rewarded and greed punished. Many offer a view of God as merciful and just by celebrating his presence in the natural order and the ways in which he presides over creation. Natural occurrences and elemental matters are given theological justification in terms of God's actions. The devil in black folklore is not evil but a powerful trickster who competes with God and often wins, offering an example of the ways in which the normative moral structure of an oppressive society could be overturned.[5]

Because Hurston was an active participant in much of what she recorded, rarely does she step back and offer analysis of what she witnesses. Her method is presentational, not analytical, or as she describes it, "between-story conversation and business." The stories are their own explanation, yet she does make clear, by her selection of anecdotes, that in African-American culture there is an undeniable spiritual essence to all aspects of living and creating. The first line of *Mules and Men,* which reads "I was glad when somebody told me, 'You may go and collect Negro folk-lore'" (3), is a biblical allusion that Cheryl Wall points out "establishes both Hurston's sense of mission and the high value she places on the material she is out to preserve" (*"Mules and Men* and Women," 662). Her biographer Robert Hemenway even describes Hurston's work in religious terms, identifying her collecting efforts as characterized by "evangelical zeal" and a "missionary spirit" (157).

Mules and Men, published in 1935, was the first popular book about African-American folklore ever written by a black scholar. It begins with a preface by Franz Boas, Hurston's esteemed mentor. Boas, in the tradition of Lydia Maria Child, Olive Gilbert, and other editors of slave narratives, serves as the accepted "authority" who grants a necessary stamp of authenticity to Hurston's work. A collection of folklore she had gathered during extensive tours of the rural South, it displays the rich imaginative life in the black folk community. Divided into two parts, headed "Folk Tales" and "Hoodoo," it begins in Eatonville and includes information about Polk County and the practice of hoodoo in New Orleans. In addition to the seventy folktale texts, she gives a series of hoodoo rituals, a glossary of folk speech, an appendix of folk songs, conjure formulas, and root prescriptions, plus a personal account of her collecting experiences. Interspersed among all of this are a folk sermon, rhymes, proverbs, and blues lyrics.

Because Hurston's recuperation of black culture was such a necessary part of her own spiritual and psychological development, a recurring issue raised by scholars is the degree to which Hurston remains objective in her anthropological reporting. There is concern over the stance she took and the level of involvement she accepted and how this influenced her writings. Were they social science documents or personal reminiscences tailored to suit her own needs? The passage from *Mules and Men* used as an epigraph to this section gives a partial answer. Essential to African-American religion and the ways in which it functioned to sustain and encourage self-expression is the belief that God and Negroes share qualities of identity, because as Hurston notes elsewhere, "even in his religion man carried himself along. His worship of strength was there. God was made to look that way too" (DT, 275). Each is described in terms of the other. The theology is based on the premise that "God never finds fault, never censures the Negro" (MM, 254). God is not only collaborative in self-affirmation but he is like the Negro in forms of expression, inviting play and adornment as essential to creative self-expression and fulfillment. Indeed, even God himself is described as one who commits to a theology of conversion and a belief in life as a process when one of the characters in *Mules and Men* remarks: "but even God ain't satisfied wid some of de things He makes and changes 'em Hisself" (MM, 129). Hurston is aware of this concept of God—at one point she calls God a "great artist" (DT, 281)—and the terms of this theology.

Her involvement in her own community's expression can be seen as a form of piety, because God "expects nothing different." Moreover, the lack of bitterness she cites as characteristic of both the Negro storyteller and God addresses the charges leveled against her for not directing attention to the oppressed state of many black people. What God has given and what blacks have done with what God has given are to be celebrated, not judged by standards not indigenous to the experience.[6] Since one theme of her work is that the folklore of the black South is an expressive system of great social complexity with profound aesthetic and spiritual significance, Hurston's subordination of issues of economic and social deprivation to achieve a specific cultural perspective is entirely intentional, and for culturally and theologically significant reasons. As Hemenway says in his introduction to *Mules and Men,* "Even in the face of an historically brutal experience, black people affirmed their humanity by creating an expressive communication system that fostered self-pride and taught techniques of transformation, adaptation, and survival. The tales of *Mules and Men* prove that human beings are not able to live without some sense of cultural cohesion and individual self-worth, no matter how hard their circumstances" (MM, xx).

The assertion of individual self-worth is necessarily bound up in a collective experience, with a moral imperative that it be shared and appreciated on its own terms. In *Mules and Men* Hurston dramatizes the process of collecting in order to make the reader feel part of the scene, enabling one to share in the communal spirit of black culture, just as if one were participating in the lying sessions on the porch of Joe Clark's store in Eatonville. She directs her descriptions away from her inner self to the works of her informants and celebrates the art of the community. She is the town prodigal who, by returning to collect the stories, rediscovers a part of herself. Her community affirms her outlook on life, and so she both presents the artistic content of the folklore and suggests the behavioral significance of folkloric events— how they affirm self, community, and Creation.

Hurston was aware that in order to gain access to the folklore she had to drop the superficial vestiges of privilege and voyeur status— her Barnardese—and stand in solidarity with the people from whom she was trying to learn. By doing such, Hurston's book becomes what Cheryl Wall describes as a "paradigmatic immersion narrative" ("*Mules and Men* and Women," 662), because Hurston is transformed, converted by that in which she participates. Joe Clark's porch in Eatonville and later Luke Turner's home in New Orleans, where she encounters Marie Leveau's spirit, are sacred, transformative places that provide her a sense of spiritual solidarity as a source of strength and identity. As she describes a visit to Eatonville, "Men sat around the store on boxes and benches and passed this world and the next one through their mouths. The right and the wrong, the who, when and why was passed on, and nobody doubted the conclusions. There were no discreet nuances of life on Joe Clark's porch. There was open kindnesses, anger, hate, love, envy and its kinfolks, but all emotions were naked and nakedly arrived at. It was a case of 'make it and take it.' You got what your strength would bring you" (DT, 62).

Hurston's belief in the value of African-American folklore was revitalized by her return to Eatonville, as she was reminded of how that belief had originally sustained her and given her strength. She emphasizes the terms of African-American theology that gave "what your strength would bring you." She was able to identify the moral wisdom within this folklore that "implies a self-sufficient set of values explaining, legitimizing, and ensuring the continuance of Black life" (Cannon, 146). In other words, Hurston realized that folktales embodied the values and beliefs of African Americans and that by preserving the folklore of African Americans, she was also preserving a method of survival and achievement and claiming it as her own source of strength.[7] Her research, her "formalized curiosity," was given voice not in academic or scientific tones, but in the tones of the very culture she was investigating. Despite its claims to be anthropological research, in *Mules and Men* one detects that Hurston avoided academic tones because she wished her audience to be not scholars only but anyone who can appreciate a story for the story's sake.

Insights into the method and meaning of *Mules and Men* can be gained from a reading of "Characteristics of Negro Expression," which appeared in Nancy Cunard's anthology *Negro*. This essay, Hurston's first attempt to summarize her fieldwork, is centered on the thesis that change and creativity are distinguishing characteristics of black American culture. In identifying key characteristics, Hurston singles out "the will to adorn" or the ways in which blacks have taken what the dominant culture has offered and ornamented it for their own use. Even the Bible "was made over to suit our vivid imagination" (MM, 5). This "will to adorn" stems from "the Negro's universal mimicry" and gives evidence of a spirit of drama that "permeates his entire self" (SC, 49). Thus "every phase of Negro life is highly dramatized," often unconsciously, and "no little moment passes unadorned" because this is "what satisfies the soul of its creator" (SC, 49–50).

Moreover, "nothing is too old or too new, domestic or foreign, high or low" (SC, 56), because blacks' adaptability expressed in folklore assumes a kind of unconscious democracy, a democracy that extends to all forms of culture and reality as well—between sacred and profane—because "the angels and apostles walk and talk like section hands" (SC, 56). For African Americans, spiritual strength derives from a sense of the ways in which a divine order is presented in mundane terms, not set apart as a transcendent reality but described and understood in terms that correspond with reality as it is experienced, not imagined. Imagination comes into play when reasons are sought for the mysteries of life—"why Negroes are black," or "how the church came to be split up"—as part of the will to adorn.

Hurston emphasizes a point made previously concerning the uniqueness of African-American religion when she says "the Negro is not a Christian really" (SC, 56), because she identifies a black system of reality that is concentrated on activity and experience, not on subtle inner reflection. Cultural and religious heroes are drawn from this world and this life. The devil and God are given equal time, since both are powerful presences in daily life and both have origins that extend beyond the rudiments of Christianity as it was presented in America.[8] In a companion essay, "Spirituals and Neo-Spirituals," Hurston emphasizes again the collaborative energy of religious and aesthetic expression and claims that "the religious service is a conscious art expression" (SC, 81).

Just as religious and artistic expression combine to create a communal vision of reality, so, too, do they participate in the individual's search for self-expression and identity. As emphasized earlier, the conversion experience is an ideal form by which to evaluate this cooperative effort. In her essay "Conversions and Visions," Hurston describes the drama of conversion as a classic example of an African American's will to adorn. Through conversion individuals internalize the community's vision and reexpress it in individual terms that authenticate self—all the while legitimating this self in the eyes of the community. In her autobiography she describes witnessing conversions and the excitement she feels in seeing this "high drama," attentive to how each convert would handle it and make it something unique (DT, 269–72). The vision that Hurston identifies as a "very definite part of Negro religion" (SC, 85) accompanies conversion and the call to preach. Each person's vision is like each person's story, bearing resemblance to all other visions but adorned with individual impressions because conversions and visions, she remarks, "have become traditional, but all sorts of variations occur" (SC, 85).

What distinguishes voluntary conversion from involuntary conversion or the call to preach is that in voluntary conversion the individual seeks the vision and goes forth "into waste places" to induce the vision. She even mentions that a cemetery "is a most suggestive place to gain visions" (85), recalling Linda Brent's vision of freedom and subsequent conversion following a trip to the graves of her parents. The call to preach, on the other hand, is involuntary. Conversion contains a mixture of internal and external struggles; the call to preach is fully external. In conversion there is a mixture of internal and external struggles because first from the outside comes the accusation of sin and then from within comes the consciousness of guilt and ultimately deliverance that, initially doubted, is accepted later. The call to preach, however, is altogether external, and "the vision seeks the man" (SC, 87).

Although both cultural patterns were identified by Hurston as part of the existing African-American historical consciousness, each pattern also lends itself to a particular reading of the writings of black women. In the writings of the nineteenth-century women previously discussed, each woman can be seen as a voluntary convert, willingly inducing a vision and seeking deliverance from God for their sins in order to create new lives for themselves. They had an intimate and deeply personal recognition of how religious faith operated in their lives. Moreover, they grappled with the internal struggle of recognizing their own sacrality while at the same time fighting the external struggle of proving themselves in societal terms that were not immediately available to them.

In the twentieth century we will see examples of women who had "involuntary visions." While attempting to make sense of contemporary reality, they were not immediately aware of the personal nature of faith and the resources it made available to them. They were, nonetheless, influenced by the external order of cultural history and found themselves "called to preach" about their identification with their cultural legacy. In both cases, women become aware of the quality of an African-American religious sensibility that Hurston describes in another essay as one that "does not crush the individual" but "encourages originality" (SC, 25).

This attitude is further reinforced in the section of *Mules and Men* pertaining to hoodoo. Hurston saw hoodoo as practiced in New Orleans as an intrinsic part of African-American religion because it, too, offered a means by which African Americans could exert control over their lives by way of a more expansive vision of themselves as active in their own redemption. It complemented what traditional forms of Christianity offered. Hoodoo was an expression of the dynamic collaboration between Old World and New World theologies. The beliefs from which hoodoo was derived were based on the premise that life was not random or accidental. Events were meaningful, and therefore human beings could understand their causes. As Lawrence Levine says, people were "part of, not alien to, the Natural Order of things, attached to the Oneness that bound together all matter, animate and inanimate, all spirits visible or not" (58–59). By understanding this premise for reality, African Americans could act to change events and alter courses. Hoodoo suited these ends by psychologically empowering all its adherents. With its curses and cures for body and soul, hoodoo offered its adherents instruments of control. Moreover, as Cheryl Wall points out, "within hoodoo, women were the spiritual equals of men. They had the authority to speak and act" ("*Mules and Men* and Women," 672). Hoodoo complemented Christianity by offering ways to undertake the human quest for transcendent knowledge and self-empowerment because both dimensions of African-American religion gave weight, indeed necessity, to the will to change, the need to act. Hurston entered into hoodoo rituals willingly, and under the providential guidance of the priestess Marie Leveau's spirit, she was completely transformed.

Hurston begins this section with a folktale, a creation myth that focuses on the human quest for the transcendent knowledge that hoodoo represents. According to the tale, the first man who attained even a portion of the knowledge—"God's power-compelling words"—was Moses, and "it took him forty years to learn ten words" (194). In acknowledgment of his knowledge, God presents Moses with the rod that becomes the emblem of his power. Throughout this tale Hurston establishes the African dimensions of hoodoo and its compatibility with the Judeo-Christian tradition (she notes the Bible is the greatest conjure book of all), themes she will discuss further in reference to the Caribbean islands' religion. She also takes great pains to distinguish the sacred qualities of hoodoo from the "voodoo ritualistic orgies of Broadway and popular fiction" (195), by emphasizing its secrecy, its private or almost Gnostic knowledge.

Hurston must undergo tests of her sincerity in order for Marie Leveau's nephew, Luke Turner, to consent to share the knowledge he has been taught by Leveau. She becomes a kind of disciple who confronts herself in various dimensions through her spiritual journey: "For sixty-nine hours I lay there. I had five psychic experiences and awoke at last with no feeling of hunger, only one of exaltation" (209). Hurston travels like a pilgrim through her culture and its religious practices to the deepest regions of herself and brings back yet another story to tell, inspired by her people's spiritual tradition.

After collecting folklore from the States, Hurston traveled to the Caribbean islands. There she discovered communities that were even less culturally diffuse. She probed areas of consciousness and culture to account for the survival of African religious mythologies and sensibilities. Each of her expeditions is linked to the others through the shared spiritual and cultural features of black communities. The link that she explored in greatest detail was voodoo. She realized that voodoo, as a cultural form, was a spiritual expression that enabled a tangible survival of the religions of West Africa. The survival of voodoo on the Caribbean islands documents a culture's insistent hold on the practices and beliefs that had defined it in Africa. Hurston compares the practices of Caribbean voodoo religion and American sympathetic hoodoo magic in an effort to show how the cultural relationships between blacks persist even when there has been forced dispersion.

One way Hurston establishes cultural continuity is by demonstrating how the phenomena of "God-in-nature" and the "in-dwelling God"—the God who was so much a part of the storytelling and descriptions of reality expressed on Joe Clark's porch—are part of an ancient and African theology. In *Tell My Horse,* her record of her Caribbean journeys, this theology is repeated, and Hurston goes on to explain that the Catholic imagery in the rituals is due to French colonialism. She focuses on the survival of the "blackness of the myth" and notes that the pictures of Catholic saints included in the practice are not African-Haitian gods in "whiteface" but approximations of the Haitian gods (*loa*). Although the *loa* became more visual, the change, as Hurston cautions, was not in their natures, only in their features. The iconic character of Catholicism appealed to the Africans' "urge to adorn," and the network of saints in this religion was a convenient vehicle in which to store the multitude of spirits that inhabited the African view of the world.

Voodoo, Hurston realized, was characterized by deeper spiritual values than what was usually transmitted in discussions of its alliance with Christianity. She presents voodoo as a religion with its own integrity but not unlike Christianity in the ways it offers a schema for creation and life that began with the assertive power of the word. For voodoo this creative act (*nommo*) was a six-day period during which God uttered magic spells and incantations. In other words, the word was magic, and Hurston conveys this belief in the second half of *Mules and Men,* where the opening discussion of hoodoo is a presentation of the creation story. Moreover, she writes about her impressions "in the logic of one who practices and believes" (Mikell-Remy, 225), not as an outsider.

Tell My Horse, written in 1938, documents Hurston's baptism and conversion to the Africanisms that gave focus to the life of Haitian and Jamaican peasants. She, like them, becomes a vehicle for the expression of cultural memories that had to be preserved and passed on by "horses mounted" by the gods. Hurston's approach in *Tell My Horse* is consistent with her personalized approach to black southern culture of which she was intimately a part. Just as in *Mules and Men,* where she requires that Floridians accept her as an equal participant in their lives while she collects folklore, so she also insists upon full induction into the voodoo cults and ceremonies in Haiti.

Structurally, the book is a winding journey through rural Caribbean communities, examining racial attitudes, religious rituals, and male-female relationships in Caribbean society. She presents her ideas as travel notes yet is intent on collecting details on those cultural aspects that have significance for herself. The cultural aspects she emphasizes have been selectively chosen from among those of importance within the African-American experience, among them the color-class hierarchy and how that is reflected in male-female relationships in general. Hurston struggles with the issue of amalgamation versus separatism as the correct choice for blacks, and cross-cultural comparisons between Caribbean and American life are found throughout her narrative. As in America, she finds the issues of color and class interwoven into all other aspects of life. Still, despite the dynamic political changes going on at the time Hurston is there, she sketches a timeless Jamaica and concludes: "I do not pretend to know what is wise and best for Jamaicans. The situation presents a curious spectacle to the eyes of an American Negro. It is as if one stepped back to the days of slavery or the generation immediately after surrender when Negroes had little else to boast of except a left-handed kinship with the master, and the privileges that usually went with it of being house servants instead of field hands. . . . But the pendulum has swung over to the side of our American clock" (17–18).

She takes hope in that "The Black people of Jamaica are beginning to respect themselves. They are beginning to love their own things like their songs, their Anasi stories, and proverbs and dances" (19–29). As before, Hurston holds up a heritage of folklore as a solution to a culture's malaise and offers a society's reverence of its folklore as an indication of its cultural health. Although many read her comments as naive and not fully in step with political realities, Hurston is well aware of such issues but chooses not to address them with any complexity.[9] In Haiti, for example, Hurston notes a cultural trend similar to what is happening in the States when she displays an awareness of both the contributions of elites to the development of their ethnic culture and the perception that they often take stands different from the masses of their own people. She documents this conflict in statements from the people. For example, she describes the desperation of a Haitian peasant who hears of the impending American occupation of Haiti: "They say that the white man is coming to rule Haiti again. The black man is so cruel to his own, let the white man come!" (92), and the deception of the upper class regarding the occupation and its causes: "we would have let them stay here longer, but the

Americans had no politeness, so we drove them out. They knew that they had no right to be here in the beginning" (106). The contradictions in Haitian culture mirror her own society, and her own situation of being a member of a growing African-American elite who is carving a place for herself within the race-conscious society of the States.

Hurston uses this understanding of class and culture conflicts as an introductory theme in her discussion of the role of voodoo in Haitian society. Attitudes toward and about voodoo have been central to the dynamics between socioeconomic classes in Haiti, and she views cultural contradictions within this historical framework. By framing her arguments this way, Hurston is once again giving a primary place in cultural history to the influence of religion. In the section on "Voodoo and Voodoo Gods," Hurston discusses African Yoruba religion as it is expressed in Haitian ritual and imagery. She instinctively recognizes the importance of religion in this culture and gives a lengthy discourse on the ceremonies and cults built around gods. The source of life and the ultimate relationship of male to female are at the center of the voodoo religion. Damballah and Eruzulie (the great high god and the goddess of love, respectively) are active and sexually symbolic, revealing truths about creation to all who seek knowledge.

In Haiti, Damballah is worshipped directly instead of through the *loa* because his influence is direct. Although there are major families of gods, each major section of Haiti has its own local variations of *loa* within those families. Voodoo becomes an extremely personalized religion that takes one out of anonymity into direct interaction with and service to supernatural forces. Voodoo, therefore, displays the same dramatic will to adorn and underscores the cooperation of community and individual desires in a way not dissimilar to African-American cultural-religious practices. Hurston shows that there is an internal coherence to voodoo itself and does not strain to examine its outward characteristics and functions in society, concentrating instead on the proper methods of performing voodoo ceremonies in order to please the gods and achieve desired ends. Political concerns do not enter this description. For example, there is no reference to Eruzulie being mulatto, or the fact that the majority of horses are females. Rather, she is convinced that one must be "mounted by the loa" to know truth, and so she joins in. The "horse" who becomes so mounted conveys the message and wishes of the god to those who would listen.

Here Hurston gains an immediacy of religious feeling and sympathy not often displayed in her anthropological writings. Yet she also steps back to offer an interpretation of what the gods say and do in words that sound like her descriptions of African-American religion from Eatonville: "Gods always behave like the people who make them. One can see the hand of the Haitian peasant in the boisterous god, Guede, because he does and says the things that peasants would like to do and say. You can see him in the market women, in the domestic servant who now and then appears before her employer "mounted" by this god who takes the occasion to say many stinging things to the boss" (232).

In Haiti, as in America, the gods are defined in images drawn from reality and experience. Likewise, she shows how Haitians use negative supernatural forces to accomplish personal goals, just as African Americans use the devil as often as God to explain life's mysteries. The Petro gods, for example, are used by their adherents for monetary and personal gain. They are capable of great harm and give their adherents the capacity to overwhelm the individual power of others, if one is able to endure the sincerity test of having the Petro god Guede's favorite drink—rum and hot pepper—rubbed into one's eyes. In all her discussions, Hurston dignifies voodoo by treating it as a legitimate, sophisticated religion—as a religion of creation and life.

Hurston was motivated by her own life experiences and a desire to bring to anthropology the perspective and awareness that scraps of memory remain and find new expression in many forms of black culture. Like *Mules and Men,* where her mission is to participate in black life and convey the order therein and to act as a voluntary preacher of her cultural faith, in *Tell My Horse* Hurston undergoes yet another transformation, a deeper conversion wrought by inducing a broader vision and understanding of black culture. She begins to tend the roots of black history and to look across the horizons of cultural experiences. As Gwendolyn Mikell-Remy states, "Hurston's 'horses' not only deliver the messages of the gods, but also show us what motivated the gods to send them in the first place" (232).

Autobiography

You can't slay a dragon with a formula.
—Albert Murray

A highly criticized and much-debated book, Zora Neale Hurston's autobiography, *Dust Tracks on a Road,* has been described by her biographer, Robert Hemenway, as "untrustworthy" because it lacks honest self-disclosure and "sacrifices the truth to the politics of racial harmony" (DT, xiii). It is generally read by Hemenway, among others, as a moral and political failure because Hurston displays an unbecoming cowardice and lack of thoughtful consideration of complex social issues. Such a reading is based on the judgment that Hurston "re-dramatizes her life for the autobiographical text, manipulating character and event." Hemenway deems Hurston as testing a "reader's good faith" (DT, xii) and does not suggest other motives for the autobiography's form and substance.

Elizabeth Fox-Genovese writes that Hurston would have "been surprised to see her multiple—and intentionally duplicitous—self-representations accepted as progenitor of the new Afro-American female self" ("My Statue, My Self," 63). Fox-Genovese goes on to develop a theory of autobiography based on the premise that black women have developed self in opposition to rather than as an articulation of their oppressed condition, using Hurston as her prime example. Yet less than three years later, in another essay, Fox-Genovese discusses the mythmaking in which Hurston engaged while crafting her autobiography and concludes that although the mythmaking satisfies her imagination and allows her to reclaim her past, the autobiography remains a "lie, nonetheless" ("Myth and History," 228).

Hurston's motives for such manipulation cannot be easily dismissed, especially if one takes into account her self-referential and comic signifying in the text. More than once Hurston alerts her reader that "I am of the word changing kind" (27). She describes the relation of her birth as "hear-say" and implies specifics do not bother her since, "it is pretty well established that I really did get born" (27). Later, in discussing love, she says, "anybody whose mouth is cut crossways is given to lying, unconsciously as well as knowingly. So pay my few scattering remarks no mind" (265). In the chapter on "Research," which she calls "formalized curiosity," she asserts that truth is a matter of degree, that hyperbole is her cultural style because, "once they got started, the 'lies' just rolled and story-tellers fought for a chance to talk. It was the same with the songs. The one thing to be guarded against, in the interest of truth, was over-enthusiasm" (197).

She gives her readers many warnings about her own text, cautioning them to defer judgment about any explicit self-referentiality. At the same time she gently mocks those who would misunderstand her when she says that anyone who signifies or plays the dozens can go "as far as your imagination leads you. But if you have no faith in your personal courage and confidence in your arsenal, don't try it. It is a risky pleasure" (187). This strategy of contributing to a myth of oneself reminds one of Sojourner Truth, whose use of dialect, posturing, and deliberate evasiveness about her age, among other things, greatly contributed to her legendary status. Like Hurston, Bernice Lowe claims Sojourner Truth "enjoyed this little game" of "intermingling fact and fiction" (127–30).

Hurston had the courage to go with her imagination, and those who accuse her of gross manipulation of facts ignore two basic justifications for her adornments. One is cultural, as she imitates the signifying and lying that went on on Joe Clark's front porch. As she says, "Life took on a bigger perimeter by expanding on these things. I picked up glints and gleams out of what I heard and stored it away to turn it into my own uses" (69). The other justification is theological, based on Hurston's spiritual belief that "Nothing that God ever made is the same thing to more than one person. That is natural. There is no single face in nature, because every eye that looks upon it, sees it from its own angle. So every man's spice-box seasons his own food. Naturally I picked up the reflections of life around me with my own instruments, and absorbed what I gathered according to my inside juices" (61).

In general, readings of Hurston's autobiography also do not take into account the kinds of issues raised by Bella Brodzki and Celeste Schenck in *Life/Lines: Theorizing Women's Autobiography* or by Susan Stanford Friedman in her essay in *The Private Self: Theory and Practice of Women's Autobiographical Writings,* edited by Shari Benstock. Similar theoretical assumptions are shared by all these scholars. They note, among other things, that women have had to adopt special strategies when confronting the world in order to free themselves from images of roles they are meant to play. Women have alternative motives and must create new myths in an effort to authenticate their lives. They are also bound by the very cultural paradigms that challenge them and write, therefore, in a state Elizabeth Fox-Genovese describes as a tension "between condition and discourse" ("My Statue, My Self," 65). Female autobiographers, Brodzki and Schenck claim, "take as a given that selfhood is mediated; her invisibility results from her lack of a tradition, marginality, fragmentation, the lack of a sense of radical individuality. Thus they reclaim the female subject despite the problematic status of self" (8). They go on to remark that "self-definition in relation to significant others is the most pervasive characteristic of female autobiography" (8). Friedman underscores this relational concept and exposes the inapplicability of individualistic models of the self to women and minorities: "First, the emphasis on individualism does not take into account the importance of a culturally imposed group identity for women and minorities. Second, the emphasis on separateness ignores the differences in socialization of male and female gender identity. From both an ideological and psychological perspective, in other words, individualistic paradigms of the self ignore the role of collective and relational identities in the individuation process of women and minorities" (34–35).

Special strategies such as those theorized here were seen in the nineteenth-century texts: when Linda Brent had to morally justify her choice of taking a lover to show that standards applied to white women are meaningless to a slave woman; when Rebecca Jackson had to justify leaving husband and family to follow her call to preach and redefine spirituality and God in feminine terms; when Sojourner Truth emphasized the range of qualities that can define women's abilities in her "Ain't I a Woman" speech. Moreover, each woman identified with and defined herself in terms of a community: Linda Brent with a family, Rebecca Jackson with a religious group, Sojourner Truth with a political movement. Hurston, however, identified with a specific cultural tradition that became her community, writ large. The more she absorbed of this community, the closer she came, if not to God per se, then to a spiritual essence that sustained her. It gave her the forms by which to write; the will to adorn and the emphasis on storytelling both structure her life while presenting formidable challenges as she, a unique and educated black woman, works within the autobiographical mode.

Dust Tracks is arranged in a loosely chronological framework, with themes superimposed on this framework. The structure moves from the general (a history of Eatonville), to the particular (Hurston's childhood, family, friends), and back to the general (discussions of religion, culture, and world politics). In the first part of the book Hurston reinforces her identity within the black community as a self-appointed cultural interpreter. Later, as Nellie McKay points out, she assumes the role of "historian-storyteller as the point of departure for her personal story" ("Race, Gender, and Cultural Context," 183) and remains faithful to the tradition of collective responsibility that Brodzki and Schenck identify as a hallmark of women's autobiography. She writes in both black folk idiom and her Barnardese. The subject of her autobiography parallels the subject matter of folklore, where combined identities are unfolded in structures of meaning. Cultural topics are discussed in chapters through which Hurston gives shape to her personal experiences. The only events of her "private" life on which she dwells are those that have deep symbolic and cultural value.

This is because, to Hurston, cultural forms are more important than specific events. The self she fashions is not a fixed essence but can be seen only through a process of active self-discovery by way of self-invention and by the means of folklore. She sets up her life as a series of venues in which she can perform and as a series of vantage points from which she can witness the rituals of life: from her childhood when she positions herself on a fence to attract passersby, to her adolescent entertainment of the cast of the traveling play she works for, to her adult watching and participating in the activities in the barbershop where she does manicures—each instance reminding one of the activities on Joe Clark's porch. She achieves imaginative transfiguration by staging events to pass on cultural forms involved in creation of identity or a culture itself. She takes a dynamic and contextual approach to culture and toward self as a fluid and changing concept and in the process inevitably reveals paradoxes in her multidimensional self. Moreover, her subjugation of self in favor of a cultural ideal is a deliberate and strategic, indeed religious, displacement of self, one that figures her in a larger cultural context. Hurston's work reflects what Bernice Johnson Reagon identifies as "cultural autobiography" in black women's autobiographies. She believes that the story of black women's selfhood is inseparable from their sense of community (81).

In "Autoethnography: The An-Archic Style of *Dust Tracks on a Road*," an essay in her book, *Autobiographical Voices,* Françoise Lionnet expands on Reagon's concept of cultural autobiography by introducing other tensions at work in *Dust Tracks*.[10] Like Benstock, Friedman, Brodzki, and Schenck, she draws attention to the difficulty women have traditionally had in struggling to articulate their personal visions and to excavate elements of self buried under dominant cultural and patriarchal myths of selfhood. She notes this led to a tendency for an autobiographical narrative to proclaim itself as fiction because patterns of self-definition and self-dissimulation are unveiled that are not consciously familiar.

Hurston offers a complex but interesting case of a female autobiographer, one who struggles to balance the need to assert and define a unique vision of self while at the same time placing and indeed subordinating her vision of self in favor of a larger cultural vision. She is not wholly successful in achieving this balance: she cites individuality and independence as reasons to refrain from confronting complex social issues, and she uses cultural tropes to evade specific details of her personal life.

Yet it is Hurston's training as an anthropologist, Lionnet suggests, that "influences the way she looks at the complex system of human relations that constitute culture." In her autobiography she makes use of formal descriptive paradigms of anthropological research and creates a self-portrait of a field-worker looking for her own roots (94).

Lionnet calls *Dust Tracks* a work of "autoethnography" because it shows "the defining of one's subjective ethnicity as mediated through language, history, ethnographical analysis." It is a "figural anthropology" of the self (99). Hurston redeems the quality of difference black Americans feel by saving their culture in the text, by speaking for this culture that is threatened by the influence of the majority culture. Hurston uses her position of fundamental liminality—as a participant and observer in her culture—to her own advantage, and thereby transforms and is transformed by the autobiographical process. Her conversion is ongoing because she sees her life as a spiritual and aesthetic experience that reason is inadequate to describe.

It is because of this perspective of Hurston's that race is not a useful category. Hurston does not privilege blackness by setting it up as an oppositional category to whiteness but by showing vitality and diversity in African-American culture in order to dispel the notion of "whiteness" as a point of reference. As Henry Louis Gates, Jr., says, although part of Hurston's received heritage was "the idea that racism had reduced black people to mere ciphers, to beings who only react to an omnipresent racial oppression," she thought this idea was "degrading, its propagation a trap, and railed against it." Her work "celebrates rather than moralizes" (Afterword, 189–91).

Hurston was not revolutionary but visionary, and like all prophets she was often misunderstood. By allowing her individuality to be expanded, by casting uniqueness in human rather than racial terms, she opens up the possibility for a more radical existential contemplation of her identity. She creates a form of self-discovery through self-invention and cultural preservation, by finding in her culture reflections of her own being. As Lionnet describes Hurston's approach, "a particular form acquires value not from its timeless origin or essential qualities but because it is related to practices that inform a mode of life while dynamically shaping reality" (128).

Such a shaping inevitably leads to contradictions for someone like Hurston, who was such an individualist. Her biographer, Hemenway, is certainly correct when he states that Hurston was, to a degree, "trapped in *Dust Tracks* by the personal identification she cultivated as one of the folk, for it limited her freedom to account for her experience as part of a larger world" (279). Yet by concentrating on the contradictions he sees in her understanding of her own success—the tension between her perception of herself as "special" and her attribution of her self-reliance, self-confidence, and independence to her familial and communal origins—Hemenway assumes that this is a unique posture for an autobiographer and seems unwilling to take into account most scholarship on the autobiographical form that is not unaware of how writers manipulate facts in order to present a certain vision of self. Judgments pertaining to "truth" in autobiography involve a slippery slope of hermeneutical inquiry. When speaking of conversion or spiritual narratives, for example, it is evident that a life cannot be presented from any perspective other than that of a convert. This event necessarily changes and influences one's recollection of events and tends to cast their significance in religious terms. Events, experiences, and impressions that, when they happened, appeared to have no special significance, upon reflection assume a miraculous character and are viewed as integral parts of the process of development and conversion.

The tension Hemenway cites is natural for a convert like Hurston and one she may not have wished to resolve. There is an honesty, indeed a kind of piety, in her ambiguous stance. A reading of Hurston's work as a "religious" autobiography is suggested by John Barbour's essay "Character and Characterization in Religious Autobiography." The classic religious autobiography, Barbour claims, attempts to speak both "to those readers whose faith and hope lies in the stability of character and to those whose optimism depends on the possibility of basic transformations of character" (324). He goes on to explain that such an autobiography serves dual needs, as it appeals to one's "deep desire for a finally complete self, based on the ideal of the unified self, and the idea of the soul" (324) while also appealing to "modern anxieties about the self, and to our awareness of the realities of character change, role-playing, and self-deception" (324).

Hurston's autobiography, therefore, can be seen as expressive of her desire to portray herself as a character of moral integrity even as she investigates the difficulty and the possible distortion or dishonesty in all attempts at self-characterization. In a sense Hurston is offering up her folk "Eatonville self" as reflective of the timeless, constant, and unified soul, and her worldly and "traveled self" as the modern woman wrestling with contingencies, change, and anxiety. Her vision of her childhood in Eatonville, although born of particular experience, assumes universal qualities that sustain her in the midst of a fluctuating and confusing world, and her faith in this timeless culture parallels one's faith in a timeless deity.

The most poignant example of Hurston's ambiguity and piety is given in her memory of her mother's death. While she lay dying, Hurston's mother instructed her to make sure that those attending her did not perform customary death rituals of removing a pillow from under her head and covering the clocks and mirrors. Hurston knew her mother "depended on me for a voice," but she was unable to fulfill her mother's wishes. She agonized over that failure for years but reflects later that "now I know that I could not have had my way against the world. The world we lived in required those acts. Anything else would have been sacrilege" (89). Hurston remembers that when her mother died she "changed a world," and at that moment of change, of conversion, Hurston realizes she is "old before her time," that her life will be a dialectic between her individuality and her respect for her culture. Her text, therefore, "acts" for her mother in a way that Hurston could not.

Although Hurston devotes a whole chapter to the subject of religion near the end of the autobiography, she distances herself from any specific claims to faith. She appears to appreciate religious worship as an aesthetic rather than a spiritual experience. She links revivals with lying sessions and reveals more evidence of the "will to adorn" by describing how the testimonies or visions were traditional but still it was "exciting to see how converts would handle them" (272). However, in the essay "How It Feel to Be Colored Me," Hurston describes her own response to a jazz orchestra in images that could be substituted for her descriptions of a convert's ecstasy. As with her mother, although Hurston cannot fully embrace the faith her father served as a preacher, she cannot escape its influence either.

"The Inside Search," the longest and most reflective chapter, shows how Hurston's childhood behavior reflects choices about her identity that would transcend socially restrictive boundaries of race and gender. Her self-representation reveals a portrait foreshadowing the woman who refused to subscribe to collective black oppression and insisted on emphasizing the inherent richness and emotional security of her nonmaterialistic culture. Hurston discusses how she resisted "the pigeonhole way of life" and "was always asking and making myself a crow in a pigeon's nest" (33–34). She goes on to explain that "I did not know then, as I know now, that people are prone to build a statue of the kind of person that it pleases them to be. And a few people want to be forced to ask themselves, 'What if there is no me like my statue?' The thing to do is to grab the broom of anger and drive off the beast of fear" (34). Hurston signifies on this need to pigeonhole and create statuary visions of life and ironically offers her text as the "statue" of the self she wishes to present to the world. She does not, however, confuse herself, her own being, with the statue she chose to construct in the autobiography.

Whether Hurston is aware of it or not, this reference to her external, society-pleasing self as a statue is reminiscent of Harriet Beecher

Stowe's *Atlantic Monthly* article on Sojourner Truth, in which she likens Sojourner Truth to a statue of the Libyan Sibyl. Reprinted in the narrative, Stowe recounts how her telling a famous sculptor about Sojourner Truth inspired him to create a statue of the Libyan Sibyl. She describes how Sojourner Truth's memory "still lives in one of the loftiest and most original works of modern art" (170–73). This tendency of a well-meaning white woman to objectify the life of a black woman is clearly an expression of the same tendency Hurston was aware her readers wished her to follow. Although it is iconic, a statue portrait of self is also limited and static, a convenient way to marginalize a person and limit her identity. One must appreciate that Hurston never intended her autobiography to be her life. She takes to her autobiography the strategy of a "will to adorn," as a way to cope with the powerlessness and vulnerability she surely felt in having to write an autobiography based on market-value needs and tastes. As Hemenway notes in his biography, Hurston's publishers insisted on this form, and although she wanted to write a novel, her need for money was so great that she complied with their wishes. Again, like Sojourner Truth, who had to "sell the shadow to support the substance," Hurston had to fashion this statuary self.

Barbour's notions about religious autobiography as applied to Zora Neale Hurston are confirmed in cultural and literary terms by Henry Louis Gates, Jr., when he notes how, in her autobiography, Hurston "constantly shifts between her 'literate' narrator's voice and a highly idiomatic black voice found in wonderful passages of free indirect discourse." This usage of a "divided voice, a double voice unreconciled," Gates goes on to claim, "strikes me as her great achievement, a verbal analogue of her double experiences as a woman in a male-dominated world and as a black person in a nonblack world, a woman writer's revision of W. E. B. DuBois's metaphor of 'double-consciousness'" (Afterword, 193).

Nellie McKay also discusses the strategy of revision in her essay "Race, Gender, and Cultural Context in Zora Neale Hurston's *Dust Tracks on a Road*." Like the theorists mentioned previously, she challenges the concept of individualism as the most important factor in Western forms of autobiography because, "for those outside the dominant group, identification with community is pervasive for the unalienated self in life and writing" (175). Group identification, she points out, is vital because it enables individuals to move beyond alienation within the dominant culture to construct meaningful lives in writing and permits the rejection of historically diminishing images of self imposed by the dominant culture, allowing marginalized individuals to embrace alternative selves constructed from authentic images of their own creation. Hurston needed her culture in the same way Rebecca Jackson needed the Shaker community and Sojourner Truth needed the community of abolitionists. Because, as Elizabeth Fox-Genovese asserts in her essay "To Write Myself: The Autobiographies of Afro-American Women," the identity of black women is grounded "in the historical experience of being black and female in a specific society at a specific moment and over succeeding generations" (161). Autobiographies by black women demand a theory that respects the distinctiveness of the group. Group identity remains at the center of the self emerging, and one's life must be perceived against a background of the historical experience.

Hurston's autobiography should be read as a cultural document rather than a factual rendering of her life. It is essentially like her anthropological writings (field notes taken from her travels) because Hurston describes her life as a series of migrations or wanderings that give her spices for her box but do not result in only one recipe. As she says in reference to a series of visions she has, "I discovered that all that geography was within me. I only needed time to reveal it. . . . no one could spare me my pilgrimage" (115).

This ambulatory quality of her life lends it the appearance of a journey, a quest motivated by the desire for education and achievement. Education was her tool, one she used at every opportunity. Even when serving as a maid for a theater group she remarks, "I had been in school all that time. I had loosened up in every joint and expanded in every direction" (141). She "wanted action," and to get it she "was driven inward" (40). For example, when she wanted a horse and her father would not give her one, Hurston imagined her own horse, her "phantasies were still fighting against the facts" (38). Her early interest in reading tales of fantastic adventure, stories of Thor and Odin, Moses and King David, shows how her fantasies helped her to improvise: "My soul was with the gods and my body in the village. People just would not act like gods. . . . Raking backyards and carrying out chamber pots were not the tasks of Thor. I wanted to be away from the drabness and to stretch my limbs in some mighty struggle" (56).

The first autobiography of a black woman who was also a creative writer, *Dust Tracks* may not reveal intimate details of Hurston's life, nor assume a politically correct stance as a polemic on racial injustice. Although she rejects the idea of her autobiography as a race-represented document, she never separates herself from the black community. Moreover, Hurston once again affirms her fluid, organic view of self as something ever changing, ever converting. In his essay "The Life of Women: Zora Neale Hurston and Female Autobiography," James Krasner discusses how in *Dust Tracks* and *Their Eyes Were Watching God* Hurston manifests "self-conscious construction" of self and story by placing emphasis on the generation of narratives rather than their completion. "Both life stories seem to be structured around a prophetic moment: The main character has a vision which is fulfilled by the end of the story" (113). Hurston, therefore, offers up her life not to reveal herself per se but to reveal her culture and to identify certain patterns and trends in the lives of black women. Her work can be placed alongside the works of women who wrote before her, and another motive behind Hurston's autobiography can be gleaned by comparing her work to the writings of Harriet Jacobs, Sojourner Truth, and Rebecca Jackson.

Like the nineteenth-century writers who, to a certain extent, served an abolitionist agenda, Hurston had legitimate concerns regarding the state of race relations in America. Although she rejected racial-group oppression as a characteristic identity trait, her preference for celebrating black strength implies a kind of racial identity and indicates a cause she attempted to serve, just as nineteenth-century black women writers cast their political and social concerns in religious terms. Moreover, as the nineteenth-century women had to struggle to assume identities and claim roles in society, to defend their integrity, so too did Hurston struggle to adapt to the opportunities her era presented and to be accepted as an equal while remaining faithful to her roots. Like the women who wrote before her, Hurston was concerned with the need to "authenticate," but this time not her life in particular (the veracity of her tale does not have the same existential consequences it did for women writing in the nineteenth century) but a certain way of life expressed in black folk communities. A reading of her autobiography must be historically contextual to make sense because, as she says, "each moment has its own task and capacity" (264).

Finally, another prominent feature identified in the writings of Harriet Jacobs, Sojourner Truth, and Rebecca Jackson is also found in Hurston's autobiography: the subversion of the autobiographical impulse for specific theological reasons. As previously shown, nineteenth-century spiritual autobiographies subverted self in order to draw attention to divine power and to identify religious faith as the source of strength, ability, and personal identity. In a similar fashion, Hurston subverts self in order to draw attention to cultural power, and to identify cultural faith as the source of her strength, ability and personal identity. Hurston even claims that she was "weighed down with a power I did not want. I had knowledge before its time. I knew my fate" (67). Her life demanded that she learn or create appropriate techniques for coping, and her dreams and visions were guiding forces in her life. If nothing else, Hurston's autobiography reveals her awareness that her visions endowed her with the imaginative ability to improvise, to realize, as Albert Murray says, that "you can't slay a dragon with a formula."

Nellie McKay believes that *Dust Tracks* is a "deliberately staged work" because Hurston knew "exactly what she wanted her readers to know" ("Race, Gender, and Cultural Context," 187). Since it was written primarily for a white audience and to meet the expectations of the dominant publishing industry, which wanted a book to promote race relations, *Dust Tracks* is bound by conventions not dissimilar from those which influenced nineteenth-century abolitionists seeking to persuade their audience. She wanted to show her life as a search for autonomy that was grounded in her belief that her identity was established as "one of the people," who nonetheless accepted "the means at my disposal for working out my destiny. It seems to me that I have been given a mind and will-power for that very purpose" (278). In the act of creating her life-in-writing, Hurston "brought to consciousness a special understanding of her own experiences at a particular moment in her own time. Factually or not, *Dust Tracks* presents a view of black female identity that justifies its existence" (McKay, 188). With a pious respect for mystery, Hurston declined to "read God's mind" and revise his plan of the universe through her own life (278). She was, however, a woman who accepted her call to "find the road it seemed that I must follow" (145), who "took a firm grip on the only weapon I had—hope" (143), and in writing about her life let her soul stand on tiptoe and stretch "to take in all that it meant" (158).

Their Eyes Were Watching God

> I have told it anew as one who was born later. I bear in me the blood and spirit of those who created it and out of my blood and spirit it has become new. I stand in the chain of narrators, a link between links; I tell once again the old stories and if they sound new it is because the new already lay dormant in them when they were told for the first time.
> —Martin Buber

In her foreword to the 1990 edition of *Their Eyes Were Watching God*, Mary Helen Washington describes the history of the book's reception and how, largely due to the efforts of Alice Walker, this novel has now come to assume an unparalleled importance in the canon of African-

American literature. She and Henry Louis Gates, Jr., who wrote the afterword, both cite Hurston's novel as the essential link in establishing a maternal literary ancestry for black women. The novel has become, in Gates's words, "a metaphor for the black woman writer's search for tradition" (Afterword, 186), because several black women writers have "openly turned to her works as sources of narrative strategies, to be repeated, imitated, and revised in acts of textual bonding" (190). This tradition, however, extends backward as well as forward, back to Harriet Jacobs, Rebecca Jackson, and Sojourner Truth, in ways literal as well as literary. As Mary Helen Washington notes, "the history that nurtured this text into rebirth . . . galvanized us into political action to retrieve the lost works of black women writers," and as the novel "affirms and celebrates black culture it reflects that same affirmation of black culture that rekindled interest in the text" (Foreword, xiv).

My attempt, therefore, is to trace this backward lineage while anticipating the future developments in black women's fiction. *Their Eyes Were Watching God* serves this function by recapitulating the concerns of early spiritual autobiographies while casting them in a novelistic style that creates a form by which future converts could come to tell new stories. The protagonist, Janie Starks, tells the story of her life—her childhood, her journeys, and her loves—to her best friend, Pheoby, and through her to the community to which she returns. As her community has helped form her, so she helps to form it. Through Janie's story Hurston creates not only a work of literary inspiration but a cultural, indeed an anthropological, document that traces the spiritual lineage of black women. As Barbara Christian states, this novel "is a classic example of the fusion of creative imagination with folk materials" that serves a transitional purpose in the literary history of black women writers by leading the way "toward the presentation of more varied and complex women characters" (*Black Women Novelists*, 57). June Jordan calls the novel one centered on love—"the prototypical Black novel of affirmation" (88).

Their Eyes Were Watching God is about Janie Crawford, who was raised by her grandmother to "take a stand on high ground" (32), and to seek the material comfort and security Nanny observed in the lives of the white people for whom she was a slave. Nanny's wish to fulfill through Janie her dream "of what a woman oughta be and to do" (31), leads her to encourage Janie into a marriage with Logan Killicks, an older, modestly prosperous farmer. The marriage proves loveless for Janie, whose ideal is different from the one her grandmother has for her. She dreams of something or someone to represent "sun-up and pollen and blooming trees." She wants "to be a pear tree, any tree in bloom" (25).

Two recurring metaphors, the pear tree and the horizon, help unify her vision. Although the horizon represents the individual experiences one must acquire to achieve selfhood, the pear tree represents organic union with another, a mystery that is revealed to her one day: "The inaudible voice of it all came to her. She saw a dust bearing bee sink into the sanctum of a bloom; the thousand sister calyxes arch to meet the love embrace and the ecstatic shiver of the tree from root to tiniest branch creaming in every blossom and frothing with delight. So this was a marriage! She had been summoned to behold a revelation. Then Janie felt a pain remorseless sweet that left her limp and languid" (24). This spiritual-natural vision comes to represent the union Janie searches for throughout her life as she reaches for the horizon. In a sense this vision is her moment of awakening to the possibility of conversion, when she becomes aware of the kind of life she wants to lead. Indeed, Alice Fannin cites this vision as Janie's "Eve-like" recognition of her own individual selfhood, as a separate creature in the garden of the world (2). Finding a bee for her blossom is not a simple romantic gesture but a symbolic action, revealing the inspiration behind Janie's travels to the horizon.

Janie, standing in a long line of self-determining black women, realizes she must "invent" herself; she cannot wait for her world to be made but must create it for herself. She finds Jody Starks, an assertive and ambitious man on his way to Eatonville, a town where a man can be his own boss. She thinks that maybe he can be "a bee for her bloom" (54) and not a "vision . . . desecrating the pear tree" (28), as Logan Killicks is. Intending to become a "big voice," Jody buys land, sets up a store, gets a post office, and becomes mayor. He wants to change Janie—to make her into the subordinate and dutiful mayor's wife and to set her apart from the community. Janie watches as the spirit of her second marriage leaves the bedroom and takes "to living in the parlor" (111). Janie discovers that with Jody she has "no more blossomy openings dusting pollen over her man, neither any glistening young fruit where the petals used to be" (112). Eventually she reacts to Jody's control by publicly challenging his manhood, and he soon dies, bitter and upset over the challenge to his authority.

Now that she is a woman of means, Janie is pursued by status-conscious suitors. She rejects her class role and falls in love with Vergible "Tea Cake" Woods, a free-spirited laborer much younger than she. Janie describes Tea Cake as a "glance from God" (161). This third marriage (appropriate since in describing conversions Hurston said "three is the holy number and the call to preach always comes three times" [SC, 86]) is without the hypocrisy and suffocation that characterized her other marriages. Tea Cake "could be a bee to a blossom—a pear tree blossom in the spring" (161). The "son of Evening Sun" (264), as Janie describes him, Tea Cake is the symbolic representation of her arrival at the horizon, when she thinks her conversion is complete. Tea Cake accepts Janie as equal, and they are open and giving toward one another. She travels with him from job to job, leaving her home and money in Eatonville. They end up in the "muck" of the Everglades, working together in bean fields. Their happiness does not last long, however, because during their escape from a hurricane Tea Cake saves Janie but in the process is bitten by a rabid dog. He slowly goes mad. While he is disoriented, he attempts to shoot Janie, forcing her to shoot him in self-defense. She is tried and acquitted by a white jury, and after returning to her home in Eatonville tells her story to her best friend, Pheoby. Janie is left with her memories of a transcendent love and an awareness that Tea Cake will "never be dead until she herself had finished feeling and thinking" (286).

Janie does not see her life as tragic but as full and rich. This is the message she brings back to her community, that "self-fulfillment rather than security and status is the gift of life" (Christian, *Black Women Novelists*, 59). For Janie, learning about living means going to the horizon of her consciousness and establishing relationships, with God as well as with men and women. Self-discovery and self-definition consist of learning to recognize and trust her inner voice, to find the source of value and authority out of which to live in the ground of her own being, while rejecting the formulations others try to impose upon her. "Increasingly, she comes to validate 'the kingdom of God within'" because "Her eyes have been watching God—the God who manifests himself in nature, in other human beings, and especially in our deepest selves" (Bush, 1036).

Janie's experiences fit into the spiritual lineage of black women in a way Katie Cannon has chosen to describe in ethical terms by identifying in the black women's literary tradition a standard of moral principles. Among the contributions Cannon makes is the revelation that "the moral agency of the characters in [Hurston's] fiction is that the protagonists are always connected with the general history of the race in the context of community." Furthermore, Hurston "shows how each generation is dependent upon the last for its understanding of moral wisdom and in turn, each new generation creates it for the next" (Cannon, 126–27). Since the attributes of femininity available to white women were useless in the pragmatic survival life-style of black women, Cannon describes their strategy of moral conduct as one of "quiet grace," an attitude that develops upon recognition of difference and the ways in which one responds to that difference. Janie realizes she is black and therefore different from the white children she plays with, in much the same way Linda Brent realizes this. "Ah was wid dem whit chillun so much till Ah didn't know Ah wasn't white till Ah was round six years old" (21). From this early age Janie is aware that there are two possible perceptions of her: the intrinsic natural image she has of herself, and the image held by the rest of the world. In doing such, she identifies the friction between self and society that underscores much of Hurston's autobiography as well.

Yet Janie also sees life as a great tree in leaf, "with things suffered, things enjoyed, things done and undone. Dawn and doom was in the branches" (20). This cosmic view is presented in *Their Eyes Were Watching God* as the drama of Janie's thirty-year search for self-fulfillment as she moves between the values of the community and the tension that arises when that community prescribes a certain life for her. Janie has her eyes on the horizon, but as for all converts, the pattern of grace that orders her life is visible only in retrospect, after experience has brought her full circle. When she returns home after losing Tea Cake, Janie accepts this loss and all other losses as part of the quiet grace that brings one to self-authenticity because, "If you kin see de light at daybreak, you don't keer if you die at dusk. It's so many people never seen de light at all. Ah wuz fumblin' round and God opened de door" (236). Janie's self-esteem and sense of spiritual fulfillment are not based on illusion or false values but on the experience of unconditional love and the realization that her identity has been sacralized through this love.

What makes *Their Eyes Were Watching God* such an appropriate book for this discussion, in a direct line with the texts previously discussed, is not only the ethical propositions it sets forth in terms of the view of African-American culture that is presented. Hurston also creates a kind of intimate spiritual autobiography that, like the examples from the nineteenth century, constitutes an archetypal quest.[11] Moreover, Janie herself is a model for female development, one who understands being as a habit of mind as much as a set of behaviors. Her quest, as Alice Fannin points out, is psychological, spiritual, "even cosmological and ontological," because Janie "goes beyond the level of all these [social and political circumstances] to an exploration of self as part of the universe and the universe as part of self" (1).

Janie's revelation beneath the pear tree and her choice of natural metaphors to describe her deepest feelings and sensations are examples of the kind of holistic development Fannin cites. Moreover, as Peter Schwalenberg notes in his analysis of time as it structures the novel, Hurston moves between qualities of timelessness as eternal vision and time as the rhythm of life that indicates and initiates change, creating a vision of reality in which transcendent order is reflected in immanent order. Maria Tai Wolff makes much the same point when she says, "Janie's search for identity is not a temporal, progressive process, but involves the representation and evaluation of a series of experiences or images . . . a lyrical formulation of the world" (30).

Hurston also establishes a connection with antecedent spiritual narratives by constructing the narrative in the form of a memoir, as a convert's recollection of the events and feelings that led to her being able to tell her story. This is a story "full of that oldest human longing—self revelation" (18). A deliberate spiritual history is fashioned by Hurston from the perspective of Janie, who has "been a delegate to de big 'ssociation of life. Yessuh! De Grand Lodge, de big Convention of livin' is just where Ah been" (18). Janie's recounting of her experiences begins with her being weighed down with false images and community values that Hurston contrasts from one generation to the next. Aware that her community is judging her—making "burning statements with questions and killing tools out of laughs" (10)—Janie tells her story to Pheoby not to justify herself only but to edify the community, realizing that as a convert who has been to the horizon and back, she is in a special position to convert others: "'tain't no use in me telling you somethin' unless Ah give you de understandin' to go 'long wid it" (18).

So Janie begins her story not by recounting only what happened while she was off for a year and a half with Tea Cake but by going back to her roots and laying the foundation for her personal change and revelations. She decides that "her conscious life had commenced at Nanny's gate" (23). Nanny Crawford, the grandmother who raised Janie, was a freed slave woman who understood marriage as the only way to escape poverty and abuse. She had suffered rape by a white slaveowner that resulted in the birth of an illegitimate child who, greatly resembling the white man, was the object of ire from his wife. Nanny runs away and hides in a swamp to protect the baby, "But nothin' never hurt me 'cause de Lawd knowed how it was" (33–34).

Nanny represents what Cannon terms quiet grace, and the necessary actions taken by a slave woman are something Janie understands, yet she still yearns for more. Following her revelation under the pear tree Janie focuses on a vision that "connected itself with other vaguely felt matters that had struck her outside observation and buried themselves in her flesh. Now they emerged and quested about her consciousness" (24). At this crucial moment of discovery, Janie is "seeking confirmation of the voice and the vision" but finding only confirmation for "all other creations but herself" (25). She has "searched as much of the world as she could from the top of the front steps and then went on down to the front gate and leaned over to gaze up and down the road" (25). While she is "looking, waiting, breathing short with impatience. Waiting for the world to be made" (25), Nanny intrudes and announces the "end of her childhood." This is a feeling shared by Linda Brent who exclaimed after she was separated from her lover, "the dream of my girlhood was over."

Speaking to Janie as a "foundation of ancient power that no longer mattered" (26), Nanny expresses her wishes for Janie in terms that define her own denied hopes and aspirations. She prays to God "for Him not to make de burden too heavy for me to bear" (27) by guiding Janie toward a husband, a "higher bush" and a "sweeter berry" (28) who will, if not love Janie at least protect her. Nanny wants Janie to have the material security and possessions that she never had. Although Nanny uses natural imagery to describe her aspirations for Janie, she herself is delineated by the tree imagery not as a living tree but a ruined one: "Nanny's head and face looked like the standing roots of some old tree that had been torn away by a storm" (26), recalling the image of the stump on the grave of Linda Brent's mother. Nanny's visions do not correspond to Janie's pear tree visions.

Here in the text Hurston inscribes a familiar slave narrative as Nanny recounts to Janie the struggles in her own life, warning Janie that blacks are "branches without roots" and emphasizing that her whole life has been devoted to ensuring that the fate of Nanny and Janie's own mother (whom Nanny named "Leafy," a symbol of her once-naturalistic vision for the future) must not befall Janie: "'Ah wanted to preach a great sermon about colored women sittin' on high, but they wasn't no pulpit for me. . . . Ah said Ah'd save de text for you. Ah been waitin' a long time, Janie, but nuthin' Ah been through ain't too much if you just take a stand on high ground lak Ah dreamed'" (31–32).

Nanny's moral code—like that of Linda Brent—developed in relation to ethical ambiguities of her experience. Houston Baker recognizes this in *Blues, Ideology, and Afro-American Literature* when he cites Nanny's story as having direct antecedents in slave narratives where the economics of slavery define effective expression in terms of property. Functional prudence was her value center for self-fulfillment. "Ah was born back due in slavery so it wasn't for me to fulfill my dreams of whut a woman oughta be and do. . . . Ah didn't want to be used for a work-ox and a brood-sow and Ah didn't want muh daughter used dat way neither" (31). She attempts to pass down this wisdom so Janie can avoid a servile role as "de mule uh de world." Nanny will never understand the scope of the dreams of a woman of Janie's generation, while Janie, in an effort to honor her ancestors, will capitulate to Nanny's advice and consequently suffer from stifling her being.

Although it is Nanny's religious beliefs that allow her to justify Janie's suffering with the principle that "folks is meant to cry 'bout somethin' or other" (42), she also reflects the solemn dignity inherent in the African-American female religious tradition and sensibility when she "stays on her knees so long she forgot she was there herself. There is a basin in the mind where words float around on thought and thought on sound and sight. Then there is a depth of thought untouched by words, and deeper still a gulf of formless feelings untouched by thought. Nanny entered this infinity of conscious pain again on her old knees. Towards morning she muttered, 'Lawd, you know mah heart. Ah done de best Ah could do. De rest is left to you'" (43).

At this point Janie has no experience and no authority other than her own intuition to refute the power of history, age, and religion represented by Nanny. Janie conflates her grandmother's experience with her own desires—"out of Nanny's talk and her own conjectures she made a sort of comfort for herself" (38)—and decides that perhaps the symbolic act of marriage can signify the kinds of changes in her life, the end of "cosmic loneliness," that she imagined while under the pear tree. So she marries Logan and waits "for love to begin" (38).

Love never begins in this marriage. Janie becomes increasingly dissatisfied with the explanation that prosperity should bring her happiness because when it comes to *things,* she "ain't studyin' 'bout none of 'em" (42). Janie values the spiritual over the material, so she returns to her own intuitions, her own naturalistic visions and realizes, "She knew things that nobody had ever told her. . . . she knew that God tore down the old world every evening and built a new one by sun-up. It was wonderful to see it take form with the sun and emerge from the gray dust of its making. The familiar people and things had failed her so she hung over the gate and looked up the road towards way off" (44).

It is when she is looking off to the horizon that she meets Jody Starks, who, although he did not "represent sun-up and pollen and blooming trees," still "spoke for far horizon" (50). So Janie throws her lot in with his and travels with him to Eatonville as his wife. Jody, however, proves to be the kind of man "dat changes everything, but nothin' don't change him" (79), and means to include Janie in his list of changes. He insists on her submission to his vision of her because "a pretty doll-baby lak you is made to sit on de front porch and rock and fan you'self" (49). Jody's vision entails a crucial separation of Janie from the town folks, setting her apart not just in life-style but in attitude. Janie can only get "so close to most of them in spirit" (74). In placing her up on a pedestal, Jody is merely performing a variation on the theme of women as the mules of the world. This isolation from the community, combined with Jody's indifference to Janie's needs, causes Janie to move to a new level of conscious sensibility, where she looks down the road toward the horizon not literally but imaginatively.

She objectifies Jody in the same way she perceives him objectifying her (and in the same way Hurston objectified herself in her creation of an autobiographical "statue"), and in their bedroom "put something in there to represent the spirit like a Virgin Mary image in church" (111). Her image of Jody

> fell off the shelf inside her . . . tumbled down and shattered. But looking at it she saw that it never was the flesh and blood figure of her dreams. Just something she had grabbed up to drape her dreams over. In a way she turned her back upon the image where it lay and looked further. She had no more blossomy openings dusting pollen over her man, neither any glistening young fruit where the petals used to be. She found that she had a host of thoughts she had never expressed to him and numerous emotions she never let Jody know about. Things packed up and put away in parts of her heart where he could never find them. She was saving up feelings for some man she had never seen. She had an inside and an outside now and suddenly she knew not to mix them. (112)

Once she achieves this separation and this ability to conduct two lives, one interior and one exterior, Janie becomes more bold; she even challenges Jody in public. Since Jody gives her nothing that she values, she preserves in herself those things that she does value and stores them up for the future, ensuring that she will have something for which to live. Janie has become aware of the sacrality of her own existence and the need to preserve it from corruption. Although she does not yet have a way to express her being in her daily life, she reconciles herself to a compromise between her grandmother's desire for her security and an attention to her own spiritual needs. She can watch as a "shadow of self" tends to the store while in her mind she goes and sits under a tree. Like Sojourner Truth, Janie "sells the shadow to support the substance."

After this new level of identity is achieved, Janie watches helplessly as Jody dies from lack of medical attention brought on by his own fears and stubbornness. She finally confronts him before he dies, accusing him of not being "satisfied wid me de way Ah was. Naw! Mah own mind had tuh be squeezed and crowded out tuh make room for yours in me" (133). She mourns him in pity, but essentially feels not loss but freedom. She sends her face to the funeral while her self rollicks with springtime. At this moment in her development she also turns on her grandmother's memory that she had "hid under a cloak of pity" (137).

In order to understand her examination of her grandmother's vision at this point in Janie's life, it is important to recall the visionary terms Hurston sets forth at the beginning of the novel. Describing a philosophy that Lloyd W. Brown calls "female transcendentalism" (39), Hurston discusses the differences between the dreams of men and women, claiming that for men "ships at a distance have every man's wish on board. For some they come in with the tide. For others they sail forever on the horizon, never out of sight, never landing until the Watcher turns his eyes in resignation, his dreams mocked to death by time." Women, however, believe the horizon is nearby and will it so because "women forget all those things they don't want to remember and remember everything they don't want to forget. The dream is the truth. Then they act and do things accordingly" (9). This passage establishes the reflectional tone of the novel, describing the perspective of a convert, one who, once a vision is seen, a dream realized, remembers life and lives only according to that position of the sacrality of being. It also serves to temper what appears in this part of the narrative as an unsparingly critical assessment of Nanny by Janie.

Nanny's vision of her own potential, although shaped and limited by her experience, was not without its own relative value and expression of sacrality. Nanny's vision reveals what Harold Bloom sees as "the vivid pathos of her . . . superb and desperate displacement of hope" (2). Nanny herself, as Lloyd Brown remarks, "is Janie's predecessor as ethnic archetype of the woman's universal situation. Having experienced both the degradation of slavery and the usual limitations of womanhood, she has also shared the correspondingly passionate dreams those disadvantages nurtured" (41). Although Janie comes to a point where she must judge the terms of what her grandmother wished for *Janie,* she cannot judge the life her grandmother led herself because it was her grandmother's strength and courage that made it possible for Janie to have the opportunity to dream at all. Nanny "managed to maintain imaginative energies" (Brown, 41–42) and dreamed in the context of what her own needs suggested: in terms of security and safety for her family, just as Linda Brent and Sojourner Truth dreamed of freedom for their children. Nanny lived through a time when ships held not just dreams but human lives as cargo. Her dreams must be appreciated in this context.

Janie, however, is a woman of a different era and with new potential. She sees the ambiguities in Nanny's heroic stance, realizing that her materialistic ambitions capitulate to the very value structures that oppressed her. Lorraine Bethel distinguishes between Nanny and Janie in the following way: "While Janie represents the Black female folk aesthetic contained in the blues, her grandmother symbolizes the Black religious folk tradition embodied by spirituals" ("This Infinity," 181). Nanny, as John Callahan asserts, represents "a black female ancestral text to be absorbed and overcome" (128). Janie, in rebelling against Nanny's definition of womanhood and moving to assert her individuality, still needed to travel the route of tradition.

> She had been getting ready for her great journey to the horizons in
> search of *people;* it was important to all the world that she should find
> them and they find her. But she had been whipped like a cur dog, and
> run off down a back road after *things.* It was all according to the way
> you see things. Some people could look at a mud-puddle and see an
> ocean with ships. But Nanny belonged to that other kind that loved to

deal in scraps. Here Nanny had taken the biggest thing God ever made, the horizon—for no matter how far a person can go the horizon is still way beyond you—and pinched it in to such a little bit of a thing that she could tie it about her granddaughter's neck tight enough to choke her. (138)

Nanny's dealing in scraps, just as Phyllis Biggs's when she fashioned a work of art as a quilt, was an appropriate and creative spiritual response of "quiet grace." Yet relationships in which she is prized possession or dutifully obedient wife or granddaughter make Janie feel as Hurston felt in her autobiography when she says: "if somebody were to consider my grandmother's ungranted wishes, and give *me* what *she* wanted, I would be too put out for words" (284). These relationships force Janie to measure her success or failure by the goal of self-actualization. They force her to confront feelings she has hidden by playing roles under a strict code of behavior. She must, therefore, "creatively reinterpret and re-present this story to escape its constraints and preserve its empowering aspects" in order to create her own (Kubitschek, *Claiming the Heritage,* 21). Hurston inscribes Nanny's tale within Janie's as a significant cultural document or legacy for specific reasons. As Melvin Dixon notes, "by integrating the early Afro-American literary form into the novel [i.e., the slave narrative], Hurston provides a cultural context for Janie's contemporary quest" (86). It is only with Tea Cake, who makes her feel vital, needed, wanted, loved, and unlimited, that she can give of herself freely and express the full sacrality of her being in spiritual, not materialistic, terms. It is then that Janie's soul "crawled out from its hiding place" (192).

Tea Cake differs from the other men in Janie's life in his ability to appreciate her for who she is and in his ability to express his feelings of unconditional love. As he reminds Janie, "you got de key to de kingdom," and he is "de Apostle Paul tuh de Gentiles. Ah tells 'em an then again Ah shows 'em" (158). Tea Cake is Janie's spiritual mentor, who by identifying himself with Saint Paul, Christianity's most famous convert and missionary, signifies the role he will play in Janie's transformation. He affirms but does not himself create her sense of sacrality. He is the catalyst that allows her to begin to love and value herself. Moreover, the values that Tea Cake holds are like Janie's in their nonmaterialistic basis. When neighbors get suspicious of their relationship and Tea Cake's intentions for Janie, she reminds Pheoby that "dis ain't no business proposition, no race after property and titles. Dis is uh love game. Ah done lived Grandma's way. Now Ah means tuh live mine" (171).

Janie admits how Pheoby could think her previous life "look lak heben" (172) and that she herself has had moments of doubt about Tea Cake. Yet she still is willing to risk a future with him because her current routine is "squeezin' all de life outa me," and "Ah wants tuh utilize mahself all over" (169). Aware of town gossip, Janie tries to set the record straight at this point in her life by assuring Pheoby of her feelings and trusting her to explain: "Ah ain't puttin' it in de street. Ah'm tellin' *you*" (172). With Tea Cake Janie is learning "new thoughts and new words said" (173). She is rediscovering life through her experiences with him and rediscovering her spiritual self at the same time. The relationship they create together is modeled on the African-American religious image of God as one who sustains life and promotes self-expression. The relationship also conveys a similar intensity because self is surrendered willingly for divine purpose. When she looks down on a sleeping Tea Cake, Janie feels a "self-crushing love" and is reborn, converted anew in and through this love.

Janie and Tea Cake pledge to do as much as they can together. They move to Florida and work together harvesting beans in "the muck." Their home becomes the center of the community, like a storefront porch, because of the energy and enthusiasm they create together. They do not live off of Janie's wealth but "live offa happiness" (210). At this point in the narrative Hurston displays her anthropological gifts, conveying the life of Janie and Tea Cake in vivid folklore images, once again establishing the importance and primacy of this mode of living and seeing. One sees storytelling rendered for its own sake and one hears the stories of the "big picture talkers," who use "a side of the world for a canvas" (85). Janie learns to "tell big stories" (200), and indeed the story she tells Pheoby is an example of the ability and vision she has acquired. With Tea Cake as her guide, Janie explores the soul of her culture and learns how to value herself within this context. Although it was by challenging her grandmother's vision that Janie understood herself as different from cultural prescription, it is through Tea Cake that she comes to view herself as culturally defined. Both modes of self-discovery are essential, however, and both reflect the reliance on others, on community, that is so characteristic of African-American culture.

Yet it is on the muck that Janie also meets Mrs. Turner, who has "built an altar to the unattainable" (215) and whose perverted sense of being is all tied up in illusory images. Her God, unlike Janie's, "demands blood" and inspires fear.[12] Mrs. Turner is drawn to Janie because of her light complexion and tries to turn her against the darker Tea Cake. Her influence poisons even Tea Cake, who, in an effort to show "who's boss," beats Janie. Mrs. Turner misses what Janie sees— a sacrality in herself as created by God and loved by Tea Cake. Just as there is a God to watch, to turn to for answers and help, so too are there false gods who need watching.

When the hurricane hits the Everglades, all "eyes were questioning God." Janie and Tea Cake reflect on death, and Tea Cake, who worries for the peril in which he may have placed Janie, is reassured by her with these words: "If you kin see de light at daybreak, you don't keer if you die at dusk. It's so many people never seen de light at all. Ah wuz fumblin' round and God opened de door" (236). As Sigrid King notes, God becomes "a name for what she has learned through her own growth and through her relationship with Tea Cake. God is the unexplainable force which Janie is constantly seeking" (694).[13] Janie reestablishes a self-authenticated concept of living in theological terms that dictate the kind of life one leads rather than the length of one's life. Those who may think they are alive, the uncon verted, are not really living until they embrace self and life's full potential. The hurricane comes to take on an almost apocalyptic symbolic significance as living and dead are inverted by the storm—inanimate objects tossed into animate motion, living things crushed and rendered lifeless by the waves. It is in this context that Tea Cake's death occurs. As he lay dying from the bite of a rabid dog, Janie

> looked hard at the sky for a long time. Somewhere up there beyond blue ether's bosom sat He. Was He noticing what was going on around here? He must be because He knew everything. Did He *mean* to do this thing to Tea Cake and her? It wasn't anything she could fight. She could only ache and wait. Maybe it was some big tease and when He saw it had gone far enough He'd give her a sign. She looked hard for something up there to move for a sign. A star in the daytime, maybe, or the sun to shout, or even a mutter of thunder. Her arms went up in a desperate supplication for a minute. It wasn't exactly pleading, it was asking questions. The sky stayed hard looking and quiet so she went inside the house. God would do less than He had in His heart. (264)

Janie neither strains for help from God nor rages over his doing "less than He had in His heart," because God has been her companion through her changes. He has given her the knowledge no one else could, and he was also the one who brought her to Tea Cake: "Ah jus' know dat God snatched me out de fire through you" (267). When she must shoot Tea Cake in self-defense, Janie calls it "the meanest moment of eternity" yet knows too that "no hour is ever eternity, but it has its right to weep" (273), a sentiment that recalls Nanny's comment that "folks meant to cry 'bout somethin' or other." So she thanks Tea Cake for the chance for "loving service" (273). Tea Cake has given her the opportunity to appreciate her own self-worth, a quality necessary to live alone without him. Her own transcendent vision can now expand on reality rather than denying it.

Janie is tried for Tea Cake's murder and confronts community hostility not unlike that which she described initially on her return to Eatonville. The people "were there with their tongues cocked and loaded" (275). Yet upon her acquittal and after the people come to understand the circumstances of Tea Cake's death, Janie is welcomed by the community, which shares her loss. It is through Janie's awareness and honest presentation of herself that the community is edified and redeemed. Unlike at Jody's funeral, where she dressed the part but did not feel it, at Tea Cake's funeral Janie wears overalls because she was too busy "feelin grief to dress like grief" (281). This time her inner and outer selves are reconciled, or rather her outer self is transcended. The substance of her grief overtakes an image of grief.

So the story ends where it begins, with Janie on the porch having "been tuh de horizon and back." She expresses to Pheoby her hope that her story will change people's minds, and she urges Pheoby to tell them her story. She also urges Pheoby not to judge the townsfolk too harshly for their opinions because they are just "parched up from not knowin' things" (285). Instead, she instructs Pheoby, "tell em dat love ain't somethin' lak uh grindstone dat's de same thing everywhere and do de same thing tuh everything it touch. Love is lak de sea. It's uh movin' thing, but still and all it takes its shape from de shore it meets, and it's different with every shore" (284).

In these remarks one is reminded of Hurston, in her autobiography, describing the natural order God created and asserting that "nothing God ever made is the same thing to more than one person." It is through understanding the quality of divinity, of the sacrality in each being, that one can identify and appreciate the uniqueness of each gift of human life. Pheoby immediately responds to Janie's story and admits, "Ah ain't satisfied wid mahself no mo'" (284). Like a worshiper inspired to convert after a particularly rousing sermon, she has grown while listening to Janie's story, just as Sojourner Truth described her own self-emancipation as having grown "so tall within." Pheoby intends to keep growing and urge the community on to new awareness as well. Janie, however, is at peace.

Janie's peace comes from confidence in her visions and in her own judgment about how she tried to realize those visions. Secure in her status as a convert, she can realistically appraise her failed dreams and the dreams that were thwarted by circumstance. As a clever convert in the final pages of the novel, Janie says to Phoeby, "Ah done been tuh de horizon and back and now ah kin sit heah in mah house and live by comparisons" (284). Experience of reality, rather than dreams, is what makes the difference because "you got tuh *go* there tuh *know* there" (285). By the end of the novel, Janie's organic vision of unity and her independent vision of herself—the pear tree and the horizon—are resolved into one image of "a great fish-net." Janie pulled this net "from around the waist of the world and draped it over her shoulder. So much of life in its meshes! She called in her soul to come and see" (286).

Although it was only men on Joe Clark's porch who told the stories, Hurston creates a way to pass on Janie's vision through her best friend, Pheoby, on whom Janie can depend for "a good thought" (19). When she trusts Pheoby to tell her story, "You can tell 'em what Ah say if you wants to. Dat's just de same as me 'cause mah tongue is in mah friend's mouf" (17), Hurston has Janie choosing a collective rather than an individual voice, just as Hurston chose a similar voice in her autobiography.[14] Janie is the teller of the tale, although Pheoby is the bearer of it. Hurston sets up a chain of shared expression similar to that seen in the writings of nineteenth-century black women writers. Rebecca Jackson claimed to be only a "pen in God's hands," writing his story, and Linda Brent and Sojourner Truth both relied on the goodwill and faith of abolitionists to get their stories told. Pheoby, like the abolitionist scribes and editors, stands within a traditional role of women who take their message back to the community. Lorraine Bethel relates the narrative method of *Their Eyes Were Watching God* to the traditional culture of black women this way: "In presenting Janie's story as a narrative related by herself to her best Black woman friend, Pheoby, Hurston is able to draw upon the rich oral legacy of Black female storytelling and mythmaking that has its roots in African-American culture" (180).

The shift in narration from first to third person that is problematic for many critics who cite it as an example of, among other things, a failure of Janie to achieve her own voice, is yet another demonstration of the power of a shared voice and also a form of spiritual dialogue where all knowledge is transmitted from revelation downward, through testifying before a community and understood in those terms. Michael Awkward affirms the power of relational narration when he asserts that Janie's self-discovery is dependent upon and indicated by her ability to manipulate language as an accomplished storyteller who recognizes the artist's responsibility to and dependence on the larger community. He also stresses the importance of Janie's silence, a concept comparable to what Katie Cannon calls "quiet grace," or women's ability to understand when words will or will not have the power to change reality. As Henry Louis Gates says in his discussion of Hurston's text as embodying "free indirect discourse," the central theme of the novel is "the quest of a silent black woman both to find a voice and then to share it in loving dialogue" (*Signifying Monkey*, 169). Janie's survival, as Alice Fannin points out, depends not only on greater self-awareness and independence but "on the vision of the self as a wondrous part of a Creation that is itself, 'wondrously and fearfully' made" (2). A convert tells her story not for herself only but to testify, to inspire faith in others as well.

In communicating her vision, however, Janie has "both a historical and a personal memory to react against in her search for autonomy" (Hemenway, 237). Much of the novel is concerned with her struggle to understand the inadequacy of her grandmother's vision as well as her community's judgments. Janie comes to realize that all souls are equal before the eyes of God and that her grandmother and her townsfolk are confused by wanting to be above others. Her grandmother, however, "was borned in slavery time when folks, dat is black folks, didn't sit down anytime dey felt lak it. So sittin' on porches lak de white madam looked lak uh mighty fine thing tuh her. Dat's whut she wanted for me—don't keer what it cost. Git upon uh high chair and sit dere. She didn't have time tuh think whut tuh do after you got up on de high stool like she told me" (172).

But as Janie reminded Pheoby before she headed off for a life with Tea Cake, her experiences with Logan and Jody demonstrated that

"Ah done nearly languished tuh death up dere. Ah felt like de world wuz cryin' extry and ah ain't read de common news yet" (172). Nanny's text was saved for Janie, giving her a response by which she could evaluate her own life and a call to her responsibility as a member of the community. As Gloria Wade-Gayles has written of women like Nanny, "We must see them first as persons with dreams and needs no less important than ours, and then as mothers who sacrificed their dreams in order to put our hands on the pulse of freedom and self-hood" (12). In ways similar to Harriet Jacobs, who rewrote her culture's plot when Linda Brent asserted her prerogative of choosing her own partner, so too does Hurston show Janie choosing how and with whom she wants to live her life. Janie changes her culture's standard plot resolution when she "re-writes" Nanny's text. This new text becomes the scripture Janie recounts to Pheoby. Janie witnesses to her community all she has learned about relationships, making everyone an heir to the same legacy.

Janie establishes her identity within the spiritual context of her relationship to her culture and the people who embody it. In that "divine" culture her faith lies. Tea Cake is part of this reappropriation of her culture, representing "an incarnation of the folk culture" (Bone, 130). When Janie eventually becomes a storyteller herself, her blossoming occurs in the context of community and her discovery of self happens in her meaningful participation in black traditions. She discovers a way to make use of her traditions, not by seeking to be classed off and attempting to sit on high but by celebrating her cultural identity. In fact, Glynis Carr believes that it is precisely Janie's ability to take advantage of an opportunity for storytelling that indicates her spiritual health and reintegrates her into her community. Her visions of self-identity, Carr maintains, do not exist in isolation, and her "discovery of personal identity is closely bound to her exploration of her cultural identity" (198–99). Carr sees Hurston as measuring Janie's "mastery of life not only by her independence but also by the depth of her involvement in a self-affirming, self-identified folk culture" (200), and by her ability to participate in that culture on her own terms.

As Hemenway acknowledges in his biography, "Janie's growth is Hurston's subject" (240). Because, as Ann Rayson phrases it, "It is on 'becoming' rather than being" that Hurston focuses her novel (1). As a convert, Janie "makes dreams truth" by remembering life as it led to her changes: as ordered, purposeful, and intentional. Her life may have not been lived that way, but we will never know because it is in her changes and the changes she wishes to effect in others, it is through her evangelical mission that we know Janie. Janie has created her life through her own interpretation and transformation of reality. As Maria Tai Wolff points out, Janie "narrates the manner in which her identity has been revealed to her. The story is structured around successive scenes of self-recognition that are Janie's repeated attempts to create a clear, satisfying picture of who she is. The events of the narrative, and the other characters, function within this structure. Janie is led to form her own dream, her own truth, from what she has lived" (29).

From her grandmother Janie receives "a text" that did not correspond to her feelings and intuitions, but she relies on experience and appropriates this text. With Jody she realizes that "her old thoughts were going to come in handy now, but new words would have to be made and said to fit them" (54–55). Later Janie learns from her life with Jody that new words were meaningless unless they were her own. She could not simply supplant Nanny's text with Jody's. Janie and Tea Cake, however, create "new words," and Janie learns the "maiden language," the language of possibility. Tea Cake offers Janie experience, out of which she can create a dream, a text, indeed a scripture. From Nanny, Logan, and Jody she receives a prepared text, a definition of her role, but from Tea Cake she receives an invitation to live a text, to make a role for herself. From this initiative of Janie's, therefore, the reader is inspired to formulate her own image, and the story becomes a revelation to all. As Janie felt upon her first vision, the reader feels like she has "been summoned to behold a revelation" (24).

The novel gives us not only a spiritual narrative of conversion but an example of one who had been called to preach. As Robert Bone points out, the style of the novel is "based primarily on the Negro preacher's graphic ability to present abstractions to his flock" (127). This places it in direct line with what Robert Stepto and John Callahan define as a classic trope in African-American writing: call and response. Callahan, for example, stresses that the narrative exists only because Hurston calls for Janie's story, and Janie responds to Hurston as narrator by being a collaborator in the telling of her story. The novel, which as Callahan explains, begins as a private autobiographical act, is transformed into "fiction, a story, by her telling it to Pheoby and thus creates a bridge, a link between Janie and the community from which she is estranged." Hurston, "by making storytelling and the narrative act collaborative and continuing, simultaneously launches a new community of values and performs a revolutionary literary act" (212).

Janie, by creating her own scripture, can respond to society's judgments while inviting its support as well. Michael Cooke, in *Afro-American Literature in the Twentieth Century: The Achievement of Intimacy,* has a similar way to chart Janie's development as he ties it into the stages or modes he perceives in African-American literature in general. In what he describes as a metamorphosis, characters in black novels move from self-veiling, into solitude, toward kinship, and finally into intimacy. These stages could also be describing conversion, where one begins in denial of sacrality, moves toward contemplation of such a state, seeks recognition from God and others, and eventually achieves a level of intimate faith. Religious conversion was the model by which many African Americans initiated themselves into free status and a new identity, and this model continues to be carried on in black literature as an expression of the belief that transformation is possible. From the position of a converted soul, as Janie is at the end of the novel, one has the spiritual elasticity needed to live a complete life and the creative inspiration to tell a tale.

Their Eyes Were Watching God portrays a creative black woman as one who recognizes her responsibility to and her dependence on her faith and her culture. As Janie communicates her vision and her discoveries to her community, so Hurston once again pays tribute to her historical and cultural legacy through the creation of Janie. The novel, as Hemenway notes, demonstrates that "Hurston alone, among all the artists of the Harlem Renaissance, understood this principle of folk process. Folk tradition is not just a body of texts, melodies, and beliefs. . . . folk tradition involves *behavior*—performed interpretations of the world which influence action—and it does not easily transfer to a print-oriented tradition. . . . there is no separation of subject and object, of mind and material in folk tradition. What appears from afar as material for the creative artist is simply behavior for the tale-teller, an activity as natural as thinking" (80–81).

So Janie moves from a private and escapist image of the pear tree to a view of communal creation and integrates her concrete experience with her transcendent vision. This is perhaps best expressed in a parable Hurston relates just before Janie sets off for a life with Tea Cake. A classic Gnostic creation myth, it resonates with the characteristics of black religion that inform so much of Hurston's writing, characteristics that, although granting God power, also squarely place responsibility for a fulfilled life on the shoulders of each individual: "When God had made The Man, he made him out of stuff that sung all the time and glittered all over. Then after that some angels got jealous and chopped him into millions of pieces, but still he glittered and hummed. So they beat him down to nothing but sparks but each little spark had a shine and a song. So they covered each one over with mud. And the lonesomeness in the sparks make them hunt for one another. But the mud is deaf and dumb. Like all the other tumbling mud-balls, Janie had tried to show her shine" (138–39).

Janie comes to see that quality of African-American religion that views redemption as ultimately upon the individual's self-understanding and the resulting freedom it provides. The title of the book indicates further the qualities of this theology. In Hebrew culture there is a saying that "the eyes of God are on us always." In African-American religion the terms are reversed, and people do not worry about God's constant judgment so much as they look to God for signs, for recognition and affirmation. As the eyes of the folk watch God during the hurricane for signs of safety, so too does Janie watch God for indications of where and how she should fit into the world. Her journey of self-discovery is an exploration of the physical, social, and spiritual world made available to her. This universal, human situation or posture before God—of recognizing a force behind reality that makes sense of human life—is what links Janie to her community. In telling her story to Pheoby, Janie mimics God, "the great artist," and makes sense of her experiences for her community, whose members keep their eyes on her as their interpreter. She has been endowed, by virtue of experience and revelation, to transform her life and make it into a parable. So Janie is in one respect a classic convert in the Christian tradition because she finds herself by losing herself, by transcending "I" through her relationships with people and Creation and God.

Alice Walker has written of *Their Eyes Were Watching God,* that "there is enough self-love in that one book—love of community, culture, tradition—to restore a world. Or create a new one" ("On Refusing to Be Humbled," 2). The kind of love Walker is describing, the kind of love Janie eventually experiences and preaches, is rooted in the African-American worldview that does not distinguish sacred from profane but sees each dimension of reality as informing and expressing the other. By reconciling the horizon and the pear tree, by blending personal needs and choices with sacrificial and unconditional love, Janie comes to understand a certain relational way of living in the world, of expressing the sacrality of her being. God is where the pear tree and the horizon converge. When she pulls in the great fishnet, Janie understands what Sojourner Truth understood when she said of God, "we dwell in Him as the fishes in the sea."

This relationship, described by Martin Buber as an "I-Thou" relationship, is revolutionary in its simplicity. By drawing attention to the religious dimensions of human personality, Buber demonstrates how dialogical relationships, in any historical or dramatic context, recapitulate and reaffirm one's relationship to a transcendent being. Such a relationship has no bounds, has no "thing" for its object, but establishes a world of relation. For "the existence of mutuality between

God and man cannot be proved, just as God's existence cannot be proved. Yet he who dares to speak of it, bears witness, and calls to witness to whom he speaks" (137). In all her works, but especially through Janie, Hurston links herself to what Buber describes as the "chain of narrators." She creates a new story out of the "old stories" and reveals her connection to women like Harriet Jacobs, Sojourner Truth, and Rebecca Jackson. She witnesses to the reality and necessity of a vision of life wherein relationships, and respect for the Thou within and as a part of the I, lead one to wholeness and a posture of keeping one's eyes on God.

4

Involuntary Converts

teach me to survive my
momma
teach me how to hold a new life
momma
help me
turn the face of history
to your face
—June Jordan

Although the autobiographical mode that characterized so many of the writings of nineteenth-century women still persists most of the celebrated black women writers of the twentieth century have found their voice in the form of novels.[1] This is not to say that the autobiographical form has had no influence on contemporary writers. Toni Morrison, for one, admits that autobiographies constitute a very large part of her literary heritage, but she is also conscious of the limitations imposed on her predecessors when they wrote in this form. Two qualities dominated nineteenth-century autobiographies: historical veracity and a didactic tone. Both were adopted in an attempt to persuade readers that all human beings are worthy of God's grace. Driven by these two imperatives, Morrison laments the loss of any description of an interior life and sees her role as a fiction writer, in part, as ripping the veil off the protected interior lives of her ancestors. She does this through the resources of her memory and by acts of imagination. This, she believes, is a way to demonstrate fidelity to her ancestors, to show "awe and reverence and mystery and magic" ("Site of Memory," 111).

Like the autobiographies that preceded them, contemporary novels often take as their theme the formation of identity, becoming bildungsromans that offer insights into the factors and interrelationships that shape individual growth. The novel form, however, offers a dimension autobiography does not by allowing for greater flexibility in describing the interplay of psychological and sociological forces that shape identity. Unlike traditional bildungsromans, the novels of black women are not animated by the same possibilities for achievement and social integration that define so much of men's coming of age because they are often denied these opportunities that would make them aware of the intellectual, emotional, and spiritual capacities inherent in their personalities.

What facilitates the unfolding of inner capacities is different for women than for men. Efforts to shape their identity are complex, fluid, and sometimes evasive and contradictory. They often include moments of disillusionment and clashes that do not always lead to immediate integration and sometimes lead to withdrawal. Typical episodes of rites of passage available to men (formal schooling, leaving home, sexual exploration, careers) are often unavailable to women, whose pattern of growth is usually defined in terms of connectedness rather than separation, by their ability to make and maintain affections and relationships. Women's developmental goals are often defined in terms of community and empathy rather than achievement and autonomy. Their novels reflect the difference between these goals and the more commonly accepted male goals of achieving selfhood. The narrative patterns in women's fictions or female bildungsromans, cited by Elizabeth Abel, Marianne Hirsch, and Elizabeth Langland in *The Voyage In: Fictions of Female Development,* include a chronological apprenticeship, a gradual development into identity by stages, and moments of awakening (what I have been calling conversions) that are epiphanic moments of recognition. Also, there is often a submerged plot that encodes rebellion (11).[2] Implied in the fictions of women is a reformulation of accepted terms of development and an appreciation of the genre as a more flexible category that can accommodate a variety of approaches to living. What women's fictions do share with the concept of the bildungsroman in general is a belief in a coherent—if not fixed and autonomous—self, and a faith in the possibility of human development.

In an essay on Zora Neale Hurston and aspects of female autobiography, James Krasner uses the opening passage of *Their Eyes Were Watching God* to demonstrate the difference between male and female ways of ordering personal history. Using Hurston's terms, he describes men as "'Watchers,' observing the fulfillment of plans, prophecies, and desires over time," while "women are creators, building up and tearing down their atemporal fictions as they go" (113). While men's life stories describe either success or failure, women's histories are "manifestly fictional; their stories describe the construction of fictions" because, as Hurston says "the dream is the truth." We can see African-American women creating themselves not only through the development of their own writing voice but also through their creation of fictions and characters who face the challenge of creating voices within the new social, family, and community relationships that our era has produced. As Lucinda H. MacKethan writes, "Women novelists of the last several generations have shaped stories about women characters who begin their quests from the position of patriarchally defined daughter, yet who proceed to discover creative power beyond traditional roles. Breaking away from parental or communal expectations creates a rupture for these women characters, not only between themselves and their families, but within themselves. Descent into self-doubt, experiences of separation from family and from self, lead to discoveries that enable these women to identify within themselves the source of their creativity" (*Daughters of Time*, 66–67). These women also discover something more than their voice, because they discover that which gives them voice, the sacred dimensions of their own being and a spiritual connection to reality that informs their search for wholeness. Part of this discovery of sacrality within themselves involves a reappraisal of their heritage and its traditions whereby they find the sacred dimensions of culture that lend substance to their search and reunite them with community. Black women come to realize that God is not above history but acts in history. Eventually, each individual is confronted with the question of what God's acts mean. One must find satisfactory answers regarding a proper response to God and discern how that response should be translated in terms of social and personal behavior based on one's experience of what characterizes God.

In portraying women converts, twentieth-century black women writers turn to the rich and varied legacy of African-American religion that incorporates Christian dimensions, African sensibilities, and hoodoo elements of sacred quests. In describing the processes and experiences that construct and shape black women's identities, they attempt to interpret faith in such a way as to ensure its continuing relevance. They reappropriate a religious sensibility and see their history as a source for theological interpretation of God's presence in the world. By looking back into the past they can visualize the reality of the future and make decisions about possibilities in the present. They can rewrite history from the perspective of women, restore women to history and history to women. They can show how religious values reflect basic perceptions, aspirations, and values of culture and individuals. Barbara Hill Rigney, in *Lilith's Daughters,* her study of women and religion in contemporary fiction, sees many modern women writers as perceiving, revising, reinterpreting, and in some cases exorcising the images and ideas of traditional religions. By challenging the "sacred" to include qualities and experiences of women, they are creating new symbols for spiritual transcendence. These women recognize that political freedom is linked to spiritual freedom and that spiritual freedom is an essential dimension of a larger quest for women to establish identities and claim empowerment. The goal of conversion for contemporary black women is to incorporate change for personal identity and to sacralize their experience of marginality by creating a new order and a place for themselves in that order.

The nature of this search requires great vision and often involves great risk and moments of rejection; it is not a smooth, uncomplicated course. Harriet Jacobs, Sojourner Truth, Rebecca Jackson, and Zora Neale Hurston all gave intimations of the tension that is created between expressing individual personality and satisfying requirements of communal experience. Each wrestled with how to locate or construct a self in the context of transcendent realities, historical-cultural specificity, and essential (female) experience. Jacobs explored the moral ambiguities that attend both Christian practice in the South and the concept of true womanhood. Sojourner Truth drew attention to the paradox of abolitionists who would not also embrace the concept of the liberation of women. Rebecca Jackson wrestled with her desire to lead a life of vision while also serving her black community over and against the Shaker hierarchy and belief in living in a community apart from the rest of the world. Hurston battled within herself and against the dominant culture over her role as a spokesperson for her race and her culture while still trying to assert her own aesthetic and spiritual prerogatives.

Toni Morrison demonstrates in *Sula* how black women do not automatically recover from the rupture MacKethan cites. They may not achieve the spiritual wholeness they seek because in many ways the culture upon which they depend for definition is also ruptured. Morrison reveals the bankruptcy of both drastic existential atheism and a timid clinging to tradition. Paule Marshall's *Praisesong for the Widow*, however, describes ways in which spiritual direction can reveal cultural continuity within the discontinuity such a rupture entails, and Alice Walker's *The Color Purple* indicates how the rupture of the very concepts of family and community can lead to the creation of new families and communities that depend for definition upon one's own perception of self and God. Each novelist offers a measure of hope and instruction, however, showing how women alienated within themselves and searching for connections can achieve reintegration that restores their inner and outer worlds to wholeness. Morrison, Marshall, and Walker all attempt to render old traditions more palatable, to remythologize religious qualities, and to find ideas and symbols that are more existentially and philosophically attractive to contemporary women. They show, in other words, how twentieth-century black women convert—how they confront issues of identity and culture to claim a distinct sense of self—just as their foremothers did. They gain a spiritual perspective that guides them through contemporary challenges.

The affinities among black women writers of two centuries exist, as Michael Awkward reminds us in *Inspiriting Influences*, "not only as a result of common sexual and racial oppression but rather . . . occur as a function of black women writers' conscious acts of refiguration and reinversion of earlier canonical texts" (4). Utilizing what Awkward cites as a feeling of an "inspiriting influence" instead of the "anxiety of influence," black women writers demonstrate a cooperative rather than a competitive pattern in their works and successfully transform "the old stories" by adding new expressive features that their times require. Judith Kegan Gardiner, in "On Female Identity and Writing by Women," emphasizes Awkward's point about how women, who develop a capacity for nurturance, dependency, and empathy, see fiction as an occasion for cooperative textual interactions. Henry Louis Gates, Jr., in *The Signifying Monkey*, establishes a similar pattern of repetition and revision in the black tradition in reference to what he calls signifyin(g), or the double-voiced presence in black discourse. These features, therefore, are cultural forms that retain the timeless spirit of African-American culture. Barbara Christian, in *Black Feminist Criticism*, sees Hurston as providing the important cooperative link, comparing her influence on contemporary black women writers to the influence of the Bible on the earliest white male colonials. Hurston, Christian states, gave women the "authority to tell stories because in the act of writing down old 'lies,' Hurston created a bridge between the 'primitive' authority of folk life and the literary power of the written text" (11). Hortense Spillers adds complexity to perceptions of tradition by seeing it as "an active verb, not a retired nominative" (Pryse and Spillers, 260), when she claims, "black women's writing community is a matrix of literary discontinuities that partially articulate various periods of consciousness in the history of an Afro-American people" (51). Black women's voices, therefore, although rooted in individual experience, extend far beyond the merely individual.

Whereas the nineteenth century reveals black women who wrote to claim membership in human community, the twentieth century reveals contemporary black women as seeking entrance into the world of humane letters, attempting to advance black women one step further and to establish a shared sense of common experience on a basis other than racism and oppression, wishing to promote more creative notions of unity among black women. In the nineteenth century, black women were more inclined to capitulate to religion and see culture as formed by religion. Their narratives reflect this perspective and remain within already established theological and social norms. Their motives, however, were not without sincerity, and in their own ways they laid foundations for future feminist speculation. Harriet Jacobs, Sojourner Truth, and Rebecca Jackson all proclaimed their allegiance to God and credited him with aspects of their development and liberation while easing readers into an appreciation of the strength and sacrality of all women.

With Zora Neale Hurston religion became an aspect of culture in the context of her celebration of aesthetic cultural forms. It was Hurston who revealed the connection between hoodoo and Christianity, and who showed the way for a more expansive and creative theological interpretation of life. It was Hurston who banished from consciousness not only the concept of a single monolithic black female identity but also the assumption that one's identity must be a fixed and permanent thing.

In the twentieth century, however, there is an attempt not only to recover cultural forms and meaning in order to bring about the recovery of the personal qualities of religion but to do so in a context of greater freedom for women. Moreover, there is an expressed intent to affirm the communal nature and traditional qualities engendered by African-American religion. Contemporary black women are attempting to discern a divine presence, to recapture "the possibility of God, as it were, for a culture which has passed beyond the explicitness of a unified religious viewpoint into an almost helplessly pluralistic era" (Killinger, 127). It is experience that becomes the ground for that perception of presence, as one encounters self from a perspective of transcending self into an encounter with spirit.

All the described modes of being and of relating culture and religion include some version of the historical model of black women as questers or converts. They vary depending on the different aspects that take prominence in influencing a particular perception. Using the terms established earlier to describe aspects of conversion, one could say that the literary heritage of black women began in a theological mode, where reality was rendered predominantly and generally uncritically in religious terms. These women were voluntary converts who responded to the search for identity in sanctified religious ways. In the early twentieth century, when liberation from formal slavery was no longer an issue to be reckoned with and the black denominational churches no longer served the all-encompassing functions they once did, perceptions of reality were rendered in a traditional mode as black women emphasized culture and the ways that religion collaborated in preserving a unique cultural form of spiritual expression. In our present era, reality is perceived with reference to the psychological mode, where black women are involuntary converts, resurrecting religious language to explain modern longings, the contemporary search for stability, and terms by which to establish identity. The conversions they effect are not literal, but literary.

Wherever emphasis falls, however, it is clear that in their history black women have adopted religious strategies for survival and for growth. They have turned to the particulars of their own experience, their stories, and found in the details of human life a basis on which to define themselves and reality, to understand the legacy of ancestral grace, and to inspire new traditions. They have uncovered the sacred in themselves and have imagined sacred power "as present in the whole complex of life, not as a power taker but as an empowerer" (Plaskow and Christ, 10). Paule Marshall, in *Praisesong for the Widow,* emphasizes reverence for ancestors and a recognition of origins as a way to ensure the spiritual and physical continuity of humanity. Her protagonist, Avey, comes to appreciate how ancestors continue to exist and act in the world and how, in the words of Luisah Teish, "not only does their energy find a home in the wood that groans, but at the proper time and under the right circumstances they can be reborn" (Plaskow and Christ, 87). Alice Walker, in *The Color Purple,* reveals how language and images used to name the sacred underlie conceptions held about God and self, emphasizing the feminist theologian Mary Daly's assertion that "to exist humanly is to name the self, the world, and God" (*Beyond God the Father,* 8). In her spiritual revision Walker seeks an inclusive concept of God that emphasizes, but is not limited to, the feminine and immanent nature of Spirit and sees it as a vital redemptive force in black women's lives. Toni Morrison, however, offers no simple solution to a black woman's search for identity. Rather, she reveals the complexities that attend such a search and uncovers basic moral ambiguities in cultural forms and ideas that stand between women and their attempts to sacralize their identity. Moreover, she shows that sacrality, like identity, is not a permanent quality but one that grows and changes throughout time and experience.

Toni Morrison (1931–)

For it is well established that if a memory is great enough,
other memories will cluster about it and those in turn will bring
their suites of memories to gather upon this focal point,
because perhaps, they are all parts of the one thing
like Plato's concept of the perfect thing.
—Zora Neale Hurston

As a writer, Toni Morrison, like Zora Neale Hurston before her, shares a commitment to preserving African-American culture. Her culture's stories, Morrison insists, must be told because when people are able to tell their story, "they are not only one, they're two, three and four, you know? The collective sharing of that information heals the individual—and the collective" (Morey, 1039). Like Hurston, Morrison believes strongly in "the collective," in community, and defines it by personal rather than political relationships. Also like Hurston, Morrison describes her ability to write and her responsibility as a teacher and an editor for other black writers in religious terms: she calls her talents "a blessing" (Naylor and Morrison, 581); describes the life of one of her characters as "a prayer" (Morrison, "Memory, Creation, and Writing," 388); distinguishes between the "holy uses" and "profane uses" of memory in creating a story (Morrison, 389); and believes that she is called upon to "bear witness and effect change . . . to enlighten and strengthen" (Jones and Vinson, 145).

Just as Hurston found great vitality, originality, and spirituality in various forms of cultural expression in black communities, so too does Toni Morrison, whose novels embody her ancestors' memory as fiction. In an interview with Wilfred D. Samuels and Clenora Hudson-Weems, Morrision describes her anger when she sees black people depicted as boring. "I have never met yet a boring black person. All you have to do is scratch at the surface and you will see. And that is because of the way they look at life" (1). To Morrison, black life does not have to be portrayed as bigger than life because it is big as life, therefore possessing its own dramatic qualities or "will to adorn." It also expresses great variety, and in each of her novels Morrison presents "a dialectic of values, alternative ways of being black, female, or human" (Blake, 188). Like Hurston, therefore, Morrison sees one of her purposes as a writer as rediscovering and preserving black culture: its history, its myths, its essence, and its presence. A certain urgency attends her reclamation because she is concerned that "the world would fall away before somebody put together a thing that comes close to the way we [blacks] really are" (Morrison, "Behind the Making," 90). Reclaiming black culture, Morrison suggests, will help to counteract the negative definitions of self that attend minority peoples and lead to a greater appreciation of the sacred qualities of life.

One project Morrison undertook between writing novels was the preparation and publication of *The Black Book* in 1974, which testifies to the belief she shares with Hurston that black history has immediate relevance. Composed of newspaper clippings, photographs, songs, advertisements, patent-office records, recipes, and other memorabilia from the collections of Middleton Harris and others, *The Black Book* is a scrapbook of black history, a literary analogue to Phyllis Biggs's quilt. Morrison conceived this book as a way to recognize the cultural contributions of "anonymous men and women who speak in conventional histories only though their leaders," to record the lives of blacks "when we knew who we were." For Toni Morrison, like Zora Neale Hurston, understanding black history and culture gives clues to understanding those influences that shape black identity, not in "forging new myths" but in "re-discovering the old ones" (Blake, 192).

It is interesting to note, however, that for all the similarities between Morrison and Hurston, Morrison states quite explicitly in a conversation with Gloria Naylor that she had never read Hurston's work until completing her second novel, *Sula*. She sees this phenomenon as a vindication, not a denial, of what Awkward cites as "inspiriting influences," as an indication that a tradition of black women's writing really exists. As she explains, "You know, if I had read her then you could say that I consciously was following in the footsteps of her, but the fact that I never read her and still there may be whatever they are finding, similarities and dissimilarities, whatever such critics do, makes the cheese more binding, not less, because it means that the world as perceived by black women at certain times does exist, however they treat it and whatever they select out of it to record, there is that" (Naylor and Morrison, 590).

Much of what Morrison selects to record in her writing are the religious qualities and influences in African-American culture. When asked by interviewer Bessie Jones how her moral vision was influenced by her religious convictions, Toni Morrison began her response by saying that although she has trouble with "institutions," she does not have "any doubts—religious doubts—and I find that at the bottom line, striving toward that kind of perfection is more interesting, more compelling. The effort to be good and just is more interesting, more demanding. And I just don't trust any judgment that I make that does not turn on a moral axis." She goes on to explain that she comes from "religious people" who relied on biblical sources to explain and describe life. "That was part of their language . . . they expressed themselves in that fashion." That biblical language, however, they combined with another kind of relationship "to something I think was outside the Bible. They did not limit themselves to understanding the world *only* through Christian theology. I mean they were quite willing to remember visions and signs and premonitions and all of that. But that there was something larger and coherent, and benevolent, was always a part of what I was taught and certainly what I believe" (Jones and Vinson, 136–37).

Morrison is suggesting a vision that has been evidenced throughout the writings of black women, an awareness that culture and religion collaborate in creating worlds and selves. Religious faith provides a framework and structure, while cultural forms allow for variation and diversity. The novel *Sula* is an example of this approach because Morrison presents the reader with what she calls "archetypes" (Jones and Vinson, 144)—the concepts of good and evil, natural and unnatural, sacred and profane—but then proceeds to unravel these concepts to reveal their complexity, all the while relying on their stature as archetypes, their mythic resonance, to explain why they have any fundamental meaning at all.[3] Like Hurston before her, Morrison often inscribes a folk story beneath her stories to lend authenticity to her rendering of black life and to show also that there is something more going on, "because some of that stuff is not only history, it's prophecy" (Jones and Vinson, 144). Morrison, by exploring the ways in which past myths of "the folk" merge with significant events of the present, creates another variation on the theme of conversion, showing how the conflict between wishing to be part of nature or society or a cultural tradition yet distinct from it reflects the inherent desire for growth in human beings.

In her novels Morrison often presents characters in transition, journeying through mysterious circumstances and personal histories to the innermost dimensions of their psyches, often leading to a triumphant discovery of selfhood. Moreover, these people are usually marginal personalities who are lacking a social, spiritual, psychological, historical, geographical, or genealogical place or center. They are in a liminal state (which the anthropologist Victor Turner describes as "betwixt and between"), where they must undertake a quest for personal and communal wholeness and fulfillment. As such they often resort to myths or sacred stories to explain their predicaments and to gain understanding.

Myth, as Toni Morrison once described it, is "a concept of truth or reality a whole people has arrived at over years of observation" (Morrison, "Behind the Making," 88). It often involves things that cannot be explained in conventional, rational terms. Morrison's fiction is populated with the supernatural, the effect of which is to dislocate the reader into seeing reality in new ways, to uncover meaning often hidden but usually revealed in mythic attempts at understanding. *Sula*, like all of Morrison's fiction, blends the natural and the supernatural in a quest for meaning.

The drama of *Sula* (1973) takes place during the years 1919 to 1965 in a community called "The Bottom," itself a kind of mythic, sacred space. Although it is up in the hills, the narrator explains its name and origin as a "nigger joke." A white farmer who had promised freedom and a piece of bottom land to his slave but did not want to part with the rich valley land, tricked the man into believing that "bottom land" was in the hills—"the bottom of heaven" (5). Eventually, however, when the valley farms have been developed into a hot, dusty town, the hills remain cool and shady and the white folks change their mind. Buildings are leveled and trees uprooted for the Medallion City golf course. Then the Bottom becomes the suburbs, and the multiple ironies of its naming and history signal the shifting relationships of value that will appear throughout the novel.

In *Specifying,* Susan Willis states that the Bottom, although it is "terminated and dramatically obliterated," nonetheless "refers to the past, the rural South, the reservoir of culture that has been uprooted—

like the blackberry bushes—to make way for modernization" (94). Willis's reference to the blackberry bushes comes from the novel, which begins with a timeless sort of opening often found in myths: "In that place, where they tore the nightshade and blackberry patches from their roots to make room for the Medallion City golf course, there was once a neighborhood" (3). Willis identifies a central problem explored in Morrison's writing as one of "how to maintain an Afro-American cultural heritage once the relationship to the black rural South has been stretched thin over distance and generations" (Willis, "Eruptions of Funk," 264). *Sula* offers an interesting example of this dilemma, Willis maintains, because it is set in the 1940s, a period of heavy black migration to the cities, when black neighborhoods were created where previously none had existed. The novel also stretches back to World War I, when blacks were first incorporated into the system as soldiers, and ahead to the 1960s, when cultural identity with the past seems to dissipate. Covering this span, Morrison develops the social and psychological aspects that characterize lives lived during periods of historical transition.

Keith Byerman, in *Fingering the Jagged Grain,* sees *Sula* from a similar perspective because of the way it probes "for origins of oppression, victimization, and social order" and offers "possibilities for negating such control" (192). He sees the community, therefore, as serving a "religious" function by establishing terms for relationships: male/female, parent/child, individual/society, good/evil. It codifies attitudes toward power and establishes rituals that attend birth and death, beginnings and endings.

It is within this context of transition and permanence that the novel explores a black woman struggling for self-realization on her own terms rather than defining herself by the terms of her community. The protagonist, Sula Peace, shares many qualities with Janie Crawford—an independence of spirit and an eventual unwillingness to conform to community standards of propriety. Sula differs from Janie, however, in that she never had to struggle to relieve herself of responsibility to someone else's idea of what "a woman oughta be"—

she was practically born rebellious, in an unconventional family that expected nothing else of her. As the narrator states, "Hers was an experimental life" (118). Sula comes to assume the unyielding personality of an outcast who refuses to succumb to the codes, values, and standards of both the dominant culture and her own immediate environment, but she is vulnerable to the loss that accompanies such isolation. By cultivating the scapegoat qualities that distinguish her from her neighbors and by choosing isolation, she is eventually defeated. Sula seems to believe that she can create for herself an identity that exists beyond community and social expectations, but her life, although existentially "authentic," is also lonely and without any enduring meaning. Her desire to be different leaves her spiritually and physically alienated, and she dies alone.

Unlike Janie, who returns home with hopes of reintegrating with her community, Sula comes home defiant and aloof after having left her community for schooling and travel. Ironically, however, Sula's very position as an outsider has the effect of uniting the community in its judgment against her: "Their conviction of Sula's evil" makes the townspeople their best selves; they begin to "cherish their husbands and wives, protect their children, repair their homes and in general band together against the devil in their midst" (117). But Sula is unable to participate in this communal bond. It is only through her friendship with Nel Wright that Sula eventually confronts the limits of measuring her worth and acts based on her own value system.

The treatment and attitudes toward Sula likewise reveal patterns of the community when she refuses its attempt to order her and submits to its embodiment of her as evil. By ignoring or deliberately violating conventions, Sula threatens assumptions by which life in the Bottom is organized and made meaningful. Having been away, Sula is a threat to the community's insulated moral order that has already been so threatened by the intrusion of the dominant society. To a certain extent the community has lost its mythology, and Sula's symbolic presence represents an opportunity for the community to retrieve it. With Sula standing as an outsider in relation to this lost community (having neither true family nor true community to give her bearings), the townsfolk can label her a witch and, by doing such, by casting all evil as her doing, regain a tenuous sense of themselves. Their response to Sula is a spiritual one, however skewed, that changes them in "accountable yet mysterious ways" (118). As Philip Royster explains: "the folk create the scapegoat by identifying Sula as the cause of the misery, which they identify as evil, in their lives. It is undoubtedly easier for the folk to anthropomorphize their misery than to examine the generation of that misery by their relation to the environment. The folk produced good in their lives, that is, loving and caring for one another, by reacting to their own conception of evil, Sula, whom they considered a witch" (164).

The concept of evil in The Bottom, therefore, is not unappreciated. The townsfolk believed "aberrations were as much a part of nature as grace" (118). African Americans, as Morrison reminds us, understand evil as having a natural place in the universe, and the folk in the Bottom recognize that nature is "never askew" and that there is a "legitimacy of forces other than good ones" (90). This is why they are so willing to see Sula as an embodiment of the evil forces that surround them. Evil, however, as Morrison explains in an interview with Robert Stepto, is not a simple concept to grasp: "One can never really define good and evil. Sometimes good looks like evil; sometimes evil looks like good—you never really know what it is. It depends on what uses you put it to. Evil is as useful as good is" (Stepto, "'Intimate Things,'" 476). Morrison does not assess evil and goodness in conventional religious or moral terms. Nor does she wholly identify good and evil with either Sula exclusively or the community. Evil is not a sin against God per se: "evil is not an alien force, just a different force" that has "a natural place in the universe. Black people did not wish to eradicate it. They just wished to protect themselves from it" (Tate, 129). In Morrison's concept, or so she seems to suggest, evil is another aspect of life, albeit a life-denying one; it is a sin against oneself or one's community, one's failure to act either responsibly (as Sula does by shunning her community) or existentially (as the community does by all too easily shrugging off its own responsibility and complicity onto Sula).

In referring to the funeral of Chicken Little (a minor character in whose death Sula shares complicity), Keith Byerman sees myth and ritual operating in ordinary experience where "the need here is to express, not to explain. The funeral is not the cause but the occasion to reaffirm a position as both victim and elect. The ritual transforms an absence into a presence, makes a private, physical loss into a communal, spiritual gain. The language of the passage, which modulates into a litany, refines the pattern by suggesting recurrence and thus permanence of structures" (196). Thus, when the women of the Bottom, at Chicken Little's funeral, do not "protest God's will but acknowledge it and confirm . . . their conviction that the only way to avoid the Hand of God is to get in it" (66), Morrison is not wholly critical of their religious position. What she seems to be suggesting is that both Sula and the pious women are wrong, that getting in God's hand is not a passive act of acceptance and that refusing to see his hand in Creation is not simply an act of heroism. Morrison, with her suspicion of institutions, challenges the townsfolk's blind piety while acknowledging their need for faith, to make sense of tragic events and to "see the lamb's eye and the truly innocent victim: themselves. They acknowledged the innocent child hiding in the corner of their hearts, holding a sugar and butter sandwich" (65).

In the African-American tradition, however, faith is action, more than a "sugar and butter sandwich" taken to quiet spiritual hunger. As Barbara Lounsberry and Grace Ann Hovet argue, Morrison is most interested in showing "the constriction and ultimate futility of any single ordering vision" (126). Morrison, by indicting at once both Sula's irresponsibility and the community's uncritical acceptance, suggests a need for a reverence for the past, but also that such reverence be based on genuine sacred qualities, not empty forms and rituals.

Full of bizarre characters and punctuated with violent deaths, *Sula* confuses many readers. The first character to whom we are introduced is Shadrack, a shell-shocked World War I veteran who founds National

Suicide Day, which twenty years later the whole community observes. Shadrack, however, through his madness orders the chaos of the community in his own eccentric way. Then there is Eva Peace, Sula's grandmother, a one-legged woman who reputedly laid her leg across a train track to collect insurance money to feed her children. She sets her heroin-addicted son, Plum, on fire and hurls herself from her third-floor window in a vain effort to save her daughter Hannah (Sula's mother), who has caught fire while canning in the yard. Sula herself lets Chicken Little slip from her hands only to watch him drown in the river. She never tells anyone. She takes and then casually discards her best friend's husband. She puts her grandmother in a retirement home. Morrison leaves her reader confused about how to perceive these characters and events, whether to applaud Eva's self-sacrifice or deplore her control; whether to admire Sula's freedom or condemn her heartlessness. Morality is always an ambiguous quality in the world of the Bottom.

Although it appears that *Sula* is constructed in a logical, chronological fashion (each chapter of the book beginning with a date), times and dates in the novel become important only through significant action. Morrison begins with a prologue that introduces the landscape of the novel and follows this with a discussion of community personalities; only at the end of the second part does she introduce her major character, Sula, and then only through her relationship to her childhood friend, Nel. The novel ends with an epilogue concerning Nel's life—Sula is already dead—and an eulogy to the Bottom, which is on the brink of vanishing. Like the time frame of a convert who reconstructs a life as naturally leading toward eventual salvation, Morrison does not tell a strict tale but highlights events that lead to a certain impression. Diane Johnson, in *Terrorists and Novelists,* describes Morrison's effect as "that of a folk tale in which conventional narrative qualities like unity and suspense are sacrificed to the cumulative effects of individual, highly romantic or mythic episodes," thus "forcing the reader to abandon criteria of plausibility" because they cease to matter (115). The significant event that organizes the novel into two parts, however, is the separation of two childhood friends. What appears one way in part 1 appears another way in part 2. Morrison explores this inverted perspective through the growth of identities and friendship between Sula Peace and Nel Wright.

Morrison claims that in writing *Sula,* she set out to explore a dimension of black life she felt was often left out of even black histories—friendship between black women. Were it not for the friendship between Nel and Sula, no story could be told (just as in *Their Eyes Were Watching God,* where Pheoby's friendship with Janie provides the occasion for her to tell her story). Morrison, by showing the feelings, actions, and thoughts of black women in America, emphasizes what Mary Helen Washington asserts when she says "few, if any, women in the literature of black women succeed in heroic quests without the support of other women or men in their communities. Women talk to other women in this tradition, and their friendships with other women—mothers, sisters, grandmothers, friends, and lovers—are vital to their growth and well-being" (*Invented Lives,* xxi).

She also shows, however, what such a friendship "was really made of," if one did an "unforgivable thing" (Naylor and Morrison, 577). By creating a relationship that involved a spiritual bonding that transcended the flesh and was much superior, Morrison makes a point about not only what women can accept of other women but what they can accept of themselves and of God. When she does the "unforgivable thing," when she seduces Nel's husband, Jude, Sula reveals her unwillingness to obey moral codes, to acknowledge Nel's reliance on him and her need to have him to help create her identity. Likewise Nel, by blaming only Sula for the transgression, refuses to acknowledge the weakness and ultimately the inability of her husband to compensate not only for what she lacks in herself but for what she lacks when divorced from Sula. From Morrison's perspective, and Sula's also, Jude was not nearly as important to Nel as Sula was. Still Morrison realizes that "if all women behaved like those two, or if the Sula point of view operated and women really didn't care about sharing these things, everything would just crumble—hard. If it's not about fidelity and possession and my pain versus yours, then how can you manipulate, how can you threaten, how can you assert power?" (Naylor and Morrison, 578).

The will to exert power on nature, humanity, or history and tradition is what seems to get in the way of creating authentic relationships and sacralized identities in *Sula*. Sacred qualities cannot be appreciated when they are used as a force to control. The examples Morrison gives of women's ability to love—from mother love that leads to infanticide, to friendship that leads to adultery—demonstrate what Morrison said in an interview with Gloria Naylor: "the best thing that is in us is also the thing that makes us sabotage ourselves, sabotage in the sense that our life is not as worthy, or our perception of the best parts of ourselves. . . . what is it really that compels a good woman to displace the self, her self, to [try] to project the self not into the way we say 'yourself' but to put a space between those words, as though the self were really a twin or a thirst or a friend or something that sits right next to you and watches you" (Naylor and Morrison, 585).

Her notion for the story, although it is developed around a friendship, began with Sula: "I got to thinking about this girl, this woman. If it wasn't unconventional, she didn't want it. She was willing to risk in her imagination a lot of things and pay the price and also go astray. It wasn't as though she was this fantastic power who didn't have a flaw in her character. I wanted to throw her relationship with another woman into relief. Those two women, that too is us, those two desires to have your adventure and safety. So I just cut it up" (Naylor and Morrison, 577). She then created Nel, whom she wanted to be a "warm, conventional woman, one of those people you know are going to pay the gas bill and take care of their children. . . . they are magnificent, because they take these small tasks and they do them. And they do them without the fire and without the drama and without all that. They get the world's work done somehow" (Stepto, "'Intimate Things,'" 475).

Together Sula and Nel represent the range of choices possible for women, each on one end of the spectrum. Each offers an approach to the task of self-discovery. Beginning when they are adolescent girls and continuing as they mature, their friendship changes in nature but remains the deepest attachment and most profound influence in both of their lives. Initially, their friendship underscores the relational quality of conversion among women: "Because each had discovered years before that they were neither white nor male, and that all freedom and triumph was forbidden to them, they had set about creating something else to be. Their meeting was fortunate, for it let them use each other to grow on. Daughters of distant mothers and incomprehensible fathers (Sula's because he was dead; Nel's because he wasn't), they found in each other's eyes the intimacy they were looking for" (52). Both only children, when they met "they were solitary little girls whose loneliness was so profound it intoxicated them, and sent them stumbling into Technicolored visions that always included a presence, a someone, who, quite like the dreamer, shared the delight of the dream" (51). Although they share dreams of adventure and unfolding selfhood, their approaches to the task of maturation are different. Nel casts her visions in traditional romantic fantasies and sacrifices her independence to conventionality as she dreams of "lying on some flowered bed tangled in her own hair, waiting for some fiery prince" (51), while Sula insists on her independence and imagines herself "galloping through her own mind on a gray and white horse tasting sugar and smelling roses" (51–52). But as the narrator hints when she says Nel's prince "approached but never quite arrived" (51) and Sula's romp on the horse is alone but "in full view of someone who shared both the taste and the speed" (52), neither path necessarily leads to personal fulfillment.

Their dreams, however, naturally reflect their circumstances, since Nel has grown up in an orderly, if suffocating, traditional household while Sula has grown up in a home of chaos and unconventionality. Nel's mother, Helene, is the kind of woman who "won all social battles with presence and a conviction of the legitimacy of her certainty" (18). Leading a tidy, organized life, Helene wished to force all creativity out of Nel as if it were a sin. So "under Helene's hand the girl became obedient and polite. Any enthusiasms little Nel showed were calmed by the mother until she drove her daughter's imagination underground" (18). Sula's worldview is shaped by her mother, Hannah, and her grandmother Eva, neither of whom can find any meaning in the domestically prescribed role for women in the Bottom. Eva's concept of love was a form of control not dissimilar from Helene's in intent, if not in expression. From her bedroom she was "directing the lives of her children, friends, strays, and a constant stream of boarders" (30). Hannah, however, "rubbed no edges, made no demands" (43) but like Eva "simply loved maleness, for its own sake" (41).

Sula and Nel come together in a friendship "as intense as it was sudden. They found relief in each other's personality" (53). At this point in their friendship, in their emerging adolescence, when each is trying to cast off the influence of her family, they are still "unshaped, formless things" (53) yet striving to find in each other that catalyst for conversion, that reflection of better self each seeks for herself. Moreover, it becomes clear that they are not as different as initially presumed.

Nel, whose grandmother was a prostitute in New Orleans, has within her background the seeds of rebellion and a dimension of independence. When she travels to New Orleans with her mother for her great-grandmother's funeral, Nel discovers, "I'm me. I'm not their daughter. I'm not Nel. I'm me. Me" (28). This revelation fills her with prayerful inspiration "I want . . . I want to be . . . wonderful. Oh, Jesus, make me wonderful" (29), and gives her the strength to cultivate a friend as different and as disapproved of as Sula. Likewise, Sula is shown as less than independent, indeed vulnerable to her need for reassurance, as when she overhears her mother remark that although she loves Sula, she "just don't like her," and Sula falls prey to "dark thoughts" (57).

A pivotal scene in the novel occurs when Nel and Sula are playing with Chicken Little and the boy drowns. Nel's first instinct is not grief for Chicken Little but a fear of being discovered when she says, "Somebody saw" (61). Sula suspects it is Shadrack who witnesses the scene and runs to his house, where he greets her by saying only "Always" (62). At this point Sula dissolves in tears; Nel, composed and rational, consoles Sula and leads her away. What emerges from this scene is a portrait of Nel (the good girl) as utterly in control, with no moral concern but with thoughts only of propriety, of her crime being discovered, while Sula (the bad girl) reveals herself as out of control and deeply anguished over her guilt.

Ultimately, therefore, Sula and Nel complement one another, support each other, and serve as each other's apprentice in their development. As Morrison says in an interview, "there was a little bit of both in each of those two women, and that if they had been one person, I suppose they would have been a rather marvelous person. But each one lacked something that the other one had" (Stepto, "'Intimate Things,'" 476). What each lacks becomes apparent only after they are separated, after Nel's romantic imagination takes over and she agrees to marry Jude and capitulate to his desire that "the two of them together would make one Jude" (83). Nel and Sula, who had become so close "they themselves had difficulty distinguishing one's thoughts from another" (83), were also women on the brink of maturity who each needed to define herself apart from her friend, to claim some aspect of identity as hers. Nel, as a woman whose parents had "succeeded in rubbing down to a dull glow any sparkle or splutter she had. Only with Sula did that quality have free reign" (83), chooses a traditional, if self-abnegating, way to assert her personality as distinct from Sula's. She does so because "greater than friendship was this new feeling of being needed by someone singly" (84). Sula, likewise, although initially excited about Nel's marriage, cannot see herself following such a path and chooses a community-abnegating course and heads out of town for college.

Sula's return to the Bottom after ten years' absence is heralded by a plague of robins, a "relatively trivial phenomenon" that the townspeople allowed to "become sovereign in their lives and bend their mind to its will" (89). This is when, in their efforts to assign meaning to natural events and preserve a sense of order, they cast Sula as the embodiment of their evil. Sula, they believed, "was laughing at their God" (115), and even Eva challenges Sula from a pietistic plane with such aggression that Sula puts her in a retirement home. Nel, however, saw Sula's return as "magic" and likened her appearance to "getting the use of an eye back," because Sula was one who could make "her see old things with new eyes" (95). Despite the passage of time, Nel still remembers that "talking to Sula had always been a conversation with herself" (95). Moreover, she admits that Sula's great gift to her—and indeed to the community—was her ability to "help others define themselves" (95). Whereas the town chooses to define itself based on Sula as evil, Nel still chooses to define herself through Sula's ability to enhance her life, to "turn the volume on and up" (95).

Nel has not yet become totally the community's daughter, but she still has been away from Sula too long and has not yet taken stock of all Sula has experienced. When Sula admits she had put Eva away, Nel is shaken. Still, she comes to Sula's support when Sula admits that she needs Nel because "You always had better sense than me. Whenever I was scared before, you knew just what to do" (101). Yet when Nel discovers her husband and Sula making love, when the "unforgivable thing" is done, all that she has felt and known about Sula vanishes. Whereas before her identity was mingled with Sula's, now it is so entwined with Jude's that she cannot accept Sula's actions as anything other than betrayal. Jude, however, is jealous of Sula and sees her as a threat to his domination over his wife. Moreover, he is a weak man who cannot fully accept his responsibilities and submits to Sula's seduction out of cowardice. Nel, however, only sees that her best friend and her husband have betrayed her and that at once she has lost the sustaining relationships that have given her an identity.

In her lonely longing she questions Jude, "how could you leave me when you knew me?" (104) and then turns her questions to God. Reflecting on the women at Chicken Little's funeral, she realizes that "they were screaming at the neck of God, his giant nape, the vast back-of-the-head that he had turned on them in death. But it seemed to her now that it was not a fist-shaking grief they were keening but rather a simple obligation to say something, do something, feel something about the dead. They could not let that heart-smashing event pass unrecorded, unidentified" (107). She is missing not only Jude but also being able to talk about it with Sula, and she is really "empty." Yet it is identifying the source of grief, the genuine loss, that is Nel's greatest problem. She cannot see at this point that she has been freed of a man who sought only to stifle and control her by a woman who meant only to liberate and wake her to her own identity. Nel can only conclude that "Hell is change" (108) and in a long, discursive prayer/ dialogue, begs "O my sweet Jesus" to explain to her how she is supposed to live with change, without love.

Sula, however, believes that "The real hell of Hell is that it is forever" (107). Sula does not understand Nel's inability to welcome capricious change and is left with a loss similar to Nel's. "She had clung to Nel as the closest thing to both an other and a self, only to discover she and Nel were not one and the same thing" (119). What Sula most loved about Nel was her faithful acceptance of her as she was, in all her complexity and arrogance. Nel had been "the one person who had wanted nothing from her, who had accepted all aspects of her" (119). Yet now "she wanted everything and all because of *that*" (119). Sula must accept that "the first person who had been real to her whose name she knew, who had seen as she had the slant of life that made it possible to stretch it to its limits," was now "one of them. . . . she belonged to the town and all of its ways" (120). Sula, like Nel without Jude, is lost because she had been "looking all along for a friend" (121) and Nel supplied that other half of herself that her idle imagination required. An "artist without a form" (121) and a self without a twin, Sula becomes "dangerous" and gives up any notion of intimacy. Unlike Nel, who chooses self-righteous celibacy, Sula welcomes sex as an occasion to join "herself in matchless harmony" (123).

Sula's experimental life is most threatened, however, when she is reacquainted with Ajax, a man who regularly visits her, bearing gifts and love. Ajax's mother, "who inspired thoughtfulness and generosity in all her sons" (126), was an "evil conjure woman" who "knew all about the weather, omens, the living, the dead, dreams and all illness" (126). His love for his mother is what attracts Ajax to a woman like Sula, yet before long Sula discovers "what possession was. Not love, perhaps, but possession or at least the desire for it" (131). It is a new feeling for Sula. The instant she expresses it to Ajax, he flees because she has forsaken the very quality in her that drew him to her in the first place. Left alone, Sula decides, "'There aren't any more new songs and I have sung all the ones there are'" (137), and before long she takes ill.

Nel, who by now has structured her identity around "virtue, bleak and drawn," as her "only mooring" (139), comes to visit Sula out of duty. They get into an exchange over Sula's transgression. When Nel accuses Sula of pretending she knows everything, Sula replies, "'I don't know everything, I just do everything'" (143). When Nel asserts that she would not do what Sula does, Sula accuses her of doing "'what every colored woman in this country is doing . . . dying'" (143). Although it is Sula who is physically dying, she sees this as incidental to the spiritual death Nel has chosen. Nel's response to Sula's arrogance is to remind her that she has nothing to show for her life, that she is lonely, to which Sula replies, "'I got my mind. And what goes on in it. Which is to say, I got me. . . . my lonely is mine.'" Unable to reach any common ground, Sula tries to instruct Nel that whatever happened between them does not matter because "'Being good to somebody is just like being mean to somebody. Risky. You don't get nothing for it'" (144–45), once again tossing the concepts of good and evil from their archetypal throne. Although each admits that once they were good friends, Sula's parting words to Nel are a kind of apocalyptic prophecy that further skews the terms of good and evil. Sula's speech reveals the fundamental dislocation both individuals and the community reflect and confronts the limitations of their respective moral visions. She says the townsfolk will love her after time: "After all the old women have lain with the teen-agers; when all the young girls have slept with their drunken uncles; after all the black men fuck all the white ones; when all the white women kiss all the black ones; when the guards have raped all the jailbirds and after all the whores make love to their grannies; after all the faggots get their mothers' trim; when Lindberg sleeps with Bessie Smith and Norma Sherer makes it with Stepin Fetchit; after all the dogs have fucked all the cats and every weathervane on every barn flies off the roof to mount the hogs . . . then there'll be a little love left over for me. And I know just what it will feel like" (146). Sula concludes by telling Nel to consider that maybe it was not Nel who was good; maybe it was Sula.[4]

Sula, who has left everything in her quest for freedom, continues to the end to repudiate what others consider responsibilities, to discard what others value. She clings to her intention that "I don't want to make somebody else. I want to make myself" (92). But in trying to make herself she also learns that although there is "no one other that you could count on" there is also "no self to count on either" (119). Her life has been a perpetual search for something she never finds because she has "no center, no speck around which to grow" (119). She laments the loss of Nel, not just in terms of what she has lost but in compassionate, relational terms by considering what Nel has lost by remembering only "how much I have cost her and never remembering the days when we were two throats and one eye and we had no price" (147). The only center Sula ever had was Nel; so after Sula dies, Morrison completes her characterization and identification with Nel when she follows Sula into the afterlife and has her remark: "'Well, I'll be damned,' she thought, 'it didn't even hurt. Wait'll I tell Nel'" (149).

Nel, who has become a wife and mother and a member of the community, not only follows but endorses the community's conventions, especially after Jude leaves. Nel, who chooses to live a life opposite to Sula's, is like the young Janie Crawford, who accepts the myths that marriage and motherhood are the only acceptable roles for women and capitulates to society's standards of "what a woman oughta be and do." By doing such she eventually becomes intolerant of Sula and denies those essential aspects of her own being that Sula once brought out in her. Although Nel may have what Sula lacks—the goodwill and respect of the community—she is without the aggressive or creative sense of self that so energizes Sula and allows her a critical distance from which to judge society's rigid standards. Nel, who survives Sula by many years, remains alone at the end of the novel and is forced to live her life with an all-too-painful awareness of what she has lost.

Even when Nel, as responsible churchwoman, visits a senile Eva Peace in an old-folk's home twenty-four years after Sula's death, she is shocked into realizing her identification with the girl who let Chicken Little drown and the woman who took her husband. This realization is precipitated by Eva's psychic knowledge of the circumstances of Chicken Little's death. Sula's speculation about who was bad and who was good, along with Shadrack's simple reminder, "Always," comes rushing back to Nel, and she remembers her secret calm and her compassion for Sula's "frightened and shamed eyes" (170). Her complicity catches up to her at last, and in a graveyard, a sanctified spot for conversion, Nel begins to understand, to change, and cries out: "'All that time, all that time, I thought I was missing Jude. . . . O Lord, Sula,' she cried, 'girl, girl girlgirlgirl'" (174). Her conversion, when it comes, occurs too late to heal and preserve those things about which she most cares, and instead of feeling joy, her grief surrounds her with no bottom and no top, "just circles and circles of sorrow."

Nel has dutifully played the obedient daughter and succumbed to society's rigid standards, paying a price for denying her own personality, but Sula has lived out her own fantasies and created her own reality, always questioning the tendency to blindly accept identity as a given, rather than something that can be challenged and changed. Yet by casting Sula's personality in harmony with Nel's, by developing her character through her relation with others—her family, her friend Nel, and ultimately her community—Morrison signifies on Sula's independent character. Sula "exists" only as she influences and is influenced by others.

The shifting perceptions of reality and identity that underscore so much of the drama in *Sula* are symbolized in Sula's distinctive birthmark, which reappears throughout the novel. It is perceived differently by everyone who sees it. To Nel it is a rose, to Jude a rattlesnake, to Shadrack a tadpole. Morrison explains that Sula's birthmark "doesn't so much define her so much as other people because other people have to get themselves together in her presence because she is not helpful in any way; so that they see in her what they wish to see not only in her birthmark but in her because she was wanton, experimental, genuinely dangerous, morally dangerous person" (Jones and Vinson, 144). Yet together Sula and Nel convey a coherent, sacralized identity; they are one woman character in two forms, symbolically representing identity fragmented by the pressures put on the people of the Bottom, by a world of shifting values.

Based on her redefinition of language from a feminist perspective, the theologian Mary Daly offers a unique way of looking at *Sula*. She explores what the novel indicates about friendship and women's spiritual health as they react to the pressures inflicted by society. Daly also offers a description of the resources necessary for conversion and an explanation of why Nel and Sula fail. As Morrison suggests in her remarks to Gloria Naylor, women possess a latent potential that they seem unable to utilize or integrate with other potentials. Morrison, to dramatize this split, presents two women, "twins" who together make up one whole woman. In her essay "Be-Friending: Weaving Contexts, Creating Atmospheres," Daly picks up on this image and sees the potential value of Nel and Sula's relationship as demonstrating qualities of "Be-Friending . . . the creation of a context / atmosphere in which acts / leaps of Metamorphosis can take place" (199). Such a context is what Nel and Sula create as children but are not able to sustain as they mature, yet it is through Nel's—and to a degree Sula's—memory of this context that an act of metamorphosis, of conversion, finally comes.

Daly admits that, "while the knowledge of female potency is certain, it is far from certain that this will be Actualized/Realized by many women under the prevailing conditions of the State of Separation. Therefore, quantum leaps of Fate—identified faith, hope and lust are in order. . . . acts of Metamorphosis . . . to strengthen and actualize spiritual capacities" (199). Nel and Sula, thwarted by cultural signals that confuse and distort their perceptions, leap too late to realize that "Be-Friending is radically connected with Be-Longing." Belonging includes not only relationships to other women and communities but also to self, being a friend to the being in oneself. As Daly continues, "Since friendship implies a sharing of activity—in a special sense intellectual activity—the necessary context will be one that awakens and encourages women to exercise their powers to full capacity" (204). Sula and Nel, in part because of family and community pressures, were unable to share on this level throughout their lives, to maintain a relationship with "no price" and transcend an "unforgivable act." Each denies herself and the other a greater level of awareness and instead faces an atmosphere of something missing or lost. Each forfeits her "latent potency"—her sacrality—and squanders an opportunity for "metamorphosis," or conversion.

In exploring women's friendships and fractured identities, Morrison is also exploring dimensions of the communal black life that provide the context for women's development. She shows what is lost or missing in a minority culture when the pressures imposed by a majority culture create rifts or wounds. These wounds in African-American culture, Morrison seems to suggest, reveal how identities become fractured when the culture upon which they depend for definition is equally fractured. Morrison is attempting to reclaim, and by extension recreate, a lost community or culture. In *Sula* Morrison shows us what is lost but does not name it, recognizing that the terms by which we identify the loss are themselves ineffective. She is also aware that whatever healing must occur will necessarily change things, and that life must be different. Any wound must be scarred over with new, tougher skin that may not be pretty but stops the bleeding. In African-American culture, as Toni Morrison insists over and again in her writings, there is plenty of living flesh to be used to make a scar, and the capacity exists among individuals and the community for great healing, once the need for healing is accepted.

As Valerie Smith describes Morrison's literary works, she "explores the interplay between self-knowledge and the social role" ("Quest for Identity," 721). Morrison "reveals the dynamic blacks who live in such towns, coming to grips with their search for selfhood in the empty, meaningless world, whether urban or agrarian, to which they belong" (Samuels and Hudson-Weems, x). This process of coming to understand self in relationship to one's history and culture is nothing less than the existential act of self-creation indicated by a conversion experience.

Where Sula fails in her attempts at conversion or self-creation is in her denial of her culture. She correctly assesses its problems and identifies its frustrated inability to keep pace with the changes in the world, but she does not fully respect its spiritual origins (and thereby hers) or its mythic attempts to order reality. She challenges collective identity without offering anything of substance in its place. Sula faces a psychological dilemma of being out of touch with her community and therefore her culture. She cannot find fulfillment either in the Bottom or in the larger society and becomes a symbol necessary for the community to reconnect with the mythic past.

The community attempts to come to grips with its identity through Sula, who embodies what Shadrack's Suicide Day commemorates: the unknown and uncontrollable in everyone's life—death, natural disaster, even their own rage at their manipulation by the external world. Sula's mythic function is complemented, enhanced, by Shadrack, whose "eyes were so wild, his hair so long and matted, his voice was so full of authority and thunder that he caused panic on the first, or charter, National Suicide Day in 1920" (12). Shadrack, who is fond of Sula, is, like her, an outsider; but he is a benevolent outsider, loosely associated with Christ when "The Reverend Deal took it up saying the same folks who had sense enough to avoid Shadrack's call were the ones who insisted on drinking themselves to death or womanizing themselves to death. 'May's well go on with Shad and save the lamb the trouble of redemption'" (13–14). Shadrack's annual ritual links this black culture with a larger mythic context and provides a link between beginnings and endings, a ritual re-creation of life.

Eva, like Shadrack, is a kind of spiritual authority who, in addition to dispensing names and identities, decides when someone should die. Her response to a dream about Plum attempting to reenter her womb is to set fire to her addicted son as his only means of achieving peace and wholeness. Plum even describes his death by conflagration as "some kind of baptism, some kind of blessing" (47). Eva, a kind of timeless character with special qualities, indicates a mythic level of reality to be reckoned with that Sula ignores but Nel eventually must confront. Because she possesses spiritual knowledge and vision—such as her dream of Plum, her dream of a red dress before Hannah's burning, her knowledge of Chicken Little's death—when Sula puts Eva in a retirement home she is symbolically rejecting her cultural past and alternative ways of looking at reality. Eva represents ancestors who, as Morrison points out, "are sort of timeless people whose relationships to the characters are benevolent, instructive, and protective, and they provide a certain kind of wisdom" (Morrison, "Rootedness," 343). But Eva, despite her ancestral power, exploits her role and tries to play God, names everyone in *her* image of them, and exerts formidable control and manipulation from her second-story bedroom, once again casting into relief the ambiguities of both individual and communal identity as sacred when power overtakes love.

Through this insistent ambiguity Morrison seems to suggest that all nonreverential attempts to control the natural forces of life, to attempt to manipulate or interfere with the cycle of life and death, are only illusions, and dangerous ones at that. Barbara Christian, in her essay "Community and Nature: The Novels of Toni Morrison," locates as a major theme of *Sula* the relationship between the characters' belief systems and their view of nature. The "necessary aspect of their central conflict," Christian states, "is their relationship to natal communities, the people who gave them life" (*Black Feminist Criticism*, 48). The characters' conduct is connected to the community's value system, a point dramatized when Morrison begins the novel by first introducing readers to the place, the Bottom, which becomes another sort of character in the novel, establishing setting as organic to each character's view of herself. The myth of the Bottom, the "nigger joke," becomes the core of the community's perceived sense of reality and establishes the community's philosophy of survival. The tradition, as Christian states, "is in the nature of the land"; bottom is top, and reality is seen from such a skewed perspective.

Christian also emphasizes that for all the community does by way of establishing traditions, there is importance and necessity in leaving, especially for women who particularly feel the effects of insularity. Like Janie, who had to leave Jody's town, Sula must leave, and even Nel has her own awakening to self when she is away in New Orleans. The women in the novel, apart from Sula, all help retain traditions although they also suffer from them and remain insulated and unchallenged. In reaffirming its oneness through its hate of Sula, the community is also blocking off creative channels, fighting the natural inclination to grow and change, and nature responds by seeking destructive channels.

Symbols of fire and water reappear throughout the novel as "powerful spiritual forces that are symbolic of the inherent complexity of the natural order" (Christian, *Black Feminist Criticism,* 54), where life and death are inextricably connected. An unfinished tunnel begun in 1927—the deferred dream of commerce with towns across the river and employment for black men—is yet another monumental symbol of how things meant to control are subject to collapse on the heads of those who build them or, in the case of the tunnel, those who wish to build them. Cedric Gael Bryant refers to the tunnel as "a myth of almost Biblical proportions, which—like the River Jordan—has the power to heal those who are sick and reclaim what is lost" (742). Another allusion recalled by this episode was documented by Dorothy Spruill Redford in *Somerset Homecoming: Recovering a Lost Heritage.* In exploring her own ancestry, Redford comes across an account by the overseer of Somerset plantation, who describes a similar scene involving recently transplanted African slaves: "At Night they would begin to sing their native songs. . . . In a short while they would become so wrought up that, utterly oblivious to the danger involved, they would grasp their bundles of personal effects, swing them on their shoulders, and setting their faces towards Africa, would march down into the water singing as they marched till recalled to their senses only by the drowning of some of the party" (132). The mass drowning that occurs when everyone follows Shadrack, therefore, becomes a kind of baptism into spiritual rebirth, and the town is tragically transfigured. Another world is immanent and constantly impinging on reality in *Sula,* demonstrating that a variety of perspectives are called for; there is no simple road to the truth.

What casts Sula as a pariah, therefore, is precisely her rejection of the values the community attempts to espouse, those things that stifle the self and aim at uniformity but also lend order and constancy. Unlike Nel, Sula refuses to marry, settle down, and raise a family. She feels no obligation to anyone. When Sula returns to town after a ten-year absence, she and Eva get into a heated exchange that, although it begins as a discussion of Sula's choice of what to do with her life, becomes a kind of theological treatise or a litany of sacred faith in the face of secular challenge. Each remark of Sula's is countered by one of Eva's that is derived from some traditional religious canon. Sula's independent claims are blasphemous to Eva, who claims "God's going to strike you!" (93). At this point Sula responds, "Which God? The one watched you burn Plum?" Each time Sula raises an independent thought such as "whatever's burning in me is mine" (93), Eva responds with an "Amen," or "Amazing Grace," as if these words had some kind of incantatory power to counteract Sula's blasphemy. The cumulative effect of this exchange, however, is to cheapen Eva's faith and discredit Sula's ambition. Nothing, it appears, even a religious faith, is immune from the distorted perspective of the Bottom.

Sula represents potential, freedom from restrictive codes, the raw energy of life, and the creative impulses of art, but she also represents all these things in a context of no responsibility and no concern. This is why the challenge she presents to the community's complacency becomes distorted and in the end she neither enlightens the community nor fully succeeds in creating or saving herself. Neither individual pursuit nor community loyalty is enough for fulfillment, yet both are necessary for any kind of fulfillment at all. Sula's attempts to live a life with no responsibility and the community's lack of faith in its own cultural resources indicate an illusory freedom from oppression for both. As Morrison explains in a conversation with Gloria Naylor, "Freedom is choosing your responsibility. It's not having no responsibilities; it's choosing the ones you want" (Naylor and Morrison, 573). Balancing the relationship between freedom and responsibility is what Toni Morrison attempts to describe as a way to survive whole. Morrison also makes the point that despite Sula's rejection of her community, it nurtured her, allowed her to live unharmed, and provided a "sustaining environment" (Tate, 130). Sula, in her desire for an experimental life, never fully appreciated or understood the value of the community's continuity and how it sustained and protected her.

Neither, however, is Nel a model for development. Like Sula, she was deprived as a child by her home environment, by growing up with a mother who personified a denial of reality. Static and conforming, Helene is to Nel what Nanny was to Janie. Whereas Eva corrupts power, Helene is hypocritical in using her power. Nel, under Helene's manipulation, never gave herself a chance to experiment, to change. Nel's marriage to Jude gave her an identity that required her to forfeit the necessary sense of self that remains important to Sula. After Sula's adultery Nel creates a new identity for herself that equates her suffering with goodness. She evades the implications of Sula's deathbed remarks and escapes responsibility for self-creation by believing she is a victim and a martyr. She cannot fully comprehend that the dualities bound up in Sula's personality reflect dualities in society, indeed nature itself. She claims a false innocence until Eva brings her into the world of history, experience, and responsibility, where she undergoes a "fortunate fall" and finally embraces the spirit of Sula. Nel's conversion comes only through the resources of her memory.[5]

To fully convert or appreciate the sacrality of identity, there must be balance. Nel and Sula represent two modes of self-definition described by Carol Gilligan, as well as the problems attendant to each: "these divergent constructions of identity, in self-expression or in self-sacrifice, create different problems for further development—the former a problem of human connection and the latter a problem of truth" (157). Yet Sula's independence and Nel's constancy must be read in the social context of the fragmented community to which they belong and for which they suffer. Separately Sula and Nel resemble the archetypes of "Jezebel" and "Mammy." They perpetuate the stagnation of identity that so limited black women's early development. Together, however, Sula and Nel whole are "two faces of the same coin" (Naylor and Morrison, 578). One can neither supplant the other nor offer a vision of a sacralized life. Aspects of what each brings to the relationship are what make life meaningful—a certain concern tempered with a certain irreverence, an independence with responsibility, a recognition of the good and the evil within and without. Sula gives Nel the courage to rebel. Nel gives Sula a sense of constancy. An identity cannot be sacralized by dismissing obligation, nor can it be sacralized by simply toeing the line. A belief in the future must be tempered with a reverence for the past, and likewise the past must not be accepted as a static, nostalgic memory but as a component of reality and a term by which one defines and grasps the present.

In *Sula*, therefore, Morrison seems to be suggesting that both the community and the individuals lack a sense of identity. Yet despite the tragedy that envelops nearly every character, she offers some hope that conversions can happen if one is open to mystery. The novel's circular narrative structure, beginning with the creation of the Bottom and ending with Nel's symbolic rebirth, indicates the possibility of recovering one's lost selfhood. Death is followed by birth, the collapse of the tunnel heralds Nel's new beginning. "The purpose of evil," the narrator mentions, "was to survive it and they determined (without ever knowing they had made up their minds to do it) to survive floods, white people, tuberculosis, famine and ignorance" (78). Heaven for the townsfolk is in their past, which the Bottom, "the bottom of heaven," symbolizes: their cultural creations, the importance of dreams, omens, and myth and ritual, indications of a spiritual heritage that transcends time.

Despite the ways that Morrison's text constantly undercuts the strength of Sula's independent identity, many critics claim Sula as a feminist role model by continuing to focus on the heroic dimensions of Sula's life, citing her as "Promethean" in her ability to transcend stereotypes. Victoria Middleton believes that it is Sula's heroism that eventually leads to Nel's final understanding of Sula as symbolic of an "awareness of otherness that is essential for self-realization." It is through Nel, Middleton asserts, and "her resistance and conversion," that readers are educated "in appreciating Sula's radically innovative experiments in living" (368). Many contend, therefore, that Sula presents a new model for black women, one that establishes new terms of heroism and veers away from the role of nurturer and caretaker to include a wider appreciation of black women's qualities. By representing change and standing outside social codes, the existential truths by which Sula transcends her culture prefigure its transformation in much the same way Janie's adventures indicate an opportunity for her community to grow.

Certainly, Sula's character points out necessary dimensions for growth among both individuals and communities. Sula, by "helping others define themselves," demonstrates what Lee Edwards, in her book *Psyche as Hero,* identifies as heroism: it is a habit of mind as much as a set of behaviors. In this study, where Edwards draws portraits of female artists as heroes, she sees Sula's heroism as performing the aesthetic function not of clarifying women's roles but of being the "epitome of ambiguity" (197). Yet within this context of ambiguity, Sula commits the sin of anarchy. As an artist with no form she is heroic but dangerous.[6] She becomes a lightning rod for society's doubts about complacency and creates a climate of moral obscurity that is necessary for growth, but she herself is without the materials to express and mediate her visions, and she can do nothing for herself.

In her discussion of *Sula,* Barbara Hill Rigney describes Sula as an ironic literary transfiguration of a Christ figure that is transcended and restored to human status. This is because Sula does not heroically choose the nature of her martyrdom and does not internalize the pathology of victimization. Moreover, as an archetypal scapegoat, Sula represents not a celebration of the heroism of black women but an indictment of society's need for scapegoats. When the community chooses to turn on her rather than choose the option to grow, Sula represents all women artists who must face times when cultural conventions impinge on the possibilities for free creation. Connecting self with society is harder for women like Sula who have been rendered invisible or are judged by select standards. Sula, by asserting the necessity for critical appraisal, fixes her visions and self on social habits that would seek to deny both. Sula is an artist whose medium is life itself, and her attempts at self-creation threaten not the profanities but the sacraments of the Bottom, itself a kind of cultural icon. Ultimately, Edwards asserts, "Sula is the dark prophet of her novel, the seer whose bleak visions make others conscious of the sins they mistook for salvation" (209–10). Unlike Janie, who reforms by way of redemption, Sula fractures through destruction, and Nel, her twin, is necessary in the text as a "revisionist critic to Sula's artistry" (Middleton, 373).

Some critics contend, however, that the text itself resists any attempt to focus on a protagonist as hero. In her essay "'The Self and the Other': Reading Toni Morrison's *Sula* and the Black Female Text," Deborah McDowell sees Morrison implicitly criticizing the very concepts of "hero" or "protagonist" by decentering and deferring the presence of Sula in the novel. By doing such she creates a work "rife with liberating possibilities" (79). By denying her story a central character, McDowell points out, Morrison banishes the concept of character as a static essence and replaces it with the idea of character as a process. Self, in Morrison's world, is not "knowable, centered, and unified" but "multiple, fluid, relational, in a perpetual state of becoming" (81).

In conjunction with the presentation and deconstruction of the heroic character of Sula, Robert Sargent sees as a major theme in all of Morrison's novels "the need for balance or wholeness. These qualities may be acquired by the characters in the novels only through an act that is analogous to one involved in the creation of art—an act of the imagination that comes from a willingness to see the world as others see it" (229). In doing such Morrison explodes stereotypes and shows variety in people, attitudes, and behaviors. Morrison, perhaps more than any other writer, shows us that there is no single monolithic notion of what a black woman is, or what she can be or do. The meaning of Sula's life has permanently altered categories of existence.[7]

Deborah McDowell has repeatedly drawn attention to the need for close scrutiny of concepts such as "black womanhood," or a "black female identity," or "black experience." She urges critics and readers alike to refrain from essentializing or homogenizing black women because of the never-static sociopolitical realities of life. She sees *Sula*, therefore, as raising questions about and complicating the concept of identity. The novel itself resists any unity other than that provided by the reader in the act of reading, an act that becomes analogous to the construction of self in the novel. Self, McDowell maintains, is fluid and formed in relations with others; so, too, identification in reading is a process of dialogue between oneself and writers, texts, characters, and the interpretative community. Morrison affirms as much in an essay in which she says that "too often we want the whole thing" ("Memory, Creation, and Writing," 388) when we should be concentrating instead on the pieces and fragments of memory that deliver meaning. Morrison's gift as a moral writer, in addition to showing that the "female personality is more complex than the dichotomies advanced by conventional moral concepts" (Banyiwa-Horne, 29), is her ability to articulate larger spaces of contradiction.[8] Robert Grant expands on the notions of Sargent and McDowell when he demonstrates how Morrison, in addition to critiquing the concept of a static, knowable self, also encodes in *Sula* a critique of the concept of black community as inherently stable and affirmative. There is difference even among community-shared cultural practices. The community must change to adapt to the needs of the people and must come to terms with the past and initiate healing. On the one hand, Morrison celebrates the black community and all it offers individuals. "At the same time, however, the community is opposed and, to all events and purposes *exposed* (overshadowed) by an independent protagonist" (91–92). In Morrison's world, just as identity may not be a stable thing, so, too, may the psychological security and cultural homogeneity afforded by a black community be seen as something that is not absolute, and may not define a positive value for each individual.

Grant's point underscores Anthony F. C. Wallace's notion of revitalization movements, where he identifies the reciprocal qualities of individual and societal growth. It makes sense, therefore, that Morrison "was interested in making the town, the community, the neighborhood, as strong a character as I could, without actually making it 'The Town, they,' because the most extraordinary thing about any group, and particularly our group, is the fantastic variety of people and things and behavior and so on" (Stepto, "'Intimate Things,'" 474). None of these approaches, however, is meant to deny the positive terms of black women's search for identity or wholeness. In fact, part of the principle of conversion I have been attempting to establish is precisely its ability to break down rigid concepts, to allow for greater flexibility and freedom in assessing self and one's relationship to others and to God. A conversion as an awareness of sacrality within implies an appreciation of diversity because that is how God created the world. Identity may still grow organically as long as it is not used to validate a specific model of black selfhood or approved notions of black experience. Morrison's novel suggests the need for a plurality of vision. Acquiring several vantage points on reality is the truly liberating act that regenerates identity and community. Morrison explodes the myth of the Western individualistic conception of self, accepting in its place the richness and complexity of a collective sense of identity. The "twinness" of Sula and Nel is what preserved their identities and enabled them to grow. As Mae Henderson might say, Toni Morrison's writing can be viewed as "speaking in tongues," testifying to the need for both unity and difference.[9]

Sula is a speculative novel in which all the important issues are raised in shades of ambiguity, all the important insights are framed as questions, and ultimately no final answers are given. It is a novel defined by religious paradox, where God is an enigma and even the town's sustaining myth of origins is a joke. By being such it embodies the principle of conversion, a disposition toward change and seeking, as the only way to find ultimate meaning. Moreover, by weaving Sula's identity with Nel's, Morrison demonstrates structurally the collective nature of human identity. Because for all her efforts to transcend the community, Sula remains an integral part of it. Morrison undercuts Sula's aspirations toward originality by characterizing her as only half a person. As Valerie Smith asserts, "Assuming identity is thus a communal gesture . . . knowing oneself derives from learning to reach back into history and horizontally in sympathetic relationship to others" ("The Quest," 732). It is through memory and remembering, as Nel learns at the conclusion of the novel, that one can be led back to intimacy after experiencing the ruptures that attend individuation. When she sympathetically embraces Sula through her memory, Nel establishes a relational affirmation of life. Memory, therefore, is an aid to recovery and a healing instrument of hope.

Indeed, memory is a central concern of Morrison's, a concept she refines and discusses over and over again in interviews and essays. For her the interior part of the growth of a writer is connected to memory—a deliberate act of remembering. It is "a form of willed creation" (Memory, Creation, and Writing, 385). Delivered in pieces that she reconstructs, *Sula,* she claims, emerged from such scraps of memory. The theme, the core of her memory around which she shaped her story, was one of forgiveness, of women who "forgive each other, or learn to" (386). Although she may have invented the thing to be forgiven, that is not what matters to her as a writer. Morrison is concerned with the nature and quality of forgiveness among women who are friends. By concentrating on such a quality Morrison draws her reader into nonliterary experience, into a world where one can feel the sensations of emerging identities and revelation. She also graphically portrays on both an individual and a communal level that moment Rita Dove discusses in relation to Saint Paul's conversion. What comes after the change to fill in the void before the new life begins? Between death and a difficult birth, the individuals and the community they inhabit must embrace change—for surely they will vanish without it—but at the same time not forsake their traditions or else they will face a spiritual death.

Morrison deliberately dislocates her reader with unorthodox people and events in order to insist we draw on other sources of knowledge to address how we should fill in the void. She points us to the kind of knowledge that comes from the realm of religion: myth, faith, and spirit. She holds out the possibility of individual fulfillment in the context of communal support and identification; through defiance or affirmation, it does not seem to matter. What matters is the response, the willingness to change, to convert to a new way of living and seeing the world in all its complexity through the eyes of memory and with the assistance of imagination. Visions lead to conversions once again. By putting good and evil in different terms, Morrison invites inquiry into the sacred and profane dimensions of human personalities and communities and offers opportunities, if not for redemption, at least for understanding. Somewhere between self-denying retreat and self-righteous disregard is Shadrack's "Always." Toni Morrison gives us a new cosmology and a new theology to interpret it and asserts once again that the dream is the truth.

Paule Marshall (1929–)

To acknowledge our ancestors means
we are aware that we did not make
ourselves, that the line stretches
all the way back, perhaps, to God; or

to Gods. We remember them because it
is an easy thing to forget. . . .
—Alice Walker

Paule Marshall, like Toni Morrison, is critical of the ways black women have been portrayed in literature and, like Morrison, attempts to correct or expand notions of what constitutes a black female identity. In an essay she published in 1966, "The Negro Woman in Literature," Marshall identifies—as Deborah Gray White has done—the two prevailing portrayals of black women as those of "mammy" and "wench." She states that in the process of being the object of these stereotypical characterizations, a black woman is "denied the complexities, the contradictions, the ambiguities that make for a truly rich and credible character in fiction" (51). She cites as the reason for such treatment of black women the "troubled and repressed conscience of the country" and sees her role as a writer, in part, as "capturing Negro life in all its richness and complexity," creating human portraits of black women that transcend such stereotypes.

Marshall's sense of authorial responsibility as it pertains to the creation of character, however, is not limited to developing richness and complexity in merely psychological terms. Commingled with her intention toward characterization is her intention to create a vision of a surrounding culture that is equally rich and varied. In this she is aided by her own history. Although she grew up in New York, Paule Marshall came from Barbadian origins and illustrates this influence in every literary endeavor she undertakes. Indeed, she cites as the single greatest influence on her career as a writer the times when she would listen to her mother and her mother's immigrant friends exchange stories in the kitchen after a hard day's labor. In the essay "Shaping the World of My Art," Marshall remembers in religious terms how the "faithful" would gather in the "sanctuary" of her kitchen and create "a kind of magic rite, a form of juju, for it was their way to exorcise the day's humiliations and restore them to themselves" (97–112). From these people Marshall learned the importance of "skillful characterization, the novelist's responsibility to make his people live and have their being on the printed page." Marshall, in other words, grew up in a home full of everyday ceremony and ritual, where life's mysteries were discussed in spiritual terms and where "conjure or roots or mojo or vodun" was a natural way of dealing with the inexplicable and unknown.

It was here also that Marshall became acquainted with the great injustices endured by blacks in America and how, by remembering their origins and celebrating heroes like Marcus Garvey, her family found ways to transform their experience. Growing up around people "who were veritable griots" (Marshall explains in a conversation with Maryse Condé), she became aware that for them "the memories of the legacy of slavery were very active. It was revealed in conversation about the daily humiliations they had to endure while working as domestics for white people." Yet when they gathered together to talk about their experiences "a healing process occurred which prepared them to face the next day" (John Williams, 52–53). Marshall early on became aware of the need, indeed the necessity, to preserve and celebrate what Amiri Baraka cites as the "strong nigger feeling," a faith in the knowledge and life bodied forth by ancestors ("Shaping the World," 104–5). This "nigger feeling," moreover, was not limited to the black American experience but indeed depended upon a pan-African vision for definition.

Marshall sees Africa as simultaneously a concrete destination to be reckoned with in literal, political terms and a spiritual homeland to which blacks must mythically return in order to develop a sense of identity. In 1977 she traveled to Africa, where she was adopted as a native daughter, an experience she summarizes with the local expression "Omowale": a native daughter has returned (John Williams, 52). Africa is a part of the emotional fabric of her world, so Marshall believes that "in order to develop a sense of our collective history . . . it is absolutely necessary for Black people to effect this spiritual return. . . . I consider it my task as a writer to initiate readers to the challenges this journey entails" (52). By viewing a spiritual return to Africa as absolutely necessary for the reintegration of that which was lost in the collective historical past of blacks, Marshall is placing an imperative of conversion on African Americans: "We (as people of African descent) must accept the task of 'reinventing' our own image, and the role which Africa will play in this process will be essential" (53). By viewing herself as a preacher, so to speak, Marshall believes she can assist

African Americans to liberate themselves from the inferiority complex imposed by a colonial system whose vestiges remain. Once this is achieved they will be able to impose their own point of view, to challenge accepted notions of black identity and present a more complex and varied portrait of black life. Because of her commitment to uniting various forms of black expression, Edward Brathwaite claims Paule Marshall as a novelist of the "African Reconnection."

It is clear that Marshall's agenda as a writer is steeped in issues of identity and the self's capacity for change and transcendence. Like Morrison, she realizes that any attention to identity involves "a concern for the role of the past—both the personal and historical past . . . that for black people to define ourselves on our own terms we must consciously engage our past" ("Shaping the World," 106) as part of the key to an understanding of one's total self. In fact, Paule Marshall is utterly evangelical on this point, convinced that a "psychological and spiritual return back over history is something Black people in this part of the world must undertake if we are to have a sense of our total experience and to mold for ourselves a more truthful identity" (107). In her writing, the past figures prominently but not to the exclusion of the present or the future. All perspectives are blended in a concept of vision, where identity is composed of elements of each: knowing from where one comes enables one to understand the present and plan for the future.

Inscribed within this vision is a decidedly nonmaterialistic prescription for undertaking self-creation. Marshall locates the acquisitive nature of society as the source of the most devastating impact on human relationships among African Americans, calling "this kind of almost blind absorption in the material [that] which makes for a kind of diminishing of life, of feeling" (Brock, "Talk," 199). In doing such she recalls the personal toll such a materialism can take, as seen in Hurston's depiction of young Janie Crawford's frustration in trying to capitulate to her grandmother's wish that she have a materially prosperous life. It is seen in the devastation suffered by communities like the Bottom, which because of the dominant society's greed are on the brink of vanishing. Paule Marshall's vision of humanity is best represented in her depiction of indigenous people of African descent who are endowed with a twofold vision, "of being able to see not only backward in time, so that, unlike most people, they have a clear memory of events long past, but by some strange faculty, forward also. They know therefore what the future holds and that, despite all they have undergone and have yet to endure, it is assured" ("Shaping the World," 111). This quality of vision, however, is what Marshall sees as missing from the lives of many African Americans, inhibiting their attempts to sacralize their identities and convert to a fuller sense of themselves. In her novels she depicts characters who, immersed in a materialistic, sometimes hostile world, find themselves in a confrontation with aspects of black cultural forms and rituals that is oftentimes neither willed nor planned. In attempting to understand the challenges an Old Worldview presents to their being and mode of living, her characters come to learn something about themselves—their personal and communal identity. Healing fragmented selves, Marshall suggests, recovering lost identities and repairing bridges of communication between people who share a common heritage, is possible only through an honest confrontation with one's past and a positive attitude toward one's heritage. Marshall creates characters within cultural and historical contexts, structures upon which they depend for definition whether they know it or not. A realization of such contexts is what precipitates conversion, and characters' identities are revealed in the "contours of individual human beings as they form and are formed by their land and their culture, and the relationship between the past and present of a specific community as manifested in its concept of time and by its rituals" (Christian, "Paule Marshall," 167).

Another related phenomenon that surrounds the quest for identity is the social transformation that occurs when one comes to terms with history and cultural legacies. Enjoined with this revelation is an equally compelling imperative to change not just self but one's world, too; to be a witness to the vision and an agent of transformation. Marshall's vision encompasses the principles of a theology of liberation wherein spiritual freedom cannot be guaranteed for one individual if it is not guaranteed for all. As Barbara Christian states, "underlying her aesthetic is a faith in the ability of human beings to transcend themselves, to change their condition, that is at the core of much Afro-American literature." Moreover, Christian continues, Marshall "creates worlds in which the necessity of actively confronting one's personal and historical past is the foundation for a genuine revolutionary process" (169). Paule Marshall demonstrates in her novels how characters and culture can transform each other and how black women, as bearers of ancestral wisdom, can witness and give voice to this transformation.[10]

Praisesong for the Widow (1983) is Marshall's third novel, forming a kind of developmental trilogy with *Brown Girl, Brownstones* and *The Chosen Place, The Timeless People*.[11] Like the other novels, *Praisesong* explores the cultural continuity of peoples of African descent as a perspective from which to judge contemporary black life in America. By focusing on the consciousness of African Americans as they remember, retain, and most especially develop a sense of spiritual integrity—as they sacralize their identities—Marshall reveals the bankruptcy of materialism as a value standard and shows how an understanding of their history—their faith and its rituals—can restore black people to wholeness. As a bildungsroman, however, it assumes an unusual form since the protagonist, Avey Johnson, is sixty years old, indicating that it is never too late to convert. But because the experiences of the protagonist constitute a gradual building on discovered truths, the narrative becomes a classic model of conversion in its most elemental form. For in addition to showing the cultural unity among peoples of African descent, Marshall's conversion narrative, by extension, shows how a conversion reveals a universal human pattern of religious experience that takes a specific form in certain historical episodes and contexts.

The title gives an indication of Marshall's intentions. For Africans, as Abena P. A. Busia informs us, a praisesong is a particular kind of traditional heroic poem. "Sung in various communities over the entire continent, praisesongs embrace all manner of elaborate poetic form, but are always specifically ceremonial social poems, intended to be recited or sung in public at anniversaries and other celebrations, including funerals of the great. Praisesongs may embrace the history, myths, and legends of a whole people or their representative can be used to celebrate communal triumph or the greatness of rulers, and the nobility of the valiant and brave, whether in life or death" (198). Praisesongs can also be sung to mark social transition. Sung as a part of rites of passage, they mark the upward movement of a person from one group to the next. Although initially Avey's rite of passage is coming to terms with her widowhood, her reconciliation takes on much greater proportions by the time her journey is done. The "whole narrative in itself acts as praisesong for the widow, with the narrator as the griot" (Busia, 199).

The novel centers on Avey Johnson, a middle-aged, middle-class black widow who has assumed the materialistic values of America and whose husband literally worked himself to death to attain the affluence they enjoyed. While on a pleasure cruise with her friends, however, Avey experiences a rupture in her consciousness precipitated by a persistent dream about a childhood memory. Years before, on annual visits to her childhood home in the South, her now-dead Aunt Cuney used to take her to a place called Ibo Landing, where she recited the legend of slaves who were said to have walked across the water back to Africa. A dream of her aunt and of that place takes hold of her consciousness in such a radical way that Avey is undone. She experiences a gradual conversion process, whereby she is "called" three times by visions and eventually assents. She comes to understand how past and present unite, how myth and history intersect, enabling her to become more fully human. Her conversion is a unifying force that overtakes her when she confronts issues of identity and culture to claim her distinct self.

Initially Avey undertook the journey to escape thoughts of her dead husband, Jerome, despite the objections of her daughter Marion that she should do something more meaningful, "go off on [her] own somewhere. Learn something" (15). Yet Avey's journey becomes, in effect, what her daughter had wished. It becomes much more than a mindless pleasure cruise when she travels to the island of Carriacou and explores her own past and rediscovers her identity as "Avatara," the name her great-aunt Cuney had insisted she use as a child. "Avey, short for Avatara" (251), finds her roots as a member of the Arada people of Carriacou, and her discovery prompts her to plan to sell her house in North White Plains, New York, and return to her girlhood home in Tatum, South Carolina, for at least part of the year so that she, like her aunt before her, could instill in her grandchildren the history and the truths of their people and their past. In *Praisesong,* as Ebele O. Eko points out, "there is a reaching back to dead ancestors and a reaching forward to unborn generations . . . [that] culminate in the essence of wholeness" (143).

Whereas in *Sula* Morrison depicts a black female protagonist split between claims of self and community, symbolically representing this split as two women who together constitute a whole and depend on one another for balance, Paule Marshall shows a woman who appears to have a positive, healthy sense of self and to have integrated herself well into the American dream. It is only when her past literally comes back to haunt her that Avey realizes the false and fragile foundation upon which she has constructed her identity.[12] Yet because of her past and its insistent and magical return to her consciousness—a movement that could be described as divine grace—Avey has within her the resources not just to fashion a sacralized identity but to create, or return to, a place wherein that identity can be nourished. Once-disparate elements of Avey's individual self come together and merge with a collective sense of self. This journey is seen, therefore, as something to which her whole life has pointed, a familiar perspective for the newly converted, and it all points back to the story of Ibo Landing.

Told repeatedly to Avey by her great-aunt Cuney on the Sea Island of Tatum, this is a sacred story that was handed down by Aunt Cuney's grandmother Avatara, who was said to have been an eyewitness. A group of Ibos were brought in chains from a slave ship, but upon stepping out on the landing they looked around—looked far into the future—and decided not to stay. They turned, chains and all, and walked on the water, singing, going past the ship and all the way back to Africa. The young child Avatara followed them in her mind. "Her body, she always usta say might be in Tatum but her mind, her mind was long gone with the Ibos" (39). This story reveals how people of African descent through their own power determined their freedom. Although their bodies might be enslaved, their minds were not. Africa, not slave America, was the source of their being.

When young Avey challenges her aunt and asks why the Ibos did not drown, her aunt, marshaling all of her ancestral authority, responds by posing to Avey the question: "Did it say Jesus drowned when he went walking on the water in that Sunday School book your momma always sends with you?" (40). Clearly, Marshall intends that this myth and the rituals that surround it be granted the legitimacy accorded Christian Scripture and worship, and perhaps even that they be respected for what they offer that traditional Christian theology does not. For Aunt Cuney, people in Tatum used to say, "made the Landing her religion" (34), because "those pure-born Africans was peoples my gran' said could see in more ways than one" (37). The story of Ibo Landing conveys linkages between past, present, and future, between Africa and the Diaspora, and for Avey personally a link to her own family and culture of which she is a privileged namesake. Avatara, whose mind was in Africa, returns five generations later to Aunt Cuney and announces that she is sending a baby girl into the family to be named after her—the avatar, or incarnation, of the gods. From the time Avey is six or seven, Aunt Cuney insists that she visit Tatum, there to stand again on Ibo Landing and hear the story.

At the beginning of the novel, however, Avey has come far from that time. Years ago she abandoned the annual pilgrimages to Tatum and instead gave herself over to the new life she and her husband, Jerome, had created to support their three daughters. During a cruise aboard a luxury liner named, none too subtly, the *Bianca Pride,* Avey is seized with some compulsion that she does not understand—"a strength born of the decision that had just come to her in the middle of the night" (9)—and packs her six suitcases and leaves the ship to be dropped off at Grenada, eventually to return to New York by the next available plane. Her actions are utterly uncharacteristic. She cannot even explain them to herself. She does remember, however, how the patois she heard a few days earlier in Martinique reminded her of the accents at Tatum. Then she had a dream, although "as a rule she seldom dreamed" (31), that is her first call to conversion. She dreams that Aunt Cuney prevented her from going to a social function and tried to force Avey to follow her: "Her body straining forward as though to bridge the distance between them she was pleading with her now to join her, silently exhorting her, transformed into a preacher in a Holiness church imploring the sinners and backsliders to come forward to the mercy sea. *'Come/O will you come . . . ?'* The trees in Shad Dawson's wood gave voice to the old invitational hymn, speaking for her. *'Come/Won't you come . . . ?'"* (42). Avey remembers how Aunt Cuney had "entrusted her with a mission she couldn't even name yet had felt duty-bound to fulfill" (42), though she had taken years to rid herself of the duty. But for some reason her aunt was back, reminding her of her mission, dragging her in the direction of Ibo Landing. In the fistfight that followed, Aunt Cuney tore Avey's party dress. When she awakes from the dream Avey is exhausted and actually feeling sore from battle and recalls feeling strange, not herself. Moreover, she begins to feel a "mysterious clogged and swollen feeling" (52), a bloat that intensifies even as she leaves the ship. The bloat, the clogged memories and responsibilities she "trained herself not to notice, or if she did, not to feel anything one way or the other about it" (47), take over her consciousness, each present scene recalling for her something in her past. From that moment on she begins to remember other long-forgotten things, effectively giving rebirth to an old "new self."

Avey arrives in Grenada at the time of the annual excursion to Carriacou, a little island nearby to which the natives return to honor ancestors. This yearly migration of out-islanders to their island home is when they unite with family members, pay homage to ancestors, and participate in rituals and dances commemorating African roots. Curious about the goings-on, and intrigued by all the excited people on the dock waiting for boats, she asks her taxi driver about the scene. He describes the industrious out-islanders as having "no crab antics" (78), a phrase that corresponds to one with which Avey is familiar: "crabs in a barrel." Unlike crabs in a barrel, which claw and fight their way to the top, the people she observes stick together and help out one another, a form of survival Avey admires. But as soon as she gets to her hotel, Avey is once again overcome with the bloat, falls into a chair, and "under her hat brim, Avey Johnson's eyes again had the wide frightened look of someone given to visions that were beyond her comprehension" (83).

She undergoes a strange and even violent emotional catharsis precipitated by an envisioned admonition from her dead husband, who scolds her for her wastefulness. This is her second call in which she remembers much of her life, including the desperate struggle upward economically and socially that separated her and her husband from the black communities and from Avey's home in Tatum, eventually costing Jerome his life. The next morning she still feels strange but wanders into a little grog shop, where she feels "a cool dark current of air like a hand extended in welcome. And without her having anything to do with it, it seemed, before she could even knock or find the voice to ask if anyone was there, the hand reached out and drew her in" (157). Inside she encounters a Carriacou islander named Lebert Joseph, who persuades her to come on the excursion.

The third call comes on the trip to the island. Despite assurances that the sea would be calm, the boat pitches and sways; Avey becomes desperately seasick and both vomits and voids her bowels, much to her humiliation. Later, at the home of Lebert Joseph's daughter, Rosalie Parvey, she is given a ritualistic bath and massage—a purification—and subsequently attends the ceremonies. It is then that she realizes Lebert Joseph is not a simple shopkeeper but an immortal, the embodiment of wisdom as he conducts the activities at the ceremony. Although he seems at once both literal and supernatural to Avey (much as Shadrack appears to Sula and Tea Cake appears to Janie), Marshall seems to suggest, by the invocation marking the beginning of this section that is a voodoo introit invoking the Dahomean god Legba—"Papa Legba, ouvri barriere pou' mwe" (Papa Legba open the gateway for me)—that Lebert Joseph is the incarnation of the Yoruba deity Legba, the trickster and guardian of the crossroads where all ways meet. Like Lebert Joseph, Legba is a lame old man in ragged clothes. A personal and much-loved god, Legba acts as the link between people and the whole pantheon of gods. He is vital to numerous rituals, both in West Africa and in the New World. Lebert Joseph, like the ancestral Avatara, contains "many linkages: Africa and the Diaspora; the carnate and the spirit worlds; the present generation, the ancestors, and the yet unborn" (Collier, 312).

The ceremonial ritual on Carriacou brings together for Avey elements from all of her life, and as she watches she also remembers key points in her life, most especially when the story was told at Ibo Landing. The drumming, song, and dance that accompany the ritual are celebrations of African roots. First in order is the Beg Pardon, in which families supplicate their ancestors' pardon for offenses committed against them during the year, intentional or not. They petition not only for themselves and their neighbors but also for relatives known and unknown scattered throughout the world. Ancestors at this ceremony have a nearly tangible presence and are even offered food and drink. Following the Beg Pardon is the dance of nations. In the moonlight and to the beat of drums, people descended from the nations of Africa dance their ancestral dances. Avey knows no dance of her ancestral nation, or even whether she has one, but she remembers another dance ritual. When she and her husband, Jay, were poor and living in a tenement on Halsey Street, old blues and jazz records would heal the hurt and humiliation that were part of Jay's job, and the two of them would dance a love ritual. But as they prospered, as Jay became Jerome (like Jody became Joe Starks, mayor), they stopped dancing.

The Creole dance is the novel's climax, when Avey, after thrice refusing, eventually answers the call and is converted. All the people dance this dance, even those who do not know their nation but can proclaim some African ancestry. The people dance in a counterclockwise circle a "rhythmic trudge that couldn't be called dancing" (246), with bodies swaying and arms uplifted, gliding forward with only the heels leaving the ground. The Carriacou Tramp, Avey realizes, is the same as the Ring Shout that she watched in Tatum years ago and wanted so badly to join. Eventually, invisible arms draw Avey into the circle of dancers, and she joins the ritual, joins the flow with a feeling that engages her entire being. The dance becomes the expression of all the aspects of her self joined with the community.

As Sabine Brock has noted, much of Avey's journey, both literal and metaphysical, is circumscribed by images of spaces she comes to inhabit, from the insulated neighborhood of White Plains or the cramped quarters of a ship, to the forests and shore of Tatum and the villages in the Caribbean. Each time she confronts a vision, reflects on her life and dreams, she makes a decision to change place—to vacate the ship and fly to New York, to wander the streets of Grenada—until eventually the memory of places, like the home on Halsey Street or Ibo Landing, causes her finally to travel to the mystical site of Carriacou. Her journey is in one sense a ritual of location, of remembering and finding a space wherein she can remember and find herself. In this sense she stands for all women, young and old, who are searching for a sacred space in which the sacrality of their being can be expressed.

This search for a sacred space, moreover, as Barbara Christian reminds us, is shaped and informed by ritual movement and form, where external space or reality is juxtaposed with memory, dream, hallucination, disjointed states of mind in which past and present fuse, where one locates where her mind should be (*Black Feminist Criticism*, 150). Structuring the sense of place and the ritualistic movement between spaces is a four-part division of the narrative: "Runagate," "Sleeper's Wake," "Lavé Tête," and "The Beg Pardon." Each title indicates not only a ritualistic process but also a change in Avey Johnson's character and context, delineating an archetypal journey into awareness. In "Runagate" she is running away from the visions that disturb her ordered consciousness; in "Sleeper's Wake" she is awakening to a shocking reality; in "Lavé Tête" she is washing away false values and ideas; and in "The Beg Pardon" she is reconciling with her heritage and her true identity.

The title "Runagate" is taken from Robert Hayden's poem of the same name, a poem that emphasizes the slave past of African Americans and their escape from bondage. Depicting a runaway slave as running, falling, rising, and stumbling on his way to freedom, Hayden's poem prefigures Avey in her unconscious run for freedom. It also serves as a reminder that one cannot erase or forget the slave experience and that attempts like Jerome's to struggle upward are a futile effort to move away from all reminders of that past, "back you know where" (88), as he used to say. Although she assumes at first she is running north to freedom and back to White Plains, Avey's plans are thwarted and she is sent farther south, literally in the Caribbean and imaginatively to Tatum, South Carolina. Symbolically, she becomes the archetypal fugitive slave because, until she can feel that pain, remember her origins, and seek to change human circumstances, whatever comfort and freedom she has acquired are simply an illusion.

When she leaves the ship, therefore, Avey is in a state similar to that of Avatara, who left her body in Tatum but took her mind to Africa: "Her mind in a way wasn't even in her body or for that matter in the room" (10). She is agitated and bewildered, full of self-doubt triggered by her daughter's criticism of the cruise that escalates when she has the vision of Aunt Cuney trying to drag her away, trying to force her to face her past, her roots, her heritage.

The second section, "Sleeper's Wake," has two meanings, marking a wake or a ritual mourning for the dead—Jerome and her own dead past—as well as an awakening from the past. Ebele Eko also suggests that this section could refer to the historic cultural and literary awakening of American blacks and by extension blacks everywhere through the Harlem Renaissance, recalling parallel developments like the Negritude movement in Senegal and the Haitian Renaissance (145). The action in this introspective section takes place entirely in

Avey's mind because her body is stranded, displaced in a Grenadian hotel. Like Linda Brent's mind when she is confined to her garret, at this time Avey's mind is free to roam, and she begins by reviewing her marriage to Jerome Johnson.

A certain poignancy attends these descriptions of young, passionate love, and Avey begins to understand how that love was transformed from a ritual joining full of meaning to a rote habit that simply maintained a level of stability, a sleeping state. Avey begins to awake from the stupor of her bourgeois mentality to a sudden realization of all she has lost, all she and Jay sacrificed in terms of happiness and life-giving values in order to acquire a house in a white neighborhood. She remembers all the

> little private rituals and pleasures, the playfulness and wit of those early
> years, the host of feeling and passions that had defined them in a special
> way back then, and the music which had been their nourishment. . . .
> Moreover (and again she only sensed this in the dimmest way) something
> in those small rites, an ethos they held in common, had reached back be-
> yond her life and beyond Jay's to join them to the vast unknown lineage
> that had made their being possible. And this link, these connections,
> heard in the music and in the praisesongs of a Sunday ". . . I *bathed* in
> the Euphrates when dawns were young . . ." had both protected them
> and put them in possession of a kind of power. (136–37)

Avey is ritualistically mourning not her husband's recent passing but his spiritual death, lamenting how the complex need to provide for a family and achieve a level of dignity and success had so overwhelmed him that he lost the sense of "the rich nurturing ground from which [they] could always turn for sustenance" (12). Her identity, like Nel's with Jude, eroded along with Jerome's and their mutual regard for each other. It was after the pressures of survival became so intense (in part because of her insecurities and desires) that Jay forfeited his sense of identity and his spiritual commitment to his family in order to provide for them. Avey describes the change in her marriage with an image reminiscent of the one Janie used to describe the change in Jody. Like Janie's image of Jody that fell off the shelf, "It seemed the china bowl which held her sanity and trust fell from its shelf in her mind and broke" (91). Avey and Jay had squandered the sacred aspects of their being for secular rewards, forsook the rituals of music and dancing that could "work their magic, their special mojo" (94) until Jay's accounting office which bore his name also bore "the whole of his transubstantiated body and blood" (88).

"Lavé Tête," the third section, begins with Avey's dream of a soiled baby who needs changing, a baby whom Avey discovers when she awakes is none other than herself, "the staleness of her own flesh in the slept-in clothes" (150). The memories of Jay have undone her. In addition, Aunt Cuney's call to come keeps returning, along with thoughts of Marion's criticism. Mourning Jay and beginning to reject her bourgeois values, Avey again responds ritualistically: a literal, bodily purge which she symbolically begins by removing her girdle, her "hairshirt" (145). The title of this section referring to the Haitain voodoo ceremony in which one is washed clean, signifies Avey's new state of mind, which, "emptied of the contents of the past thirty years" the preceding night was now "like a slate that has been wiped clean, a tabula rasa upon which a whole new history could be written" (151).[13] Purification or a repentance of sins and a pledge to lead a righteous life, moreover, is a traditional stage of conversion, a necessary step in the entry to a new sacralized identity. Like the black women converts before her, Avey must cast off the identity ascribed to her—or that she thought she must assume—and rediscover the sacred qualities inherent in her own being.

Once again Marshall gives prominent place to a ritual, this time a cleansing ritual that is more than bodily cleansing but a shedding off of a false image. For much of this section Avey is as a child, "slow and clumsy as a two-year-old" (151), an image that will reappear in Alice Walker's novel and to a certain extent describes Sula and Nel at the time when their identities were most secure and unencumbered. Her childlike feelings of wonder and pleasure are carried over from her memories of early in her marriage with Jay, when the things that were important to her "would have counted for little in the world's eye. To an outsider, some of them would even appear ridiculous, childish *cullud*" (136). Avey strolls through Grenada "with a child's curiosity" (154), like a convert starting to see the world anew, for the first time. What she feels as a woman now is like what she felt as a child in Tatum:

> And the threads went out not only to people she recognized from the neighborhood but to those she didn't know well, such as the roomers just up from the South and the small group of West Indians whose odd accent called to mind Gullah talk and who it was said were as passionate about their rice as her father. . . . The threads streaming out from her even entered the few disreputable types who occasionally appeared in their midst from the poolrooms and bars. . . . Then it would seem to her that she had it all wrong and the threads didn't come from her, but from them, from everyone on the pier, including the rowdies, issuing out of their navels and hearts to stream in to her as she stood there. . . . for these moments, she became part of, indeed the center of, a huge wide confraternity. (190–91)

Here she also encounters Lebert Joseph, the paternal figure who guides her in her development. Lebert is, like Aunt Cuney, "one of those old people who gave the impression of having undergone a lifetime of trial by fire which they somehow managed to turn to their own good in the end; using fire to burn away everything in them that could possibly decay, everything mortal. . . . Old people who have the essentials to go on forever" (161). Lebert Joseph is what Eva could have been had she not lived in the Bottom. Avey's ancestral parents, Aunt Cuney and Lebert Joseph, are guiding her to a "deeper state of being that was always potentially hers" (Christian, *Black Feminist Criticism*, 155). Lebert Joseph, like Aunt Cuney before him, "possessed ways of seeing that went beyond mere sight and ways of knowing that outstripped ordinary intelligence (*Li gain connaissance*) and thus had no need for words" because he "saw how far she had come since leaving the ship and the distance she had yet to go" (172).

Also figuring prominently in this section are memories of Avey's that emphasize communal rituals: the New York blacks' annual boat ride up the Hudson and the church of her childhood. Eventually, Avey joins the communal ritual the present offers her and boards the *Emmanuel C* (another boat named none too subtly after Christ). As the boat sets sail the image reminds her of a Catholic parade on a feast day of their saints, and "for no reason, not understanding why, she caught herself thinking: it had been done in the name of the Father and of the Son" (195). Uncomfortable and feeling sick on the journey, Avey is helped by the women also making the journey. They remind her of the women in church, "the presiding mothers of Mount Olivet Baptist (her own mother's church long ago)" (194), who also helped the congregation cross over: "From there their powerful 'Amens' propelled the sermon forward each Sunday. Their arms reached out to steady those taken too violently with the spirit. And toward the end of the service when the call went out: '*Come/ Will you come . . . ?*' and the sinners and backsliders made their shamefaced calvary up to the pulpit, it was their exhortations which helped to bring them through" (194). This church, as Velma Pollard reminds us, "is one of a number of religious bodies with recognizably non-European behaviours found throughout the Caribbean and among blacks in America" (295). Also, by helping Avey through this initiation process, the women's actions echo, "in a very vivid way, the African communal involvement and deep empathy with young initiates during their rites of passage" (Eko, 144). Avey then remembers a childhood Easter Sunday—the occasion of Christ's rebirth—and the preacher's sermon when he admonishes that "the shameful stone of false values" (201) prevents the bright light of the soul from shining. It is at this point that Avey becomes sick and Marshall compares her crossing in the *Emmanuel C* to the Middle Passage, as Avey has "the impression as her mind flickered on briefly of other bodies lying crowded in with her in the hot airless dark. Their suffering— the depth of it, the weight of it in the cramped space—made hers of no consequence" (209). In this entire section Marshall weaves impressions of black life and culture drawn from points as far apart as Harlem, South Carolina, Africa, and the Caribbean, each image relating to an experience in another location, underscoring the relational nature of black identity.

The ritual that concludes the book and serves as the title for the fourth section is "The Beg Pardon." As the name implies, this is the final stage in the growth process of awareness, when the cultural prodigal comes home to beg pardon of her offended ancestors.[14] In a sense this ritual is meant to accomplish what Aunt Cuney's ritual of taking Avey to Ibo Landing and telling her Avatara's story every year accomplished: a reverence for the past and the wisdom of ancestors. Before any ceremony can begin, however, Avey's body is cleansed in a bathing rite performed by Rosalie Parvey, also a widow, where "all the tendons, nerves and muscles which strung her together had been struck a powerful chord and the reverberation could be heard in the remotest corners of her body" (224). At last her body and mind have come together, and although "she was feeling more dazed and confused than ever, yet there now seemed to be a small clear space in her mind" (187). She is ready to observe the ritual. The Beg Pardon is a ceremony that "combines rituals from several black societies: The Ring Dances of Tatum, the Bojangles of New York, the voodoo drums of Haiti, the rhythms of the various African peoples brought to the New World" (Christian, *Black Feminist Criticism*, 157). Avey realizes that "it was the essence of something rather than the thing itself she was witnessing" (240). She also comes to the revelation that in the dance there is an acknowledgment of the pain of the past, "the theme of separation and loss," and that: "the unacknowledged longing it conveyed summed up feelings that were beyond mere words, feelings and a host of subliminal memories that over the years had proven more durable and trustworthy than the history with its trauma and pains out of which they had come. After centuries of forgetfulness and even denial, they had refused to go away" (244–45). Eventually Avey begins to dance, as she did with her husband and as she did as a child in

Tatum: "the shuffle designed to stay the course of history" (250). When the old people bow their heads in her direction, Avey finally recognizes herself as and reassumes the name Avatara. This symbolic gesture alludes to the African practice of *nommo*, whereby the correct naming of a thing brings it into existence. By becoming Avatara, by assuming the convert's pose of humility before divine and ancestral power, Avey has finally become herself.

By developing her story around this four-part structure, Marshall reveals the ordered and ritualistic aspects of life and development that often go undetected. Avey's growth through stages, her conversion after several calls, reflects the pattern Jaochim Wach cites in his comparative study of religions. All religious experience, Wach claims, manifests itself in three basic modes of expression: thought, action, and association. Avey follows these modes of expression in nearly sequential order as her thoughts (sometimes expressing themselves as dreams or visions) inspire her to act, however unconsciously, until eventually the cumulative result of all her thoughts and actions results in her ability to associate Tatum with Carriacou, Harlem with Africa, Lebert Joseph with Legba, and finally Avey with Avatara.

In an early essay Paule Marshall sums up her family's belief in God by describing his essential attitude in the phrase "God don' love ugly and He ain' stuck on pretty" ("From the Poets," 28). She sees this phrase as especially apt considering the way her family recognized, and in their language used, the fundamental dualisms of life to explain reality. When they described something as "beautiful-ugly" or called each other "soully-gal," Marshall believes, they were expressing the idea "that a thing is at the same time its opposite, and that these opposites, these contradictions make up the whole." She distinguishes this perspective from a Manichaean type of dualism wherein evil and good, spirit and flesh are separate and in opposition. In *Praisesong,* when the narrator is describing Thomasina Moore, one of Avey's traveling companions, as having black skin "that was the near-white of a blanched almond or the best of ivory," she comments that this color is "both sacred—for wasn't it a witness?—and profane: '*he forced my mother my mother / late. One night / What do they call me?*'" (19).

The ability to balance the forces of life, to see spirit in flesh and to recognize both good and evil intentions in every act, is what enabled Marshall's family, indeed all her ancestors, to survive. It is the same principle that underscores Marshall's insistence on drawing black women characters as full of complexity. Moreover, this concept is one that appeared in Hurston's anthropology, when she rendered black theology and culture in terms of God and the devil; in her fiction, where she showed a crafty God who had to be watched at all times; and even in her autobiographical assessment of herself as a woman of contradiction. It is the very same principle Morrison embodies in the reflexive twin characters of Sula and Nel, as in the novel *Sula* she entwines and unravels the concepts of good and evil to the point of mystifying complexity.

For Marshall, however, such a dual nature seems perfectly simple. That is why, in her fiction, she will not criticize African Americans, like Jerome, for their success-oriented goals, nor blindly romanticize black rural life, as seen in South Carolina or the Caribbean. Marshall, like Morrison, sees spirit as strength, not power, but whereas Morrison reveals what becomes of spiritual strength when it is used as a force of power, Marshall chooses to reveal how spiritual strength empowers. Such spiritual strength she locates in cultural roots and urges not a superficial tracing of lineage and a simple location of one's ancestral source but an effort to glean from one's historical past those values that have proven viable and sustaining. In this sense, as Dorothy Denniston reminds us:

> Africa remains, to a large extent, symbolic, but it is accepted, without question, as the central referent. It becomes, in short, the common denominator of the collective, black experience. As for the black woman, who carries the additional burden of learning to be comfortable with her strength, Marshall presents not a dismissal of the male but an affirmation of the female. She seems to acknowledge, along with Bonnie

Barthold, that "the source of [the black woman's] common celebration
is large enough to accommodate the ambiguities they carry within themselves" and that "their complexity reduces neither their strength nor
their capacity to celebrate that heritage." (45)

By marking Avey's beginnings and endings, Marshall moves her
readers toward an exploration of a more cyclic nature of time as perceived by traditional African societies. Contrary to the Western notion of death as the termination of life, death becomes for the people
of Carriacou a celebration of the continuity of life, something Avey
comes to appreciate through her memory of both Avatara and Aunt
Cuney. As she moves back in time and space, through memory, myth,
and ritual, Avey also moves forward in consciousness, recapitulating
also the Christian pilgrimage guided by the principle that it is by losing oneself that one finds oneself. So Avey, by discarding her artificial
forms, journeys back to herself. As Missy Dehn Kubitschek says, "her
true self is reborn" (*Claiming the Heritage,* 18).

Marshall demonstrates in general terms the survival of African cultural forms. In particular terms, she shows how these forms can influence the lives of contemporary women. African culture teaches that
body and spirit are one, that memory cannot be achieved unless there
is a reciprocal relationship between an individual and her community.
Avey comes to effect this kind of integration through a ritualistic
movement. African culture, like the dead ancestors it celebrates, is the
"living dead," because the departed one is "alive in the memory of
those who knew him in his life as well as being alive in the world of
spirits. . . . he is in a state of personal immortality" (Mbiti, 32).

This status of living dead is what Sula eventually comes to assume
for Nel, or so one can speculate at the end of the novel, and also what
marks a point of comparison for all the writers here discussed.[15] The
complexity and creativity with which Marshall insists black women
must be depicted, the shaping of individual personalities within the
communities she describes, stretch back to the nineteenth century and
cause us to consider Sojourner Truth, Harriet Jacobs, and Rebecca

Jackson as ancestors. These women showed how black women can, indeed must, be strong yet still retain vital female qualities. In addition, they showed how women can discover and be empowered by the sacrality within themselves to effect physical and spiritual change for themselves and for their community. By revealing how black women can control their lives and accept the responsibility of defining themselves by using the resources available to them to create (whatever the form or object or activity), Marshall makes Avey part of the lineage of Rebecca Jackson and Sojourner Truth, who preached to present and future generations. She places herself in the tradition of Harriet Jacobs and Zora Neale Hurston, the "chain of narrators" who wrote that it would not be forgotten. All these women are connected to the ordinary women like Phyllis Biggs, the quilt maker, and Marshall's mother and her friends, for whom simply talking in the kitchen was a creative and spiritual response to life and history.

The connections are not only temporal but geographical as well. Just as Hurston attempted to reveal to blacks the variety and wealth of their spiritual and cultural traditions in the Americas, so Marshall expands on this vision to include Africa, showing a cultural unity that joins black people of the Sea Islands of the southern United States to the black people of the Caribbean and of Africa, by implication all diaspora people. Moreover, Marshall ennobles and heightens the significance of both Christian and folk rituals by constantly placing them side by side in Avey's consciousness. Together the distinct elements of Avey's religious heritage collaborate to create a vision of spiritual unity. Marshall obviously does not see a conflict between African and Christian theologies but freely moves between and through them, employing images from each to describe Avey's sensations and feelings, all the while pointing out the importance and endurance of religious symbolism and meaning in a quest for understanding. Although an act of imagination may be necessary to conjure up this unity, it is, nonetheless, not imagined but real, "the result of cultural retentions from a common ancestor, one or other of the kingdoms of the African continent from which the black populations were taken" (Pollard, 286).

Although Marshall, it may be said, understates dissimilarity to highlight similarity, the craft with which she renders her characters enables them to retain a distinct personality that emerges as separate from, if part of, their communal identity. Her characters suggest universals without losing deeply personal qualities that make them memorable as individuals. Her reasons for understatement are decidedly didactic: to rescue blacks from what she believes is a colonial-induced sense of inferiority and to avoid the trap, as Hurston did, of portraying black lives as "solely defined by racism" (Brock, "Talk," 195). Or, as Susan Willis describes it, Marshall's "task has been to articulate the difficulties of being in two worlds at once and the need to unite the Afro-American cultures of North America and the Caribbean" (*Specifying*, 53). Marshall wants to bear witness, much as the ex-slave narrators did, to her history and her heritage. Although she dwells not on the horror of her community's past but on its grace, she nevertheless points to the need to recognize the horror and humiliation as the only means by which to transcend them. The centuries-old hurt inflicted upon blacks cannot be healed in isolation but only through an awareness and acceptance of community. As the narrator comments in *Praisesong*: "Its source had to be the heart, the bruised still-bleeding innermost chamber of the collective heart" (245). Marshall shows black culture as more than unrelieved suffering and more than miracle of collective triumph; she shows it as both at once.

The character of Avey represents both the temporal and the geographical journey Marshall urges African Americans to undertake. Avey moves through several levels of consciousness and must confront each and comprehend each surrounding aspect of reality: myth, history, ritual, and finally ontology. She realizes, unlike Sula, that one cannot escape origins but that understanding origins is the first step in integrating a divided self; of spiritually coming home. Marshall seems to suggest through Avey, as Toni Morrison does through Sula and Nel, that selves are not innately divided but that societal pressures fracture selves and separate carnate and incarnate worlds. Conversion into wholeness, therefore, is not a luxury but a necessity. Moreover, she suggests that the work is not ended with conversion.

As Avey becomes, through her final intentions to return to Tatum, an extender of myths, so Marshall accepts as her responsibility as a writer, and indeed the responsibility of all people of African descent—the imperative to keep traditions and connections viable. Marshall makes Avey's story and personal experience a symbolic means of access to the history of black people in the New World. She "lifts her character out of the individual and particular of a purely autobiographical mode and achieves by way of symbolic representation a means of expressing both the deep sensitivity of individual experience and the concerns of a much larger community. . . . [Her] great talent as a writer is her insightful portrayal of individual characters as they articulate the complex of a community's actions and desires" (Willis, *Specifying*, 54).[16]

Marshall suggests a visionary sense of renewal for individuals by way of a recovery of culture, much the same project Hurston and Morrison defined for themselves. Her novel is a literary epiphany, a call to an awakening. She does not pretend it will be easy. Avey's conversion involved long, painful, and humiliating struggles. Every shred of remembered experience Avey wrestles from her past is won at great expense. Why she would endure this kind of physical and emotional suffering can only be explained as grace. Nothing we are told about Avey's character suggests she would have been so willing to endure what she does, only that when the call came she was obliged to answer. Moreover, the pain Avey experiences is necessary.

As Marshall suggests by weaving antebellum legends into her contemporary tale, slavery must be confronted and retrieved for individuals to affirm their selves, just as the Old Testament prophets had to remind the Israelites of their bondage and exile. When Avey undertakes her journey it is a symbolic reversal of the journey that the slaves took to America and a refiguration of the journey the Ibos took back to Africa. In this sense the meaning of slavery is overturned and by reversal becomes a metaphor for the articulation individuals achieve for naming their newly acquired racial consciousness and liberation. Moreover, Avey's own suffering is diminished, its meaning modified by the knowledge of her heritage.

Storytelling, sacred ritual, music, and dance—all the significant cultural forms of African-American expression are shown in *Praisesong for the Widow*. In this novel, therefore, Marshall reenacts the coming into being of not only an individual personality but a social reality. She does so in a context that attempts to preserve a sense of the multidimensionality of individuals while showing the community as a coherent center for self-definition. Many may contend that Marshall's view of the black community "writ large" is naive and largely ineffective as a source for identity in these days of pluralism, when so many young blacks are seeking a self-definition not circumscribed by a minority culture. She might be seen to be going against the grain of current thinking, in which assimilation is seen not as a denial of true self but indeed as a genuine means of self-authentication and preservation. Moreover, the source of cultural identity she describes as Africa presents political and cultural complexities that the novel cannot reproduce fully or even prescribe for everyone. Yet Marshall has the unshakable confidence of a convert and seems largely untroubled by such accusations because, to her, the vastness and diversity of Africa, the fact that people of African descent constitute a majority, not a minority, is much of her point. A recognition of this cultural and historical reality, on the part of both blacks and whites, she believes, offers the beginnings of a movement toward general human and social change.

Reclaiming one's self and one's community is a reciprocal endeavor, as the distinctiveness of the individual affirms continuity of the whole and the celebration of the whole ensures the survival of the individual. Abena P. A. Busia sees the theme of the novel framed in Lebert Joseph's question to Avey: "And what you is? What's your nation?" (15). Avey, and hence readers who follow her in her journey, learns to recognize and reassemble cultural signs that point toward individual fulfillment. Reclaiming one's sacred stories is a form of self-recognition and spiritual healing. By juxtaposing material acquisition with cultural dispossession as a metaphor for the history of a woman and a people, Marshall reveals how the demands of the past can be transformed into a gift for the future. The praisesong that was to initiate Avey into a new life as a widow becomes an homage to her homecoming. Places become iconic with meaning—Ibo Landing, a shrine—and life's movements become rituals of worship. As Keith Sandiford states, "*Praisesong* reaffirms authorial faith in the efficacy of cultural survivals, whether as discrete individual beliefs or collective ritual practices" (371).

Marshall shows how faith is not a luxury but an essential aspect of life, and that however long it takes, however hard won, faith can be found through conversion. Avey appears to have no choice but to convert; she is chosen by Avatara to carry on the legacy Aunt Cuney was guarding, and she must answer the call. Through this divine intervention, Marshall seems to suggest that all individuals, whether they are aware of it or not, really have no choice either. If they are to sacralize their lives they must (like Avey when she leaves the ship) leave behind the materialistic perspective on reality they have assumed and enter into the realm of myth, where interactions between living and dead, expressed in dreams, memories, rituals, and ceremonies, derive from religious beliefs.

Like Morrison, Marshall stresses the durability of archetypes but seeks to reinvest them with a meaning she finds relevant. Whether or not Avey serves as a heroine in the way Morrison would not fully allow Sula to be is a question to be explored. Clearly, she fits the pattern of heroes described previously. Moreover, Avey does not symbolize the stereotypical portrayals of black women Marshall so clearly abhors. But in her own way Avey, too, dislocates the concept of character or protagonist from its perch by the collective nature of her journey—the help she receives along the way—and the very ordinariness of her being. Like the figures from the nineteenth-century narratives, she is representative, not extraordinary. She is made extraordinary only through ancestral and mythic association, in the same way all Christian souls are made extraordinary through their belief in the sainthood of believers. Full of the inspiriting influence Awkward cites as characteristic of black women writers, Marshall shows individual spiritual growth through human interaction as opposed to psychic evolution accomplished in solitude. Female forces—Aunt Cuney, the women on the boat or in the church, her own daughter, and Lebert Joseph's daughter Rosalie—are crucial to Avey's growth. Even Lebert becomes female during the dance, as "out of his stooped and winnowed body had come the illusion of height, femininity and power" (243). Female forces act as midwives for Avey's rebirth, just as Paule Marshall herself was ushered into a recognition of her own identity by the women at her mother's kitchen table.

The novel, which ends with Avey's renaming of herself, an act crucial to feminist and African theologies, also ends with Avey imagining herself telling her grandchildren the sacred story of the Ibo's walk back to Africa, underscoring Marshall's imperative that in the quest to find self one must also pledge to renew society. The quest for a sacralized identity, Marshall reveals, is not an isolated incident in a convert's life but a lifelong commitment and a continuous modification of identity, for oneself and for future generations of converts. Because, as Lebert Joseph says of the Old Parents, "We has to understand and try our best to please them" (165) for the sake of the "grands and greatgrands . . . who don' know nothing 'bout the nation dance!" (168).

Alice Walker (1944–)

> If the concept of God has any validity or use, it can only be to
> make us larger, freer, and more loving.
> —James Baldwin

Whereas in their writing Toni Morrison seeks to clarify archetypal concepts and Paule Marshall seeks to reinvest myths with meaning, much of Alice Walker's work has involved the redefinition or even the invention of new words to describe her perception of reality. Her most familiar and now widely used term is "womanist," which first appeared in her collection of essays, *In Search of Our Mothers' Gardens*. Attempting to correct or expand on what she perceived as an exclusionary term, feminist, Walker derives womanist from the African-American idiom "womanish" and comes up with the following definition: "A black feminist or feminist of color. From the black folk expression of mothers to female children, 'You acting womanish,' i.e., like a woman. Usually referring to outrageous, audacious, courageous or *willful* behavior. Wanting to know more and in greater depth than is considered 'good' for one. Interested in grown-up doings. Acting grown up. Being grown up. Interchangeable with another black folk expression: 'You trying to be grown.' Responsible. In charge. *Serious*" (xi). Walker goes on to describe a womanist as "a woman who loves other women, sexually and/or nonsexually. Appreciates and prefers women's culture, women's emotional flexibility (values tears as natural counterbalance of laughter), and women's strength," and continues by stating that such a woman loves men but is "committed to the survival and wholeness of entire people." A womanist, moreover, loves music, dance, food, the moon, "*Loves* the spirit . . . *Loves* struggle. *Loves* the Folk. Loves herself. *Regardless.*" She concludes her definition by saying, "Womanist is to feminist as purple to lavender" (xi–xii).

What Walker intends through this new term is not a capricious playing with language. Rather, she attempts to show that when certain terms like "feminist" are used, they invoke a meaning and carry a connotation that may not be fully expressive or inclusive. There is a shade of essential difference, "as purple to lavender," to which Walker wants to draw attention. She emphasizes that although she may share the concerns and goals of the feminist movement, her agenda as a feminist is literally colored by her experience—that her needs and desires and forms of expression are different and must be acknowledged. As she says in an interview, "I wanted a word that was visible in itself, because it came out of my *own* culture" (DeVeaux, 122). By drawing her definition of womanist from a folk idiom, Walker is invoking the principle of inspiriting influence, demonstrating the reality and necessity of a historical community of black women in America. Because of her belief that "folklore is at the heart of self-expression and therefore at the heart of self-acceptance" (LW, 32), Walker is revealing a perception of reality available to anyone who strives to understand and appreciate her heritage.

What Alice Walker does for feminism by way of redefinition, she also does for several other terms and concepts that play an important role in contemporary life. In defending the rights of gay men and women, for example, she refers to herself as "homospiritual" (LW, 163), in order to emphasize that although she may be heterosexual in her sexual orientation, she identifies with and supports the choices of others to claim their own sexual identity. In speaking of the planet and the strength she derives from nature, Walker calls upon people to recognize that they are "coconspirators"—from the Latin *conspirare* (to breathe together)—with the natural world, and to protect and defend this collaborative strength (LW, xx). Walker also invokes the concept of conspiracy in recent journal entries in which she addresses her thoughts to one she sometimes identifies as the "Great Spirit" (LW, 95) and acknowledges her conspiratorial relationship to that spirit. "There is no doubt in my mind," she asserts, "that I am blessed. That you are present in the cosmos and in me and that we are breathing together—conspiracy. I see now what is meant by faith and the giving up of self to the spirit. I thank you for your gifts. All of them. I see you are trying to teach me all the time. I think of this when the lessons hurt. I love you" (LW, 52). Although she seldom uses the word *God*, it is clear that Walker is addressing her thoughts and identifying herself through a concept of divinity.

Walker's reluctance to use the word *God* is not a form of blasphemy but, again, another necessary redefinition on her part that in this context is an overt display of piety. Her respect for religion is deep. Although she realizes it was given to "pacify" the slave, "he soon transformed it into an antidote against bitterness, making it at once something simple and noble" (MG, 16). As a writer Walker admires and models her own work on literature in which the author is "on the side of Christ, the oppressed, the innocent, those who search for a kind of salvation," and creates characters who can "always envision a solution, an evolution into a higher consciousness on the part of society, even when society is in the process of killing them for their vision. . . . they are generally more tolerant of mystery, believing everything is inhabited by spirit" (MG, 250–51).

Although she often invokes Christian images and concepts, Walker is careful to qualify her religious beliefs, claiming she needs "a wider recognition of the universe" (Bradley, 30) than she finds in formal religion. In the tradition of feminist theologians, Walker describes her life as a "journey from the religious back to the spiritual" (Preface, xi). In an interview with Claudia Tate, she says she wishes to deconstruct the notion of God in the same way she deconstructed the notion of feminist. She is trying to rid "consciousness and unconsciousness of the notion of God as a white-haired British man with big feet and a beard. As a subjected people that image has almost been imprinted on our minds, even when we think it hasn't. It's there because of the whole concept of God as a person. Because if God is a person, he has to look like someone. But if he's *not* a person, if she's not a person, if *it's* not a person. . . . Or if it is a person, then everybody is it, and that's all right. But what I've been replacing that original oppressive image with is everything there is, so you get the desert, the trees; you get the birds, the dirt; you get everything. And that's all God" (Tate, 178–79).

Walker's theology or reenvisioning of God, which she describes as a "pagan transformation" (Preface, xi), has evolved during her career as a writer into something closely akin to animism. She believes all things are inhabited by spirit and surrounded by a mystery to which she believes one must be open because it "is deeper than any politics, race, or geographical location" (O'Brien, 193). By blending Native American, Hindu, Buddhist, and African forms of spirituality with her Christian upbringing, Walker derives her own unique form of religion. This is not to say that her religion is exclusionary or utterly solipsistic. Indeed, Walker is evangelical in her writings, over and over again encouraging people to acquire a deeper sense of their own sacrality and the sacrality that surrounds and inhabits everything. For God she substitutes the "Great Spirit," sometimes simply the word *Universe,* which she always capitalizes, and most recently she has described God as the "Ultimate ancestor," the "Great Mystery," "All That Is," and "That Which Is Beyond Understanding But Not Beyond Loving" (Preface, xi–xii). In a recent essay, "The Universe Responds," Walker describes how she has come to appreciate the value of prayer as "the active affirmation in the physical world of our inseparableness from the divine; and everything, *especially* the physical world is divine." She goes on to state, in paraphrase of Christian Scripture, that one need only "knock and the door shall be opened. Ask and you shall receive. Whatsoever you do the least of these, you do also unto me—and to yourself. For we are one." And she concludes with the assertion that "'God' answers prayers. Which is another way of saying, 'The Universe responds'" (LW, 192).

One way Walker believes the universe responds to her is by giving her talent as a writer. She thinks of the place she writes as "holy" and considers her work a "prayer" (LW, 47). Writing helps her collaborate in her animistic theology by permitting her "to be more than I am. Writing permits me to experience life as any number of strange creations" (Tate, 185). She directly relates her role as a writer to her role as a believer, placing herself in a mystical prophetic tradition wherein she is a vessel for Spirit. At the beginning of her novel *The Color Purple,* for example, she credits the Spirit, "Without whose assistance / Neither this book / Nor I / Would have been / Written"; she concludes the novel with "I thank everybody in this book for coming" and signs it "A.W., author and medium." Moreover, she credits her ancestors in the same way she credits various present spirits. Her honor for Zora Neale Hurston as a spiritual foremother is well documented in her writings, as are many other artists, musicians, and reformers, among them both men and women and people of all colors.[17] She sees them all as "spirit helpers" (LW, 97) and describes her joy of "being *with* a great many people, ancient spirits, all very happy to see me consulting and acknowledging them, and eager to let me know, through the joy of their presence, that, indeed, I am not alone" (MG, 13).

In addition to Hurston, Walker credits two other women already here discussed, Rebecca Jackson and Sojourner Truth. She credits Jackson with telling her "much about the spirituality of human beings, especially of the interior spiritual resources of our mothers" (MG, 78). Sojourner Truth she sees as kin since their names are alike: Sojourner = Walker and Truth = Alice (which means truth in ancient Greek). They share not only names, Walker claims, but also a "mystical bent," as Sojourner Truth's life conveys a "cloak of authority" to Walker. Sojourner Truth is therefore an "incarnate" to Alice Walker, revealing to her a "feeling of being loved and supported by the Universe in general and by certain recognizable spirits in particular," which she describes as "bliss. No state is remotely like it." She goes on to explain that "perhaps that is what Jesus tried so hard to teach: that the transformation required of us is not simply to be 'like' Christ but to *be* Christ" (LW, 98).

Although historical and cosmic figures play a significant role in Walker's spiritual and literary life, she, like Paule Marshall, also identifies as a primary influence in both spheres her maternal guide. As the eighth and last child born to Georgia sharecroppers, in "In Search of Our Mothers' Gardens," and throughout her work, Walker pays homage to her mother and other women like her, who elevated their lives and creative activities to the level of art. She sees her role as a writer as an extension of the work her mother engaged in: the fashioning of quilts, the putting up of food, the growing of gardens. She sees no distinction between "high" or "low" but rather celebrates the creative impulses of black women in whatever form or context they are expressed. For Walker believes that to be "rich in spirituality" is "the basis of Art" (MG, 233). Women like her mother, therefore, were "Creators," who order the universe in the image of their personal conception of beauty. Alice Walker affirms that "guided by my heritage of a love of beauty and a respect for strength—in search of my mother's garden I found my own" (243).

Walker is not content, however, to allow her heritage to nourish only her aesthetic sense. She sees her art, her spirituality, and her sense of social justice as intertwined and makes no distinction between the sacred and profane nor the uses to which she can put her talent or even simply her present notoriety. Implicit in Walker's theology of incarnation of spirits and transformation of individuals is a principle of conversion, of recognizing the sacrality within and thereby becoming Christ or "more self" (LW, 98). Walker firmly asserts that even as a writer you have to "save your own life first" (Bonetti), convert, and become appreciative of your own unique identity or else you have nothing to give. Once that is achieved, she says, a writer realizes that "it is in the end the saving of lives that we writers are about . . . we do it because we care. We care because we know this: the life we save is our own" (MG, 14). To describe this shared sense of corporate identity and responsibility to change, Walker would probably substitute "revolutionary" for the term "convert" because it means essentially the same thing—simply growing and changing. As she says in an interview, "I believe in change; change personal and change in society. I have experienced a revolution (unfinished, without question, but one whose new order is everywhere in view) in the South. And I grew up—until I refused to go—in the Methodist church, which taught me that Paul *will* sometimes change on the way to Damascus, and that Moses—that beloved old man—went through so many changes he made God mad" (MG, 252).

For her, however, the real goals of a revolutionary outlook—the perspective of a convert—are the least glamorous stuff. They are spiritual and practical needs being satisfied. She is convinced that as an artist she is "the voice of the people," and she is "also The People" (MG, 138). An early participant in the civil rights struggle, Walker views her involvement in the movement as grounded largely in an awareness of the religious consciousness of her people: "I have fought and kicked and fasted and prayed and cursed and cried myself to the point of existing. It has been like being born again, literally" (125). Once "converted," Walker has since publicly taken on and spoken for a variety of causes and concerns, addressing issues pertaining to the plight of Native Americans, urban violence, nuclear armament, ecological awareness, prison reform, and the mistreatment of animals. She considers herself a "world citizen" (Bonnetti) who views her activism in the same way she views her art, as conveying a sense of universal identity. In her most recent collection of essays, *Living By the Word,* for example, Walker sees past a concern for the individual and even communities of women to concentrate on more global concerns—the health and longevity of her culture and the world.[18]

Walker uses the perspective of her inheritance—a black woman writer with a legacy of slavery—to characterize the entire planet as enslaved. As she says, we must realize that we are "not only the descendants of slaves but also the descendants of slave *owners*. And that just as we have had to struggle to rid ourselves of slavish behavior, we must as ruthlessly eradicate any desire to be mistress or 'master'" (LW, 80). As a writer, therefore, she feels connected to all writers—whatever their race, gender, or national origin—by virtue of a universal imagination because while writing their own story they are also "writing one immense story—the same story, for the most part, with different parts of this immense story coming from a multitude of different perspectives" (MG, 5).

As she said in an interview following the publication of *The Temple of My Familiar,* Walker believes that "the real temple of the spirit is not a church or a synagogue, but freedom" (Britt, B1). Her mission is to use this freedom to uncover the sacrality of life, even if it means sometimes exposing its defamation and abuse. Walker does not shy away from controversy and has become for many, especially black men, a symbol of racial divisiveness because of her stark, uncompromising portrayal of brutality sometimes inflicted by black men on black women.[19] The controversy bothers her not because she is hurt by readers' judgments but because of her frustration over people's inattention to what she actually does say and write. Some of this she ascribes to the contemporary climate, although she still seems bemused that "a book that begins 'Dear God' would [not] immediately have been identified as a book about the desire to encounter, to hear from, the Ultimate ancestor" (Preface, xi).

As she explains in an interview with Charlayne Hunter-Gault shortly after the novel's publication, she does not "make up brutality . . . but I write about it because it is a very strong reality in all of the communities of the planet. . . . I don't agree that the people in *The Color Purple*—the men—are negative. Mainly because they grow and change and develop. . . . You have to write what you see and what you experience" (12). For more often than not Walker shows not just sin but redemption, demonstrating in her narratives the transformative properties of love and a life lived in the Spirit. Again, in her response to Hunter-Gault, she asserts that "the main focus of the novel . . . is theology. . . . what is really important is our relationship to the universe, you know, and what—that Celie's struggle is not so much with Mister in the end as it is with developing her own connection to the universe and the cosmos. It's a spiritual book, you know. It's a religious book. All my books are religious books" (13). Walker reemphasizes the theological content of the novel in her preface to the tenth anniversary edition when she describes the book's intent as "to explore the difficult path of someone who starts out in life already spiritually captive, but who, through her own courage and the help of others, breaks free into the realization that she, like nature itself, is a radiant expression of the heretofore perceived as quite distant Divine" (xi).

In describing Celie's transformation, Walker is referring to that concept of conversion that emphasizes embracing the sacrality of being as the goal of conversion. Walker emphasizes the spiritual content of her books over and against the harsh depictions of violence because she is aware that she has inherited "a great responsibility, as well, for we must give voice to centuries not only of silent bitterness and hate, but also of neighborly kindness and sustaining love" (MG, 21). Walker believes that through their struggles, which deepen their self-knowledge and love, black women can come to claim their own lives. As Barbara Christian states, "Her works confront the pain and struggle of black people's history, which for her has resulted in a deeply spiritual tradition" ("Alice Walker," 258).

The Color Purple (1982), with the various controversies surrounding it, remains Walker's best known and most highly praised and awarded book. Like her other novels, this work spans generations and interweaves personal stories with a constant flow of history. It is informed by folklore that provides not only the idioms of speech but the source of her ideas. Like Hurston, Morrison, and Marshall, Walker believes that in the extra-academic world of folklore, "a people's dreams, imaginings, rituals, legends . . . are known to contain the accumulated collective reality of the people themselves" (Christian, "Alice Walker," 259). The grand sweep of history and its effects interest her less than the relations of people to each other and how, as coconspirators, they sustain one another. As Trudier Harris says, "she employs folklore for the purposes of defining characters and illustrating relationships between them" (3). For although she began the book with the intention of writing a "historical novel," the history she wanted to depict "starts not with the taking of lands or the births, or the battles, and the deaths of Great Men, but with one woman asking another for her underwear" (MG, 356). She wanted to reveal what she inherited from her upbringing: "a sense of community . . . the solidarity and sharing a modest existence sometimes bring" (17), as well as a "compassion for the earth, a trust in humanity beyond our knowledge of evil, and an abiding love of justice" (21).

The action occurs between 1916 and 1942 in the Deep South. During this period black status remained almost unaltered since Reconstruction. An epistolary novel, *The Color Purple* consists, for much of its length, of letters addressed by the principal character, Celie, to God. The core of the book is not unlike Rebecca Jackson's journal in its intensely personal and intimate focus. But whereas Jackson records her spiritual musings to honor God, Celie writes to him simply because God is the only being with whom she can freely communicate. As her sister Nettie described it, "I remember one time you said your life made you feel so ashamed you couldn't even talk about it to God, you had to write it, bad as you thought your writing was" (122). Although not explicitly described until late in the novel, this God comes to be viewed by characters and readers alike as a God best described by the words of an old gospel song: "He may not come when you want Him, but He's right on time."

Initially Celie is not prepared to articulate her ideas about God to anyone but God; yet as she grows and develops in relationships with others, as she converts to an awareness of her own sacrality, she becomes able to express her understanding of the remote God whose presence has sustained her. Moreover, the epistolary form, the presentation of Celie's letters to God as an ongoing dialogue, offers a unique improvisation on the conversion narrative form. Although later Celie reflects on her growth and makes judgments about her spiritual development, early in the text we are witnesses to the changes as they develop organically. Unlike most conversion narratives that are constructed *after* conversion to show how a life inevitably led to conversion, Celie's letters show us how that process actually occurs as it happens. Still, they convey a sense of coherency and pattern. Later in the novel there are letters to Celie from her separated younger sister, Nettie—letters that Celie's husband withholds from her for many years after they were written—and finally there are a handful of letters from Celie to Nettie, who lives in Africa. The novel ends with a final letter of thanks to God.

Her communications to God begin when Celie is fourteen. Poor, barely literate, Celie has been raped and twice impregnated by her stepfather (whom she believes to be her real father). She is told that her children are dead and then she is forced into a loveless marriage to Albert, or as she refers to him initially, Mr. ——. Albert is a widower with four children and is in love with a vivacious and independent blues singer named Shug Avery. Celie is merely a servant and an occasional sexual convenience, all the more convenient because she is unable to bear more children. When Albert's oldest son, Harpo, asks Albert why he beats Celie he replies, "Cause she my wife" (30). For a time Celie accepts the abuse stoically: "He beat me like he beat the children. Cept he don't never hardly beat them. He say Celie, get the belt. . . . all I can do not to cry. I make myself wood. I say to myself, Celie, you a tree. That's how come I know trees fear men" (30).

Celie regards herself as already ruined: "I don't know how to fight. All I know how to do is stay alive" (26). She makes possible, therefore, the escape of her sister from this existence with the hope that at least she might have a chance for a better life with a missionary group in Africa. During the course of the novel, however, Celie frees herself from her husband's repressive control and experiences a variety of new sensations. Her growth is charted by a series of expressions introduced by "For the first time in my life. . . ." Bolstered by her hopes for her sister, Nettie, and the contact and support of other women, among them Albert's mistress, Shug, Celie's "first time" experiences become a part of her daily life; she eventually leaves Albert and moves with Shug to Memphis, where she starts a business designing and making clothes.

It is Albert's real love and sometimes mistress Shug Avery and his rebellious daughter-in-law, Sofia, who provide the emotional support for Celie's personal evolution. She learns what Alice Walker claims her own life taught her: "How to be shocked and dismayed but not lie down and die" (MG, 37). In turn, it is Celie's new understanding and confidence in herself that eventually lead to Albert's reevaluation of his own life and a reconciliation among the novel's major characters. Conversion for Celie, and indeed for many of the characters in the novel, incorporates change for personal identities and sacralizes the experience of marginality by creating a new community and a place for each individual within that community.

A plot summary can in no way reflect the subtle interactions among the characters, nor account for the novel's intense emotional impact. What makes the novel so affecting is the choice of narrative style, which without the intrusion of the author, forces intimate identification with the protagonist Celie. Especially effective is how, as the novel progresses and Celie grows in experience, her observations become sharper and more informed. The letters take on authority, and the dialect assumes a lyrical cadence of its own. The girl who initially knew only "how to survive" becomes a woman who can honestly and eloquently reflect on her own life and the lives of others. Moreover, as her sensibilities develop, so too do her spiritual qualities. She can for-give Mr. —— and appreciate him as Albert, her companion in old age. "Here us is, I thought, two old fools left over from love, keeping each other company under the stars" (238). Celie, who says at one point in her letters, "long as I can spell G-o-d I got somebody along" (26), achieves something akin to Frederick Douglass, who in his nar-rative shows the achievement of literacy as directly linked to his achieve-ment of political liberation and spiritual salvation.[20]

Several literary critics, among them Mae G. Henderson and Lindsey Tucker, have remarked on how Walker's choice of an epistolary form creates opportunities for Celie's characterization that a more tradi-tional form of fiction would not allow. Henderson and Tucker both point to the fact that the epistolary form is effective in part because it has been a convention used mostly by women. Citing work by Josephine Donovan and Janet Todd, they show that as a "semi-private" genre used primarily by women because of their inferior education and be-cause such writings were not expected to be published, the epistolary form grants a unique and valuable portrayal of women's lives. Tucker emphasizes the importance of Celie's letters to God as an indication of her being impelled to articulate experience, of a woman's need for language and voice whatever her circumstances ("Emergent Woman, Emergent Text"). Henderson, however, points to the significance of relations between women and the ways in which Walker's choice of an epistolary form formally links the portrayal of such friendships to the development of an epistolary novel ("Revisions and Redefinitions"). In other words, the narrative technique of the epistolary novel suits its subject because fictional friendships between women grew out of the ideal of the confidante—the correspondent in the epistolary novel. Citing the epistolary form as one of the only forms of expression avail-able to women, who historically have been denied access to popular and commercial print media, Henderson shows how Walker, in her own words, "liberated [Celie] from her own history" (Henderson, 14) and consequently gave voice to all women like Celie. Moreover, by doing such, Henderson asserts, Walker transposes the black oral mode

into the Western epistolary tradition, enhances it with vernacular qualities, and achieves a universal kind of integration.

Henderson also compares what Walker did with *The Color Purple*
to what Harriet Jacobs did with her narrative by turning the senti-
mental novel on its head. Just as Jacobs drew on the codes and conventions of the novel to appeal to readers, so, too, does Walker; yet
both resist the tendency to subscribe to the dictates of that form and
instead liberate it from its confining strictures (14). Tucker makes a
similar point when she draws an analogy between *The Color Purple*
and the entire genre of slave narratives, where the first-person mode
of discourse places the narrator as a central figure and thereby helps
to "repossess subjectivity by means of the 'I' or, as Susan Willis expresses
it, 'to wrest the individual black subject out of anonymity, inferiority, and
brutal disdain'" (83). Henry Louis Gates, Jr., in *The Signifying Monkey*,
also locates Celie's letters to God within the African-American tradition
deriving from the slave narrative, a tradition in which the act of writing is linked to a powerful deity who "speaks" through Scripture and
bestows literacy as an act of grace (239). In addition to being the story
of one woman's conversion into selfhood, *The Color Purple* is also
about a woman "breaking silence, acknowledging female influence,
and preserving cultural . . . characteristics" (Cheung, 162).

The novel begins, however, with Celie describing for God in graphic
terms the brutality she has been forced to endure. Significantly, at this
point Celie cannot even write "I am" but crosses out this declarative
and substitutes "*I have* always been a good girl" (11). She asks God
for a sign so that she might "know what is happening to me" (11).
She appears at this point in her spiritual development to see God as
someone with whom to barter, that if she is good perhaps God will
explain why her life is the way it is and change it. Her early and undeveloped perceptions of God are not dissimilar from those expressed
by Sojourner Truth before her conversion.

At this point, too, Celie first becomes acquainted with the image
of Shug Avery when her picture falls out of Mr. ——'s billfold. Celie
is instantly attracted to and captivated by Shug, keeping the picture

and dreaming of Shug as her only means of escape. By introducing the image of Shug so early, Walker is indicating something about her eventual presence in Celie's life. Although it begins as symbolic fascination with another sort of life, it soon becomes incarnate, an embodiment of all Celie dreams.

Taken out of school, Celie is "given" in marriage to Mr. ——. The abuse her stepfather inflicted on her is taken up and intensified by Mr. ——. Meanwhile, Nettie surreptitiously instructs Celie and tries to convince her of her own talents and give her the confidence to fight Mr. ——. Celie continues to dream of Shug, and soon Nettie comes to live with Celie and Mr. —— because her stepfather's advances have become too intense. Celie's life becomes bearable with Nettie around. Mr. —— soon begins to show interest in Nettie, causing her to leave at Celie's insistence. In a typical expression of immature faith, Celie speculates that if she were dead at least she would not have to work.

Celie continues to think of Shug Avery; when she shops for cloth for a new dress she tries to imagine what color Shug would wear and decides (in the novel's first reference to the title) that "She like a queen to me so I say to Kate, Somethin purple" (28). Mr. —— won't allow that, however, so Celie must choose a drab navy blue. Eventually the tedium and difficulty of Celie's life are broken when she learns Shug Avery is coming to town. Her enthusiasm nearly matches that of Mr. ——, who cannot wait to see his beloved mistress.

Occurring simultaneously are the love and marriage of Harpo, Mr. ——'s eldest son, to Sofia, a woman with a level of determination and strength as strong as what Celie imagines Shug's to be. Sofia transforms Harpo from what Celie calls "a trifling nigger" (29) into an industrious and affectionate father and husband. Harpo, however, is uneasy with his new life not because it displeases him but because it shames him among other men who assert their strength through the dominance of women. Celie, in what she calls a "sin against Sofia's spirit" (45), counsels Harpo to beat her. When Sofia finds out and confronts Celie, she admits she told Harpo to beat Sofia because she was jealous of Sofia for doing what she cannot, namely fight. Celie is overcome with shame, describing the feeling as "the Lord done whip me a little bit" (46). Eventually, however, she and Sofia change the talk around and begin to talk like friends, sharing their experiences and a sense of solidarity born of their bearing the abuses of men.

Like Nettie, Sofia counsels Celie to be strong and fight back, but Celie only retreats to her faith and says that the Bible instructed her to honor her father, despite his abuse, and that although she "have to talk to the Old Maker," she knows that as her husband, Mr. —— must be obeyed. She consoles herself again by asserting that "This life soon be over. . . . Heaven last all ways" (47). Celie, the model church-woman admired by the preacher as someone "faithful as the day is long" (48), has a very simple view of how faith operates in her life. God is a refuge, an audience; similarly, faith is a promise that whatever suffering is endured in this life will be rewarded in the afterlife. Yet when Celie goes to church and encounters the parishioners and preacher criticizing Shug as a "nasty" woman, taking "her condition for his text" (48), Celie utters to herself the first challenge to her received theology and thinks, "Somebody got to stand up for Shug" (49). This time, however, she chooses to remain silent.

Before long, however, Mr. —— brings Shug to his home; Celie is called upon to care for her and gladly accepts. For the first time in their married life she and Mr. —— share a similar feeling in their mutual concern for Shug, a feeling that intensifies when Mr. ——'s father comes to chastise his son for taking in Shug. Celie describes it as "the closest us ever felt" (59), and when Shug is well enough to join the circle of her and Mr. ——, Celie exclaims to God, "For the first time in my life, I feel just right" (61). At this point in the narrative Walker begins to prepare her readers for the eventual redemption of all characters by establishing the terms by which that can occur. Mutual regard and love for Shug give her and Mr. —— a sense of solidarity and understanding, while Celie is also given an appreciation of qualities he possesses, even although he never chose to express them before. Also, as Celie and Sofia grow in friendship (they work together a quilt pattern called "Sisters' Choice"), Sofia confides that Harpo possesses a sensitivity unique in men, a love of cooking and other domestic chores. Walker is showing through Sofia's strength and Harpo's sensitivity that men and women are happiest, most successful, in sacralizing their identities, when they do not assume prescribed roles but find and encourage the qualities within that most reflect their sense of identity.

At this point, however, Harpo is not sufficiently confident or flexible. Sofia eventually decides she must leave him. Harpo's response is to busy himself building a juke joint, applying to it an industry he was never able to sustain for Sofia and their children. The juke joint becomes successful when Shug, recuperated from her illness, agrees to perform there. During one of her performances Shug sings an original tune she names for Celie, who "scratched it out of my head when I was sick," and Celie remarks that for the "first time somebody made something and name it after me" (75).

The longer Shug stays, the closer she and Celie begin to grow until eventually Celie confides to Shug that Mr. —— (known to Shug as Albert) beats her. She fears that if Shug leaves he will resume the beatings. Shug assures Celie she will stay until she is sure Albert will not beat her, and during the course of her visit introduces Celie to the pleasures of sexuality. For Celie sex has been a form of violence, an act to be endured. She never knew it was something she could not only control but enjoy, nor that it was a genuine form of self-expression. By showing Celie how to masturbate, and later by actually engaging in lovemaking with her, Shug further empowers Celie.

Sofia returns to the community but ends up in jail when she challenges the mayor's wife. The story of Sofia's fight and incarceration is related to Celie by Squeak, or Mary Agnes, Harpo's new girlfriend. Celie rushes to Sofia's aid and nurses her in prison as best she is able. Sofia admits to Celie that her incarceration has changed her and now, "Every time they ast me to do something, Miss Celie, I act like I'm you. I jump right up and do just what they say" (88). Celie is chagrined by the realization of what she was (and in many ways still is) through the transformation of Sofia. With Shug and Squeak, Celie plans a way for Squeak to spring Sofia from jail. The plot is foiled, and in the process Squeak is raped by the guard, who is also her uncle. The act, however, of trying to do something empowers Squeak, who, at Shug's urging "if you can't tell us, who you gon tell, God?" (95), relates the events at the jail and subsequently insists from that moment on that she be called Mary Agnes.

As relationships grow and develop between women—principally Shug, Celie, Mary Agnes, and Sofia—each woman sustains and encourages the other. But Shug introduces a man into the picture. Having been away in Memphis for a time, Shug returns to visit Celie and Albert and introduce them to Grady, her new husband. Once more Celie and Albert share similar feelings when they encounter Grady as a competitor for Shug's affection: "He look like the end of the world. I know I don't look no better" (105). Still Shug makes time for Celie and they spend hours alone talking until eventually Celie confides her life story to Shug, all the hurt and abuse, the sorrow particularly of her separation from Nettie. When Celie admits that "Nobody ever love me" (109), Shug replies, "I love you, Miss Celie"; soon her affectionate consolation turns into a gentle and passionate expression of affection, and Celie feels and acts "like a little lost baby" (109).

Shug spreads her confidence to Mary Agnes, too, encouraging her to sing at Harpo's juke joint, but her most significant act is her retrieval of letters Nettie has written to Celie. Albert has been hiding them for years. At this point the novel switches and the text becomes a series of letters from Nettie to Celie; the reader encounters them as Celie does, in one large dose after years of absence and many changes. Nettie describes how she is taken in by missionaries Samuel and Corrine, who take her to Africa with them. Although she relates many interesting stories about life and culture in Africa, Nettie's greatest gift to Celie is the revelation of their own personal history. Nettie learns that Samuel and Corrine's adopted children are, in fact, Celie's children, stolen from her at birth. Moreover, Celie learns from Nettie that the man they call "Pa" was not their biological father but a stepfather.

Nettie also introduces to Celie concepts about African culture and spirituality that begin to take hold of Celie's imagination. Although Celie and Nettie are both Christian, Nettie's experience in Africa teaches her things about her faith and her race that she had never known before. She shares this knowledge with Celie and grants her a broader sense of vision when she tells her facts about Egyptian civilization and the black ancestry of the Ethiopians they read about in the Bible. The pictures in the Bible, Nettie asserts, "fool you" into assuming all the people from the Bible were white. In fact Christ, she suggests, described in the Bible as having "hair like lamb's wool" (126), was probably black, too.

Nettie also informs Celie that their present condition as heirs to slaves was due to their "own sisters and brothers" loving money more than their kin and selling them into slavery. Devastated by this knowledge, Nettie nonetheless describes for Celie the hope for the future she envisions through the settlement of Liberia, founded by ex-slaves as a place to come home to Africa. Moreover, through the course of her letters Nettie begins to notice not just discontinuities but continuities as well, how African designs resemble quilt patterns, how the dancing and singing she observes appear familiar, and that the Uncle Remus story she told has its original version in Africa. Nettie functions for Celie similarly to how Lebert Joseph functions for Avey, as a source of ancestral knowledge and corrective wisdom who opens Celie up to an awareness of the vitality, endurance, and strength of black identity and culture.

After reading many of the letters Celie resumes her correspondence with God but in a different tone. Angered by the revelation of Mr. ——'s deception and confused in her faith because of what Nettie has told her, Celie confides to Shug that she could kill Mr. —— for hiding Nettie's letters. When Celie claims it is hard to fight the impulse to want to hurt Mr. ——, Shug replies in language Celie once invoked for Sofia: "Hard to be Christ too. . . . But he manage. Remember that. Thou Shalt Not Kill, He said. And probably wanted to add on to that, Starting with me. He knowed the fools he was dealing with" (134). Celie counters by saying Albert is not Christ, nor is she, to which Shug replies that she is somebody to Nettie and to her. So dazed by all the new information, Celie addresses a final letter to God and accuses him, "You must be sleep" (163). Celie plans to leave Albert and join Shug in Memphis.

More letters from Nettie are read by Celie, further complicating her sense of spiritual identity when, for example, Nettie introduces the thought that the roofleaf, the basis of worship among the Olinka tribe, "is not Jesus Christ, but in its own humble way, is it not God?" (142). Although Nettie has grown to respect and admire aspects of African culture, she also notices practices that subordinate women—such as forcing them to endure excessive labor or denying them education—similar to what she saw in America. Olivia (Celie's child and Nettie's charge) undertakes to secretly educate one girl, Tashi, just as Nettie had done for Celie, who was also unable to participate in formal schooling. Yet Tashi's father, like Celie's, interferes and forbids Tashi to learn. Nettie realizes that Olivia, like Celie, must learn "to take her education about life where she can find it" (150). Yet Nettie also observes the close ties between the Olinka women, how they would do anything for one another, recapitulating the kind of female solidarity already evidenced in Celie's community.

From this point on Celie begins to address letters to Nettie, not God, because as she tells Shug, "What God do for me?" (175). She proceeds to relate to Nettie a theological exchange between her and Shug where Shug defines for Celie a concept of divinity different from the one to which Celie had been subscribing, but one which closely parallels much of what Nettie has been writing to her. Celie is shocked by Shug's faith, but Shug insists she has it even though she "don't harass it like some peoples us know" (175). Celie, however, is so angry at God, her confidant over these many years, that she doubts he ever listened to her, because if he had, "If he ever listened to poor colored women the world would be a different place" (175). Despite Shug's accusations of blasphemy, Celie continues: "All my life I never care what people thought bout nothing I did, I say. But deep in my heart I care about God. What he going to think. And come to find

out, he don't think. Just sit up there glorying in being deef, I reckon."
She admits, however, "it ain't easy, trying to do without God. Even if
you know he ain't there, trying to do without him is a strain" (175–76).

Shug replies to Celie by explaining that although she is conscious
of being a sinner, she is also aware that she feels loved by God and
does the best to please him by pleasing herself, things that do not
necessarily include going to church. Shug reckons that God wants her
to be happy and have a good time because she never felt God in a
church, "just a bunch of folks hoping for him to show. Any God I
ever felt in a church I brought in with me. And I think all the other
folks did too. They come to church to *share* God, not find God" (176).
Celie grows increasingly curious about Shug's theological speculations;
when Shug asks her what she thinks God looks like, Celie provokes
Shug to laugh by replying, "He big and old and tall and graybearded
and white" (176). Shug realizes (in the words of Michael Awkward)
that "Celie's problems with God arise not from God's absence but
from her acceptance of a White Christian conceptualization that prevents her from searching for divine presence 'inside you and inside
everybody else'" (159).

Shug proceeds to deconstruct the "white" biblical image of God
that she found served only to oppress her and substitutes instead a
concept of divinity that corresponds to her experience of sacrality in
the world: "Here's the thing, say Shug, The thing I believe. God is
inside you and inside everybody else. You come into the world with
God. But only them that search for it inside find it. And sometimes it
just manifest itself even if you not looking, or don't know what you
looking for. . . . God ain't a he or a she, but a It. . . . Don't look like
nothing, she say. It ain't a picture show. It ain't something you can
look at apart from anything else, including yourself. I believe God is
everything, say Shug. Everything that is or ever was or ever will be.
And when you can feel that, and be happy to feel that, you've found
It" (177–78). Shug goes on to explain that her concept of divinity
developed out of her experience of nature, when she realized that if
she cut a tree, her arm would bleed. She also continues by connecting

her love of God to her love of sexual feeling, asserting that you "praise god by liking what you like," because "God love admiration." God, Shug says, "just wanting to share a good thing. I think it pisses God off if you walk by the color purple in a field somewhere and don't notice it. . . . People think pleasing God is all God care about. But any fool living in the world can see it always trying to please us back" (178). Celie connects this feeling of God wanting to be loved to her own experience and to what she read in the Bible. She is still confused and angry, but her eyes begin to open. It isn't until she begins to make some decisions for herself, determine her own fate and find creative outlets for her sacrality within, that Celie fully appreciates all Shug has been telling her about God.

She begins by confronting Mr. —— at a family dinner, saying to him that he is "a lowdown dog. . . . It's time to leave you and enter the Creation" (181) and announcing her intention to go to Memphis with Shug, Squeak, and Grady. Her valediction as they depart is "I'm pore, I'm black, I may be ugly and can't cook, a voice say to everything listening. But I'm here. Amen, say Shug. Amen, amen" (187). On her own for the first time in her life, Celie soon establishes a business designing and making what she calls "folkspants," and for the first time since she has been writing either to God or to Nettie, she signs her letters with her name and her corporate identity.

Finally happy with "love, work, money, friends and time," Celie is confronted by another woman about her vernacular speech but decides that it is expressive of who she is and that "only a fool would want you to talk in a way that feels peculiar to your mind" (194). Each step toward independence and self-sufficiency empowers Celie so that when she returns home to see Sofia, released from jail, she does so as the new Celie, not the woman whom the beaten-down Sofia came to resemble. She also encounters a new Albert. Clean-shaven and industrious, Albert began his self-improvement, Sofia reports, when he finally relinquished to Celie the rest of Nettie's letters he had been holding. She exchanges more letters with Nettie and reports to her that the house their stepfather had occupied was in fact

their true father's house which has been deeded to them. Celie prepares the house for Nettie's return and agrees with Shug that "you
doin' all right, Miss Celie. . . . God know where you live" (217).

Meanwhile, Shug falls in love with another man. Celie's heart
breaks, and she asks Nettie to pray for her. Eventually, Albert comes
to fill the empty place left by Shug's departure and consoles Celie,
who believes Nettie has died. He becomes the "only one understand
my feeling" (229). Celie begins to realize that she no longer hates Albert
and continues to write to Nettie as she did God because "Maybe, like
God, you changed into something different that I'll have to speak to in
a different way, but you not dead to me Nettie. And never will be"
(230). She realizes the importance of relationships and what people
share by virtue of experience; she values the love she and Albert share
for Shug; and she admires his attempt to make something out of himself and the way he "appreciates some of the things God was playful
enough to make" (230). Albert is a true convert who now expresses
to Celie sensations similar to hers: "I'm satisfied this the first time I
ever lived on Earth as a natural man. It feel like a new experience"
(231). Ever inclusive in her portrayals of human life, Alice Walker does
not hesitate to include men in her paradigm of conversion, indicating
that the healing power women can have on other women extends to
men as well.

Other transformations take place in the lives of Celie's friends as
Sofia confronts her white charge with the pain of living without her
own children, and eventually Celie hears from Shug, who has become
reacquainted with one of her sons. Reflecting on Shug's life, Celie de-
scribes her admiration for her much as Janie described herself for
Phoeby: "What I love best bout Shug is what she been through, I say.
When you look in Shug's eyes you know she been where she been,
seen what she seen, did what she did. And now she know" (236). Shug
has been to the horizon and back, and by telling what she knows, to
Celie and others, inspires them in the same way Janie's story made
Phoeby grow ten feet higher. Evidence of this is given especially through
Albert, who says to Celie, "I thank God he let me gain understanding

enough to know love can't be halted just cause some peoples moan and groan," a lesson he has learned through experience because if you can stay alive "everybody bound to git some of that sooner or later" (237).

As time passes, Celie and Albert come to exchange their deepest thoughts, fears, and hopes, among them theological concepts on the order of Shug's. Celie expands on what she has learned from both Shug and Nettie. She tells Albert, "I think us here to wonder, myself. To wonder. To ast. And that in wondering bout the big things and asting bout the big things, you learn about the little ones, almost by accident. But you never know nothing more about the big things than you start out with." Albert replies, "The more I wonder, the more I love" (247). Celie and Albert have both learned that divinity is a given, expressed in a variety of small, special ways, from the color purple in a field to just sitting on the porch together sewing. Although Celie believes Nettie has died, her letters continue to appear. In them she expresses a similar expansion of her spiritual concepts. She says God is different to her now, "More spirit than ever before, and more internal. Most people think he has to look like something or some-one—a roofleaf or Christ—but we don't. And not being tied to what God looks like, frees us." She goes on to say that when they return to America she and Samuel intend to found a new church that has no idols but "in which each person's spirit is encouraged to seek God directly" (227).

The novel concludes with Celie's return to writing God a private prayer of gratitude. Only this time she amends her invocation to in-clude "Dear God. Dear stars, dear trees, dear sky, dear peoples. Dear Everything. Dear God" (249). In doing such she creates, in the words of Mae Henderson, "a liturgical lection affirming the rites, rituals, and experiences of the Black community" (Henderson, "Revisions and Redefinitions," 18) and a call to worship that unites her Christian up-bringing with the new sense of spirituality acquired through Nettie and Shug. The occasion of this final letter to God is the unexpected grace of Nettie's return to Celie along with Samuel and Celie's children, Olivia and Adam. She thanks God for the magical return of her family on a secular holiday of independence, the Fourth of July.

Overcome by the presence of her sister, Celie can barely move or speak, but eventually they find each other and "totter toward one nother like us use to do when us was babies" (250). For the first time Celie introduces Albert by his given name, not Mr. ——, and the whole community of extended family assembles for a celebration. Celie's last lines to God, upon realizing all the time that has passed, are "I don't think us feel old at all. And us so happy. Matter of fact, I think this the youngest us ever felt," and signs the letter "Amen" (251). Celie and Nettie, who come together late in life like children, have lived and now understand the words of the Scripture in Peter's first letter. They have been "rejected by men but in God's sight chosen and precious"; therefore, "like newborn babes," who have "long[ed] for the pure spiritual milk," they "put away all malice and all guile and insincerity and envy and all slander," because they know "that by it you may grow up to salvation; for you have tasted the kindness of the Lord" (I Peter 2:1–4).

Some readers may contend that this ending is too unrealistic to accept. The coherent resolution of all the characters' lives may seem to undercut the realistic portrayal of black life.[21] The novel fails only if one ignores not only the challenges and sacrifices accepted and overcome by all the characters, major and minor, but also the perceptible movement of grace in the narrative. Walker herself subscribes to a belief in the "impact of supernatural grace on human beings who don't have a chance of spiritual growth without it" (MG, 53). The reunion and reconciliation that end the novel are expressive of the new concept of deity introduced by Walker, a deity that embraces and consecrates all forms of existence. Energized by Shug in particular, Celie moves from a "theology of self-denial" (Henderson, "Revisions and Redefinitions," 15) that validates her inferior status to a theology that "allows a divine, self-authorized sense of self" (Henderson, 16). Shug, a self-invented character not unlike Sula, transforms Celie from a woman of passivity and self-resistance into a receptive and responsive woman. In turn, Celie helps Shug to become more nurturing and thoughtful, and together they create, by participating in the sacralization of one another's identities, a friendship Nel and Sula were unable to sustain. Likewise, they effect on their community a transformation through redemption, not destruction, as witnessed in the Bottom.

The changes that occur in the lives of all the characters center on themes typical of black women's writing but especially important to Alice Walker the writer. Her novel reveals a vast network of communal relationships in which female bonding is the dominant and connecting link. It emphasizes the need to remove oppressive and rigid gender roles that often lead to violence and to create new paradigms for male-female relationships. It elevates folk forms of expression like sewing and cooking to art forms and shows how these forms are expressive throughout the diaspora of black people. Finally, it demonstrates how people can reclaim the past and participate in the transformation of the future.

Celie's letters are, as Mae Henderson has observed, a refiguration of the Apostle Paul's letter to the Philippians. Although Celie addresses her letters not to the church but to God, she is like Paul in prison. Both affirm a belief in death as a blessing for the faithful. Also like Paul, she writes amid persecution in the hope of divine deliverance. In Philippi, Paul's church was formed as a result of the efforts of a small group of women, just as Celie's community is sustained by Sofia, Squeak, Shug, and other women. Lydia, a dealer in purple cloth, was Paul's first convert, followed by his jailer. Celie succeeds in the conversion of her jailer, Mr. ———, after being converted by a dealer in purple, Shug. Consistent with Walker's frequent attempts at redefinition, Henderson also asserts that in rewriting Paul's Letter to the Philippians, Walker subverts the more popular Pauline letter to the Ephesians in which Paul prescribes in detail the duties of wives and servants to husbands and masters.

Another religious category in which to place Walker's novel is that of a text for a liberation theology. Celie begins with an inherited theology that is traditional and limited in its scope and associated primarily with the church and the Bible. Her faith is institutional and hier-archical. Initially, Celie even imagines the crucial scene in which Mary Agnes attempts to liberate Sofia from jail in terms of deus ex machina: "But I think about angels, God Coming down by chariot, swinging down real low and carrying old Sofia home. I see 'em all as clear as day. Angels all in white, white hair and white eyes, look like albinos. God all white too, looking like some stout white man work at the bank. Angels strike they cymbals, one of them blow his horn, God blow out a big breath of fire and suddenly Sofia free" (96).

Celie's inherited theology, in which God figures as a white man, functions to keep her in her place and does not address even the larger issues of social justice represented by Sofia's unfair imprisonment. Celie does not identify herself as oppressed, only powerless. Yet by witnessing Sofia's strength and by learning through Shug and Nettie, Celie finds a liberating concept of God that serves to free her from her false image of herself. She envisions an image that sacralizes her identity and in turn sacralizes all of creation. Once she recognizes her condition of oppression and can acquire the orientation to which lib-eration theologians subscribe of viewing life from that perspective, she can see, in turn, that oppression emerges not individually but collectively.

Corresponding to these principles of a liberation theology is a cer-tain reading of the Bible wherein God is seen as an image reflective of self, emphasizing either one's race or gender, or in the case of Alice Walker, to see God as Spirit. Also crucial to a liberation theology is an emphasis on praxis, the integration of reflection and action, evidenced first in Celie's letters to God and later in her attempts to liberate her-self and to interact with other women in their liberation. Writing is, in a sense, Walker's own form of praxis. She says in an essay, "only when Celie comes in from the cold—do I come in. And many of you as well" (LW, 66).

More than any other theologian, Delores S. Williams has drawn attention to *The Color Purple* as a source for feminist and liberation theologies.[22] She sees the text as affirming a belief that women's lib-eration is the key to the redemption of society. Moreover, this social redemption depends upon changing notions about the maleness of God and other structures of power. Williams also draws attention to the fact that although black women writers celebrate African-American culture and folk idioms in their work and derive spiritual strength from their traditions, they also reveal how that culture may work against black women's liberation struggles. Just as Sula had to leave the Bottom and Janie had to leave Jody's town in order to gain a perspective on their respective communities, so, too, did Celie have to leave for Memphis.

What is crucial to Williams, however, is what feminist theologians in general assert, and that is affirming the primacy of women's experience in constructing a theology. The writing of black women clearly describes experiences not generally known to many and as such offers a source by which to broaden and deepen feminist understanding of women's experience, including their oppression. Celie's letters, in effect, rewrite history and create a new history by which to interpret God's actions in the world. Through their stories in which women are seen as acting as moral agents for one another, black women come to heal their wounded self-concepts and through solidarity create new relationships, community identities, and a concept of family that is inclusive of all creation.

In an early essay Walker asserts that prophecy is "our only hope— in a culture so in love with flash, with trendiness, with superficiality as ours we must acquire a sense of essence, of timelessness and of vision . . . to point the direction of vision and at the same time to follow it" (MG, 8). The vision that Walker alludes to is not unlike the vision Hurston writes of in her descriptions of the conversion process wherein the ability to imagine a new life—as Celie does when she first encounters the name, then the image of Shug—makes the creation of that life possible. Alice Fannin describes Walker's vision as "a sense of wonder," seeing it as descriptive of the spiritual quest Celie undertook: "an exploration of self as part of the universe and the universe as part of self" (1). Celie, Fannin continues, comes to recognize that she is "a unique entity in the plenitude of Creation and that her place, however finite, is an integral part of a mysterious and wonderful working process that created, and is always creating and recreating, an infinite universe" (2).

With Walker's casting Celie's conversion and identity in terms of a perpetual re-creation, Hurston's concept of identity as a fluid form once again comes to prominence. Deborah McDowell, who has shown how Morrison undercuts identity as a stable thing through her character-ization of Sula, makes a similar point with reference to Alice Walker. Celie's letters show text as the production of self, rather than a reflec-tion of self, and identity as textually constructed, not a pregiven entity. Such a dynamic conception of identity, McDowell asserts in "Reading Family Matters," resists any notion of a single identity to be positively represented in fiction and defuses many of the criticisms leveled against Walker and her portrayal of African-American life.

In Alice Walker's *The Color Purple* we see once again conversion as a process of sacralizing identities in such a way that it underscores the relational, metamorphosing nature of identity and fixes it on a more organic, natural model of growth. Crucial to Walker's concept of conversion, however, is the notion that individuals and communi-ties can have freedom from fixed roles and that, indeed, even God can be liberated from a confining image, but what endures as a source of both identity and divinity is a permanent Spirit, a ground of Being that not only tolerates change but encourages it. Celie learns the power of naming not just herself, but God.[23] She also moves from silence—letters addressed to a correspondent who cannot answer—to voice, where she is able to talk to God in all forms at all times, simply by living. Although Celie has necessarily altered her concept of God, as Lucinda H. MacKethan points out, even the remote, patriarchal God had served her in a way as "a listener whom she creates out of her own need. God keeps her alive in giving her ideas and feelings a shape and a place to go" (*Daughters of Time,* 104). Celie's growth and development depend largely on her having a view of God and change only as she comes to understand the terms by which divine accessibility creates human possibility.

Like all the writers here presented, Alice Walker gathers up the historical, spiritual, and psychological dimensions of her ancestors' lives and creates a legacy to them. Self-expression, like God's creation, generates its own imperative to see the sacred in the secular, the divinity in the royalty of the color purple that grows unnoticed in a field or in a mother's garden. Celie's story is indeed one of a black woman acquiring "a new spiritual awareness, a rebirth into strong feelings of Oneness" (Preface, xi). The epigraph Walker chose for the second part of *In Search of Our Mothers' Gardens* is a saying attributed to Jesus in *The Gnostic Gospels:* "If you bring forth what is within you, what is within you will save you. If you do not bring forth what is within you, what is within you will destroy you." This epigraph obviously informs much of Walker's own philosophy. It finds an interesting parallel in Petru Dumitriu's *To the Unknown God.* There he writes: "But I have not tried to weigh Evil and good against one another. I know well that they are incommensurable, asymmetrical, not enemies, but strangers one to the other, not like light and dark, but like an equilateral triangle and the colour purple" (77). The color purple, it seems, which embodies the sacred and the secular, the good and the bad in fragile harmony, has as many forms as God, and that is precisely Walker's point in *The Color Purple.*

5

Visions

No one shows a child the Supreme Being.
—Ashanti proverb

Let the children come to me, do not hinder them; for to such
belongs the kingdom of God. Truly, I say to you, whoever does
not receive the kingdom of God like a child shall not enter it.
—Mark 10:14–15

In 1875, eight years before her death, Sojourner Truth claimed to actually have grown younger. Her editor, Olive Gilbert, noted that Truth's "eyesight, for many years defective has returned," and that her "grey locks are being succeeded by a luxuriant growth of black hair without the use of any other renovator than that which nature furnishes" (xiii). Rebecca Jackson made no such actual claim, but she does say that after conversion she "became as a little child just born into the light, beginning to learn the way of God" (275). Harriet Jacobs was eulogized by Reverend Grimke as a woman "with great strength of character," with which "there was also combined in her a heart as tender as that of a little child" (Smyth, 37).

In tracing a literary tradition among black women writers, genre is not always the most useful tool. Female African-American novelists of the nineteenth century more often than not created characters who had to bear the burden of being exemplary standards. The autobiographical writings of Harriet Jacobs, Sojourner Truth, and Rebecca Jackson, however, seem less restricted by this burden. The freedom to create themselves that they found through religious faith makes their works the spiritual and literary antecedents of the writings of Morrison, Marshall, and Walker. Indeed, their freedom was so unconditional (in spiritual, if not actual, terms) that these women all returned, in some fashion, to a younger life. To conclude this cultural study of conversion experiences in the writings of black American women, therefore, I chose two epigraphs to emphasize several related concepts.

First among the reasons is to underscore a similarity between African and Christian faith and to show how religious forms of expression, although they may not be universal, are universally significant. Each phrase describes a posture one must take before God, emphasizing that in childlike innocence and trust one can reasonably accept what one already feels: that there is a God listening to individuals and watching over human history. Secondly, this childlike posture is one we have seen explicitly described in the conversions of Morrison's, Marshall's, and Walker's protagonists. Nel, sobbing on Sula's grave and realizing after years the love she squandered, remembers Sula and herself as children, when they "used each other to grow on," and cries, "We was girls together." Avey, as she makes the difficult passage to Carriacou, back to her past and to her true self, experiences not only a childlike wonder and curiosity but a child's humility and helplessness, thereby opening herself up to healing and growth. Celie, whose growth and development are charted by a series of childlike "for the first time in my life" experiences, finds in her old age as a convert that "this is the youngest us ever felt."

By presenting stunning examples of the Gospel imperative that the "last shall be first," these contemporary black women writers have created complexity in their characters precisely by distilling them to their essential simplicity. This childlike posture in relation to a parental divine suggests a pattern witnessed in the writers Morrison, Marshall, and Walker themselves, where each sees as part of her mission and as vital to her vision a recuperation of the past—a reconnection to African-American origins and the beginnings, the childhood, so to speak, of their history that nourished and strengthened them. They know what bell hooks asserts when she says that in the African-American religious tradition "ancestor acknowledgment [is] crucial to our well-being as a people" (hooks and West, 77). History gives topic and substance to their writing because they look back not with simple nostalgia and not with an imperative to cast off the things they already know and have experienced. History is important to them because they possess a vision wherein they allow their contemporary sensibilities to be informed by history, thereby to rewrite or correct false assumptions about black women and also to provide more opportunities for black women in the future. They know that memory can be a basis by which to let "one's true self surface" (Naylor and Morrison, 572), and that it can help heal past indignities. They take the literal conversions of women like Harriet Jacobs, Sojourner Truth, and Rebecca Jackson and transform them into the literary conversions of Nel, Avey, and Celie. Each writer understands that in order to convert, to sacralize identities and transform communities, two ingredients are essential and inseparable: a sense of self and a sense of culture.

Morrison reveals the terms of conversion through the dramatic and symbolic split of her female protagonist into two characters, Nel and Sula. Although Nel understands the necessity of cultural values in sacralizing one's identity, Sula understands the importance of finding and expressing one's own particular sacrality. Each woman lacks and needs what the other possesses, and each, therefore, is unable to fully convert on her own. Although the survivor Nel does eventually convert by the resources of memory and painful recognition of Sula, she does so too late to give back to Sula what she gained from her, so her identity will always be, to a degree, fractured. Avey, on the other hand, converts in time to give back something to her grandchildren. As a woman with a properly defined sense of self, she comes to realize the false image she has created only when she accepts that it has no cultural foundation. Only when she reacquires a sense of a spiritual and cultural identity and responsibility, when she takes again her childhood name, Avatara, do the core components of her self—her strength and self-reliance—enable her to lead a sacralized life. Finally, Celie, who grows up in a distinct world of black culture that nourishes her and enables her to survive, can fully appreciate the gifts of this culture and the community that expresses them only when she develops a strong sense of her own identity and realizes more fully her participatory role in the development of that culture. She realizes that understanding self is the precondition for transformation on any level.

Each change effected in these women is born of a recognition of a sense of sacrality that is apart from them and yet also part of their own interior selfhood. They recognize what Harriet Jacobs, Sojourner Truth, and Rebecca Jackson learned long ago—that what they were perceiving as sin or a blight on their characters was really an affair of an ideology of manipulation imposed by oppressors. They realized through their encounters with a world that humbled and thwarted them and sought to defeat them that they could indeed survive by gaining a depth of self-acceptance and love of God that enabled them to keep intact a sense of human dignity. They sacralized their experience of marginality by creating a new order and a place for themselves in that order, by confronting the complex relationship of identity and culture. Religious faith expressed through cultural forms, a sense of the sacred in the profane, and a recognition of self-love, self-reliance, and self-awareness sacralized these women's identities and in turn created sacred stories to be passed down to the generations.

Black women's writing, as Chikwenye Okonjo Ogunyemi states, is "a gospel of hope" that "ensures larger horizons" (79) because it involves not just an encounter with the past but a need also to reverse the present order. The sacred stories of black women's lives offer us what Sharon D. Welch calls a "feminist ethic of risk," wherein they pass on a moral wisdom that assumes responsibility for and offers requirements for social transformation by recognizing that the past must be confronted and healed before any significant change can take place. Part of this healing involves a conversion—a reconsideration of the concept of God, reenvisioning God in terms that more closely parallel the organic, metamorphosing concept of identity they have found descriptive of themselves. By recognizing divinity or sacrality as a plurality—inclusive of all forms of life and expression—black women cast the character of God in terms that are inherently relational. History— both personal and communal—and natural processes can be seen not only as worthy of worship but as providing orientation, focus, and guidance to life. Black women, therefore, understand that in order to see how God has permeated their history they must view God not as a transcendent being of perfection and completion but as immanent, an incomplete power that is always changing and growing as they themselves are. These prophetic women see divinity as a resilient, healing power, and sacred qualities embedded in all aspects of life.

Religion provides a center for exploring women's lives, a critical perspective on and alternatives to the ways that women, and black women in particular, have come to be judged. Religion has functioned to empower and challenge black women, not to oppress and render them passive. Through religious faith and by naming the sacred within them that sustains them, women are able to name themselves. It is then that they are "given" a story to tell. By confronting and transforming customary forms of spiritual reflection, women offer new points of religious connection. Moreover, they demonstrate that spiritual speculation is a natural, accessible, and necessary constituent of human growth and not a luxury reserved for the intellectually gifted or the financially prosperous. Black women know this because they are inheritors of a cultural tradition that blends folk wisdom, African retentions, European influences, and Christian morphology into a vision of wholeness. Black women writers and the stories they tell, therefore, serve a redemptive presence in our cultural life by revealing the recovery of spiritual resources as a necessary constituent of human growth. Another way to put it is to say that these women theologize life by showing the sacred as a dimension of life and life itself as a declaration of sacred identity. And they "call" their readers to some transformative "response."

Religion and literature, therefore, can be viewed in African-American history as two chief expressive forms for resisting oppression and affirming self-worth, with culture as the common ground that preserves and redefines religious and literary identities. Religion, which embodies the truth, and literature, which embodies the beautiful, are cojoined—the sacred and the secular in cultural harmony—to embody the struggle for liberation and integrity that characterizes African-American history. In the writings of Harriet Jacobs, Sojourner Truth, and Rebecca Jackson we see religion and literature collaborating in the struggle to authenticate the personality and the humanity of black Americans. As persuasive and creative rhetorical tools in the hands of Zora Neale Hurston, religion and literature point to new directions for change, complicating and energizing the aspirations of African Americans. Hurston's struggle to locate a contemporary, critical-reflexive self and also find herself in her own history leads us to the fiction of Toni Morrison, Paule Marshall, and Alice Walker, who write as a form of cultural renewal and a recovery of origins—literally reinscribing the past—while also demonstrating the vitality and originality of African-American creativity. They do so mindful of the paradoxical situation they face of "being drawn to the black church and at the same time being unable to fully embrace it" (James Evans, "African-American Christianity," 208).

Yet as Alice Walker emphasizes in her preface to the tenth-anniversary edition of *The Color Purple,* "no one is exempt from the possibility of a connection to All That Is" (xi). Writings by contemporary black women embody an answer to the postmodern condition precisely because of their respect for origins, for what created them and still survives: an ability to give voice to oppressed peoples and offer a prophetic critique of society; a pragmatic spirit derived from traditional African religions that do not separate sacred and secular; a desire for wholeness and freedom expressed through their stories of the integration of inner and outer dimensions of lives; a tolerance for other revelatory stories in the search for what is authentically human and a corresponding belief in difference without domination; and their contribution of new models for community that are based on the idea of covenant—mutual trust and integrity. These terms in some sense also characterize two centuries of writing by black women in America that affirm the sacrality of being and describe the experience of encountering "That Which Is Beyond Understanding But Not Beyond Loving," while saying "I see and hear you clearly, Great Mystery, now that I expect to see and hear you everywhere I am, which is the right place" (Walker, Preface, xi–xii). Although we may acknowledge and appreciate the discontinuities and complexities of these works for the new insights they afford, we may also recognize that the ways in which black women writers perform a truly revolutionary act come from their refusal to accept the notion that they have become too sophisticated to believe and from their faith in themselves and in their ancestors— by their holding a vision of life as sacred and committing themselves, through conversion, to a scripture of change.

Notes

Several works frequently cited in the text have been identified by the following abbreviations:

Works by Zora Neale Hurston

Dust Tracks on a Road—DT
Mules and Men—MM
The Sanctified Church—SC

Works by Alice Walker

In Search of Our Mothers' Gardens—MG
Living By the Word—LW

1. Conversions

1. One of the first studies to relate African-American religion and literature was Benjamin Mays's book *The Negro's God as Reflected in His Literature* (Boston: Chapman and Grimes, 1938). In it he describes how the idea of God functions in Negro literature as a way to support or give adherence to traditional compensatory patterns of development and also how ideas of God were interpreted by African Americans to support their growing consciousness of a need for social and psychological adjustment.
2. A good example of this return to "sacred texts" can be seen in the abundance of contemporary writings that employ the motif of slavery. Deborah E. McDowell's essay "Negotiating between Tenses: Witnessing Slavery after Freedom—*Dessa Rose*," in *Slavery and the Literary*

Imagination, ed. Deborah E. McDowell and Arnold Rampersad (Baltimore: Johns Hopkins Univ. Press, 1989), 144–64, discusses this trend.

3. The psychologist James Fowler refers to something similar when he discusses "master stories," or stories that disclose the ultimate meaning of our lives. See: *Stages of Faith: The Quest for Human Development and the Quest for Meaning* (San Francisco: Harper and Row, 1981).

4. Evidence of "dropping a veil" can be found in the fact that Harriet Jacobs wrote under the pseudonym Linda Brent; Sojourner Truth's narrative was dictated to and edited by a third-party scribe; Rebecca Jackson's journals were private and written only to describe in detail her visionary life, not her actual life. Still, it is interesting to consider Toni Morrison's comment in light of Lydia Maria Child's introductory remarks to Jacobs's narrative. Child claimed that Jacobs's text was unique in its time precisely because before it appeared, "this peculiar phase of Slavery has generally been kept veiled. . . . I willingly take the responsibility of presenting them with the veil withdrawn" (xii).

5. In her book *Mythic Black Fiction* (Knoxville: Univ. of Tennessee Press, 1986), Jane Campbell discusses the mythic qualities of black writing. She asserts that myth is an especially effective form for blacks because of its ability to move an audience to consciousness and to voice culture's most profound perceptions. Campbell diverges from the concept of myth I invoke, however, when she cites the literary mode of romance as the predominant device for presenting black historical fiction.

6. One can assume that Genovese meant to include women in his formulation of moral experience, although he uses only the noun "Men." Other such examples of the use of "men" or "man" to indicate the human community will appear throughout this text in various quotations. Although I judged it intrusive to draw attention to each instance, I am hopeful my audience will read such usage of *men* as inclusive of women also, for that is how I intend such references to be read.

7. As Elizabeth Higginbotham and Sarah Watts have demonstrated in their essay "The New Scholarship on Afro-American Women," *Women's Studies Quarterly* 1&2 (1988): 13–21, most African-American history, such as that written by Blassingame, Genovese, and Raboteau, is male dominated and does not distinguish between feminine and masculine forms of spirituality or other cultural expressions.

8. In *Claiming the Heritage: African-American Women Novelists and History* (Jackson: Univ. Press of Mississippi, 1991), Missy Dehn Kubitschek explores how the development of identity, particularly in relationship to community, has frequently been described through quest patterns. She discusses three preexisting models: the universalist

model of Joseph Campbell; the racial model of Robert Stepto; and the gender model of Carol Christ. She shows how black women's writings encompass and transcend these models.

9. In this examination of African-American religion I am dealing with the qualities and aspects of faith, not the development of the institutional black church. Most of my research is based on the Southern black religious experience since even though black denominations were founded in Northern cities, the essential quality of black religion in America stems from the South.

10. Although the relationship between African and African-American religion is now an accepted principle, it should be remembered that E. Franklin Frazier, one of the first scholars to write on the Negro church in America, downplayed the possibility of African retentions in African-American religion and emphasized the otherworldly dimensions of slave religion in particular, despite the research of DuBois and Woodson that gave evidence of African antecedents. Frazier did, however, contribute greatly to our understanding of the primacy of religion in black life and how Christianity functioned as a new basis for social cohesion as it was adapted to social and psychological needs.

11. As Elizabeth Fox-Genovese and Eugene D. Genovese point out in their essay "The Divine Sanction of Social Order: Religious Foundations of the Southern Slaveholders' World View," *Journal of the American Academy of Religion* 55.2 (1987): 211–33, the slaveholders held an equally solid worldview but one predicated on the belief in "hierarchy, particularism, and the necessarily unequal interdependence of society's members."

12. In "Culture and the Phenomena of Conversion," *Gospel in Context* 1.3 (1978): 4–14, Donald R. Jacobs gives an example from an East African setting of how conversion is a culturally controlled experience. Also, Orlando E. Costas, in "Conversion as a Complex Experience," *Gospel in Context* 1.3 (1978): 14–40, gives a personal case study to show how forms of conversion vary in accordance with cultural situations, specifically noting how socioeconomic and political factors affect this personal experience. His thesis is rooted in the tradition of liberation theology that describes religious conversion as interrelated to conversion to the world of the poor and disenfranchised of society.

13. Olive Stone, in her essay "Cultural Uses of Religious Visions: A Case Study," *Ethnology* 1 (1962): 329–48, gives an example from the River Island community in which converts "have seen in their sought visions those things which their culture has taught them to expect," resulting in a strengthening of unity and cohesiveness in the community.

14. In his essay "Religious Conversion and Community Development," *Journal for the Scientific Study of Religion* 18.3 (1979): 252–60, Paul

R. Turner demonstrates the relevance of religion to social development and how conversion became the catalyst for community development—quantifiable improvements in the quality of life—in a
Mexican Indian municipality.

15. "Conversion: Evaluation of a Step-Like Process for Problem Solving,"
Review of Religious Research 13.3 (1972): 178–84, by John Seggar
and Philip Kunz, is an attempt to perform a quantifiable study of the
personal changes effected by conversion. This is a rather "cookbook"
approach that reduces the phenomenon to a casually appropriated
method for dealing with problems. Unfortunately, it is representative
of many conversion applications.

16. An example of a similar approach can be seen in Roger A. Straus's
essay "Religious Conversion as a Personal and Collective Accomplishment," *Sociological Analysis* 40.2 (1979): 158–65, in which he
distinguishes between the passivist view of conversion as something
that happens to the person and the activist view (which he promotes),
where conversion is viewed as the accomplishment of an "actively
strategizing seeker interacting with the others constituting a religious
collectivity." In other words, conversion is an accomplishment on the
seeker's part, rather than the effect of social, psychological, or other
forces. Also like Pratt, Straus emphasizes that the act of conversion is
not terminal but one that insists on further change.

17. In "The Process of Change: Sacred and Secular," *Journal of Psychology
and Theology* 5 (1977): 103–9, Cédric Johnson tries to answer the
question of whether or not personal change and conversion are the
same things. He comes to the conclusion that in any discussion of the
process of change, both psychology and theology see the person as
less than their potential and as possessing a need for growth, change,
and self-actualization. Therapy and religion offer different answers,
but not necessarily antithetical ones.

18. James A. Beckford, in his essay "Accounting for Conversion," *British
Journal of Sociology* 29.2 (1978): 249–61, states that accounts of
religious conversions are situated in social contexts that lend them
meaning and that they do not represent an objective view of reality
because they are cast only in terms of available linguistic resources.

19. Lucinda H. MacKethan's essay "From Fugitive Slave to Man of
Letters: The Conversion of Frederick Douglass," *Journal of Narrative
Technique* 16.1 (1986): 55–71, is an elegantly presented example of
the conversion trope found in many narratives. She demonstrates how
Douglass categorizes his life and his writing in sacramental contexts,
beginning with baptism (where letters are seen as symbols); through
conversion (where the power of naming is established); and confirmation to ordination (where he joins literary culture as a full member).

20. Although much of what Collins argues is useful, I would argue with her claim that conversion is an exclusively patriarchal term that, when used, reinscribes an oppressor mentality (see 202–3). The term conversion, like much else available from traditional theologies, can be transformed by way of a reformation of thought, and this is precisely what I believe the religious experience of African-American women suggests.

21. Jacquelyn Grant, in her essay "Black Women and the Church," in *But Some of Us Are Brave,* ed. Gloria T. Hull, Patricia Bell Scott, and Barbara Smith (New York: Feminist Press, 1987), notes how "Black church*men* have not dealt with the oppression of black women in either the Black church or the Black community" (144–45). She claims that unless black women are included as divine agents in the concept of liberation theology, it will be inauthentic.

22. In her recent essay, "Sexism as Original Sin: Developing a Theacentric Discourse," *Journal of the American Academy of Religion* 59.4 (1991): 653–75, Mary McClintock Fulkerson asserts that fuller treatments on behalf of feminist positions on sin are still needed. Fulkerson maintains that feminist discourse about sin offers "an important contribution to our theological understanding of historically specific forms of *human* waywardness, not simply of one kind of sin (sexism)" (653).

23. Susan Faludi, in *Backlash: The Undeclared War against American Women* (New York: Crown, 1991), draws attention to how Gilligan leaves herself open to misinterpretation that may, under the backlash, cause real harm to women. See 327–32.

24. James Cone, in his book *For My People: Black Theology and the Black Church* (Maryknoll, N.Y.: Orbis Books, 1984), cites his own "conversion" (134) to the issues of women's equality in society, church, and the doing of theology.

25. For a historical survey of urban and rural black churches, their influence and development, see the thoughtfully written and carefully researched *Black Church in the African American Experience* (Durham, N.C.: Duke Univ. Press, 1990), by C. Eric Lincoln and Lawrence H. Mamiya.

2. Voluntary Converts

1. The assertion of each woman's right and necessity for self-definition takes on additional meaning when one considers that in the nineteenth century women were not being granted ordination and the authenticity of the call of women was frequently put to a test. Jacquelyn Grant discusses these issues in the previously cited essay.

2. Andrews also draws attention to the fact that black autobiography in America did not start out offering an image of black selfhood, but that as the genre developed, selfhood became increasingly identified with individuality.

3. Valerie Smith, in *Self-Discovery and Authority in Afro-American Narrative* (Cambridge: Harvard Univ. Press, 1987), diminishes the experience of conversion by asserting that in black conversion narratives the writers appropriate a rhetoric that denies the value of independence of mind and will. I intend to show that this is a false assumption of the character of conversion as experienced and described by most African Americans.

4. John Barbour makes a similar point in more general terms by his refusal to distinguish between "religious" and nonreligious autobiographies. Using the language of H. Richard Niebuhr, Barbour asserts that in autobiography "the self's character is interpreted as a response to the formative and shaping action of God or whatever the writer holds sacred." See his "Character and Characterization in Religious Autobiography," *Journal of the American Academy of Religion* 55.2 (1987): 307–27.

5. In *Witnessing Slavery: The Development of Antebellum Slave Narratives* (Westport, Conn.: Greenwood Press, 1979), Frances Smith Foster states that the search for spiritual identity in slave narratives was "complicated by a desire to use incidents in the narrator's life as examples of the experiences of many others like him" (5), focusing more on race than on individual identity. The tension between being a symbol or an individual, she claims, is a basic quality of slave narratives. Although I acknowledge that this dialectic exists, I hope to show the ways that black women resisted this symbolizing tendency while at the same time deconstructing the very symbols themselves.

6. In the essay "'Together and in Harness': Women's Traditions in the Sanctified Church," *Signs* 10.4 (1985): 678–99, Cheryl Townsend Gilkes details the involvement of nineteenth-century black women in the church hierarchy of independent black congregations and shows how their work provided great energy for the social-reform movements of the time. By doing such, Gilkes hopes to demonstrate that "religion and religious activity have been the most important spheres for the creation and maintenance of tradition." Indeed, the church was for a long time the one place where black women were accorded dignity and respect. Yet as significant as was black women's involvement in the church structure, I am attempting here to describe a religious loyalty or attachment of a much more personal nature—what came ontologically before their decision to become involved in a

church—and also to show how such involvement was not the only indication of religious feeling among African-American women.

7. Valerie Smith, however, believes that Jacobs's "freedom to reconstruct her life was limited by a genre that suppressed subjective experience in favor of abolitionist polemics" (*Self-Discovery and Authority,* 28). Also, Frances Smith Foster, in *Witnessing Slavery,* believes that the secularized use of religious tropes was employed for didactic purposes and in an effort to win the sympathy of the reader (83). I believe, however, that this does not deny that religious sincerity played a part.

8. According to Daniel Shea, the polemical agenda of slave/spiritual narratives like Jacobs's differs from the Puritan conversion narratives of the same time because the Puritan narratives were essentially an exercise in assuring one's own salvation, not the salvation of a people. See his *Spiritual Autobiography in Early America* (Princeton: Princeton Univ. Press, 1968).

9. William Andrews discusses the implications of this paradox—not being able to tell all the truth for fear of offending readers and being denied the opportunity to establish fully a text's veracity—in his essay "The Novelization of Voice in Early African American Narrative," *PMLA* 105.1 (1990): 23–34.

10. In his essay "Dialect and Convention: Harriet A. Jacobs's *Incidents in the Life of a Slave Girl,*" *Nineteenth-Century Literature* 45 (1990): 206–19, Andrew Levy compares Jacobs's dialect to slave dialect and shows how both developed out of a need to mediate between deference and self-assertion. The language "appeared superficially guileless and deferential to non-speakers, but clarified ambiguity and double meaning through context and tone to speakers."

11. William Andrews, in *Sisters of the Spirit* (Bloomington: Indiana Univ. Press, 1986), shows how the mother or the maternal black figure plays the predominant heroic role in many slave narratives, setting up the pattern of mother inspiring daughter by example—the paradigmatic pattern for African-American women's writing. Joanne Braxton, in "Harriet Jacobs' *Incidents in the Life of a Slave Girl:* The Re-definition of the Slave Narrative Genre," *Massachusetts Review* 27 (1986): 379–87, states that Jacobs's text offers "as a counterpart to the articulate hero, the archetype of the outraged mother."

12. In her essay "My Statue, My Self: Autobiographical Writings of Afro-American Women," in *The Private Self,* ed. Shari Benstock (Chapel Hill: Univ. of North Carolina Press, 1988), 36–89, Elizabeth Fox-Genovese claims Jacobs "endows herself with a pedigree of physical, mental and moral comeliness," by which she reflects "either her assimilation of 'white' values or the determination to play to the

prejudices of her audience." This results in what Fox-Genovese calls a "confused picture of the relation between the identity and behavior of Afro-Americans." Fox-Genovese, although surely pointing out a crucial paradox in the testimony of slave women, seems to be neglecting the spiritual resources that transcend whatever character and will a slaveowner can break.

13. Deborah Gray White's study of female slave life in the South, *Ar'n't I a Woman* (New York: Norton, 1985), gives examples of passive resistance and dissembling tactics practiced by female slaves to avoid hard labor or unwanted pregnancies.

14. As astonishing as it seems, as recently as 1990 the defense of the "Christian" character of slaveholders was upheld by Thomas C. Parramore in his essay "Harriet Jacobs, James Norcom, and the Defense of Hierarchy," *Carolina Comments* 38.2 (1990): 82–87. In this essay Parramore defends Norcom (Dr. Flint) by pointing out his professional and civic deeds and his devotion to his children, and by casting into doubt the authenticity of Jacobs's recollections. Jacobs, Parramore asserts, "must stand condemned for an overwrought and libelous portrait of her former master." Although he agrees that Norcom may "have been guilty at some point of lewd or at least suggestive remarks or actions toward his attractive slave girl," he dismisses this harassment as understandable since "the coy and languishing eye of a household servant, cast in innocence or otherwise, might no doubt act as powerfully upon Norcom as that of any other comely woman." In Parramore's eyes, Jacobs stands guilty of having "[spun] . . . a web of alleged deceits and cruelties" about Norcom. In a defense now familiar to those of us who witnessed the nomination hearings of our recent supreme court justice, Parramore excuses Norcom's sexual harassment on four counts: by emphasizing his medical vocation, his civic and familial love and duty, and by describing his personal ambition and standards of perfection; by remarking on the temptation presented by the physical attractiveness of his victim; by objectifying the victim as less than human (i.e., as a preying spider spinning webs); and by perpetrating the notion that the victim's testimony is a malicious lie. Parramore's article makes sadly ironic Rosemary Bray's comments in "Taking Sides against Ourselves," *New York Times Magazine*, 17 November 1991, where she suggests that "*Incidents in the Life of a Slave Girl* would have made more instructive reading for the Senate Judiciary Committee than *The Exorcist*."

15. Deborah Gray White discusses the dimensions of slave mothers' anxiety over their children's safety in *Ar'n't I a Woman*, 95.

16. In a letter written to Amy Post while she was writing *Incidents*, Jacobs

credits God with giving her "a soul that burned for freedom and a heart nerved with determination to suffer even unto death in pursuit of that liberty which without makes life an intolerable burden." See *We Are Your Sisters,* ed. Dorothy Sterling (New York: Norton, 1984), 79.

17. Smith goes on to show that other modes of confinement she endures are still choices Linda makes herself, such as choosing to be an unwed mother rather than submitting to her master. Thus, "each moment of apparent enclosure actually empowers Jacobs to redirect her own and her children's destiny" (30).

18. Jacobs also encountered frustration and resistance in her dealings with Harriet Beecher Stowe, who rather than wanting to help Jacobs sought to include her story in *The Key to Uncle Tom's Cabin.* See Jean Fagan Yellin's article in *The Slave's Narrative,* ed. Charles T. Davis and Henry Louis Gates, Jr. (New York: Oxford Univ. Press, 1985), for a full discussion of Jacobs's encounters with Stowe.

19. It is significant to note, however, that Jacobs chooses not to live in the house and sells it immediately, perhaps because the weight of memories was too heavy or because she had already developed a home and an active life up North.

20. For information regarding the circumstances of Harriet Jacobs's place of burial, I am indebted to Mary E. Lyons for sharing all her careful research that went into the writing of *Letters from a Slave Girl* (New York: Charles Scribner's Sons, 1992). She credits the staff at Mount Auburn cemetery in Cambridge, Massachusetts, for generously providing details and assistance.

21. In another example of the power of the word and the African-American faith that did not distinguish between spiritual and political freedom, Sojourner Truth recounts the time when President Lincoln showed her a Bible that was presented to him by "the colored people of Baltimore." The Bible bore a large plate of gold, representing a slave with his shackles falling from him in a cotton field, stretching out his hands in gratitude to President Lincoln for the freedom of slaves. See *Narrative,* 78–79.

22. For an interesting analysis of the various images of Sojourner Truth, see the essay by Kathleen Collins, "Shadow and Substance: Sojourner Truth," *History of Photography* 7.3 (1983): 183–205.

23. A discussion of the issues raised by an "as told to" autobiography can be found in H. Porter Abbott's article "Organic Form in the Autobiography of a Convert: The Example of Malcolm X," *CLA Journal* 23.2 (1979): 125–46. Abbott also discusses the "organic cohesiveness" that derives directly from the author's experience of conversion.

24. The speeches Montgomery verifies are the following: a speech in 1851

before the Women's Rights Convention; the 1852 Mob Convention
in New York City; the 1867 American Equal Rights Association
convention in New York City; and the 1871 Address of Community
to the Eighth Anniversary of Negro Freedom in the U.S. in Boston.

25. The transcription of quotations attributed to Sojourner Truth appears
in the narrative in an appalling and insulting dialect. There is no
evidence to suggest that Sojourner Truth spoke in the "dialect" Olive
Gilbert attributes to her. Sojourner Truth was raised speaking Dutch
and even after she learned English spoke with this strong accent her
entire life. To correct this editorial intrusion, I have transliterated
Sojourner Truth's words into "standard" English.

26. One example of Sojourner Truth's symbolic status within the African-
American community is described by Esther Iverm in the December
1988 issue of *Essence*. She discusses "The Sojourner Truth Adolescent
Rites Society," which conducts seminars that show how rituals—rites
of passage, naming ceremonies—can be used to address problems
young people face by emphasizing African values and fostering a
strong sense of identity, morality, and culture.

27. Although it has been demonstrated how Harriet Jacobs crafted a
relationship with her white female readership, according to Esther
Terry, Sojourner Truth's narrative does not present much data for a
shared experience. She goes on to claim, however (citing Harriet
Beecher Stowe as an example), that Sojourner Truth's wit impressed
people but overall she was considered an "oddity." See "Sojourner
Truth: The Person behind the Libyan Sybil," *Massachusetts Review* 26
(Summer/Autumn 1985): 425–44.

28. Sasson gives more details than I provide here, tracing specific biblical
allusions and motifs and also making a persuasive metrical argument
for Jackson's writing being patterned after black preachers.

29. Information regarding Rebecca Jackson's place of burial and details
concerning Shaker customs were provided for me by Geraldine Duclos
in June 1992 when I telephoned her at her office at the Free Library
of Philadelphia, where she is head of the theater collection.

3. Called to Preach

1. In his introduction to *Jonah's Gourd Vine*, Larry Neal discusses
specifically how in this novel Hurston exposes the reader to two
"distinctly different *cultural* attitudes toward the concept of spirituality." One he cites (as I have done) as having its roots in the formerly
enslaved communal society and "showing no clean-cut dichotomy
between the world of spirit and the world of flesh" (26), and the
other as a rigid blend of Puritan concepts of the white evangelical

tradition that did emphasize this dichotomy. Reprinted in *Zora Neale Hurston,* ed. Harold Bloom (New York: Chelsea House, 1986).

2. Judith Robey's article "Generic Strategies in Zora Neale Hurston's *Dust Tracks on a Road," Black American Literature Forum* 24.4 (1990): 667–81, offers a reading of the autobiography that shows that the movement of "I" in the text from one existential mode to another has a correlate in generic movement from myth to picaresque to essay. Robey attributes this generic shift to Hurston's ongoing attempt to deal with her audience but finds the strategy ultimately unsuccessful in empowering the author.

3. Neal continues in this article to describe how the Harlem Renaissance failed in two essential categories of form and sensibility because there was no "encounter and subsequent grappling with the visceral elements of the black experience but rather a tendency on the part of many of the movement's writers to pander to the voguish concerns of the white social circles in which they found themselves." Hurston, he claims, is an exception to this trend.

4. Sojourner Truth admits that she was called a "white folks nigger" by fellow slaves on her plantation because of her hard work and desire to please. See *Narrative,* 33.

5. For examples of allusions to biblical incidents, see the tales of how the woodpecker got his red hair and why the possum has no hairs on its tail that are related to incidents on Noah's Ark (MM, 111–13). To read about the field hand who became an herb doctor, see Father Abraham (SC, 15–18). Two stories that describe moral virtues are the tale of a cat that eats nine fish, all the food that a starving family and its dog possess. All eventually die of starvation except the cat, which dies from eating too much (MM, 130–32); and the story of the man whose dedication to the freedom of mockingbirds is rewarded with their loyalty (MM, 102–3). An example of God's presence in creation can be seen in the story of the rattlesnake and how God gave it rings to rattle as a warning of danger (MM, 105–6). Theological justification of natural occurrences is described in why waves have whitecaps (MM, 138–39). The role of the devil can be appreciated in the story of how the devil tricks God and man with the help of woman (MM, 33–38).

6. Theresa R. Love's essay "Zora Neal Hurston's America," *Papers on Language and Literature* 12.4 (1976): 422–37, gives a comprehensive reading of Hurston's treatment of folk materials in relation to her political agenda at the time.

7. For a full discussion of how *Mules and Men* is a narrative of a successful quest for *female* empowerment, see Cheryl Wall's essay "*Mules and Men* and Women: Zora Neale Hurston's Strategies of Narration and

Visions of Female Empowerment," *Black American Literature Forum* 23.4 (1989): 661–80. In this essay Wall demonstrates how "Hurston's narrative strategies allow her to represent first, the ways in which women are relegated to subordinate roles in the culture she otherwise celebrates and, second, the means by which women in that culture gain access to creative expression and power."

8. Hurston's own imaginative extension of this concept can be seen in her rendering of Moses and the Israelites in *Moses, Man of the Mountain* (Urbana: Univ. of Illinois Press, 1984).

9. Marion Kilson, in her essay "The Transformation of Eatonville's Ethnographer," *Phylon* 33.2 (1972): 112–19, detects, midway through Hurston's career, a shift in perspective from relativism to critical commitment, particularly in discussions of race.

10. Alice Deck, in "Autoethnography: Zora Neale Hurston, Noni Jabavu, and Cross-Disciplinary Discourse," *Black American Literature Forum* 24.2 (1990): 237–56, also uses this term and insists Hurston's work creates a new kind of autobiography whose aim is to demonstrate the basic humanity of blacks to readers outside the community.

11. Mary Jane Lupton, in "Zora Neale Hurston and the Survival of the Female," *Southern Literary Journal* 15.1 (1982): 45–54, describes this journey motif in terms of *The Odyssey,* citing the pattern of tensions created between the call to adventure and the return to the homeland. Missy Dehn Kubitschek, on the other hand, uses the schema outlined by Joseph Campbell in *Hero with a Thousand Faces* to describe the quest motif in the novel in "'Tuh de Horizon and Back': The Female Quest in *Their Eyes Were Watching God,*" *Black American Literature Forum* 17 (1983): 109–15. Finally, Sigrid King, in "Naming and Power in Zora Neale Hurston's *Their Eyes Were Watching God,*" *Black American Literature Forum* 24.4 (1990): 683–96, charts Janie's development through stages of naming, from named to renamed to unnamed.

12. In her essay "The Influence of Voodoo on the Fiction of Zora Neale Hurston," in *Sturdy Black Bridges,* ed. Roseann P. Bell, Bettye J. Parker, and Beverly Guy-Sheftall (Garden City, N.Y.: Doubleday, 1979), Ellease Southerland discusses how the culmination of Hurston's folklore is the form it gave her religious thought. She cites Hurston's description of Mrs. Turner's love for Janie as influenced by voodoo symbols and rituals.

13. Gay Wilentz, in the essay "Defeating the False God: Janie's Self-Determination in Zora Neale Hurston's *Their Eyes Were Watching God,*" in *Faith of a (Woman) Writer,* ed. Alice Kessler-Harris and William McBrien (Westport, Conn.: Greenwood Press, 1988), demonstrates several other readings of God, including one that

portrays him as a "capricious slave master," reminding readers of the "duality of the Christian God for blacks" (235).

14. In *Dust Tracks* Hurston employs the same phrase when discussing her friendship with Ethel Waters. Hurston, who admired Waters's religious faith as well as her "homely philosophy that reaches all corners of Life," states: "I am her friend and her tongue is in my mouth. I can speak her sentiments for her" (DT, 245). Recycling phrases and images was not uncommon for Hurston, and this is but one of many examples found throughout her works.

4. Involuntary Converts

1. In her book *Speaking in Parables: A Study in Metaphor and Theology* (Philadelphia: Fortress Press, 1975) Sally McFague comments on the relationship between autobiography and fiction. She writes: "The truth of an autobiography is not the imitation of details or external facts but the consistency of the ordering pattern or master form in relation to the person's encounter with the world. As with a novel, it is not the flashes of insight that count but the total cumulative effect, and this is an achievement of a high aesthetic and interpretive order" (156).

2. Carol Christ proposes a similar pattern in her book *Diving Deep and Surfacing* (Boston: Beacon Press, 1980), where she delineates a four-step cyclic pattern for women's spiritual development: emptiness, connection, awakening, and integration.

3. For another reading of archetypes in *Sula* see Stephanie A. Demetrakopoulos's essay in *New Dimensions of Spirituality* (Westport, Conn.: Greenwood Press, 1987), where the author analyzes Morrison's novel through a framework of both Christian and Greek goddess figures.

4. For a thoughtful reading of issues pertaining to moral conduct cast in terms of contemporary women-centered psychology, see the essay by Diane Gillespie and Missy Dehn Kubitschek, "Who Cares? Women-Centered Psychology in *Sula*." *Black American Literature Forum* 24.1 (1990): 31–48. Joseph H. Wessling offers a different kind of psychological analysis in "Narcissism in Toni Morrison's *Sula*," *CLA Journal* 31.3 (1988): 281–98. He describes Sula's personality with reference to the clinical term *narcissism*, which is a pathological tendency characterized as "an unhealthy level of self-regard which interferes with, undermines, and even destroys inter-personal relationships." Sula is not alone in her narcissism, for Wessling believes Nel suffers from the narcissism of spiritual pride.

5. Rebecca Jackson subscribed to the Shaker belief that conversion of souls was possible even after death. Morrison, by following Sula into

the afterlife and seeing Nel converted in old age, gives us cause to speculate that perhaps Sula was converted as well by Nel's redemptive act of confession, just as all their actions in life impinged on one another's being.

6. For a discussion of the heroic qualities of Sula in the context of the epic form, see Karen F. Stein's essay "Toni Morrison's *Sula:* A Black Woman's Epic," *Black American Literature Forum* 18.4 (1984): 146–49. Morrison, she claims, uses ironic reversals of epic expectations to create a new definition of heroism that will encompass the lives of black women.

7. The three Deweys, orphans taken in by Eva—who do not resemble one another but who are all given the same name and who "spoke one voice, thought with one mind" (39)—represent a further complication of identity.

8. Naana Banyiwa-Horne, in "The Scary Face of the Self: An Analysis of the Character of Sula in Toni Morrison's *Sula*," *Sage* 2.1 (1985): 29, shows how Morrison explores the conventional ramifications of the binary concepts of good and evil as they affect the manner in which women are perceived in society.

9. Mae Henderson, in the brilliant essay "Speaking in Tongues: Dialogics, Dialectics, and the Black Woman Writer's Literary Tradition," in *Changing Our Own Words,* ed. Cheryl A. Wall (New Brunswick, N.J.: Rutgers Univ. Press, 1989), 16–37, reads *Sula* from two critical perspectives: the dialogics of Bakhtin and the dialectics of Gadamer. She unites these two perspectives to show the qualities of both contestation and consensus that she believes underscore the simultaneous difference and identity that constitute a black female literary tradition. She further expands on these terms by casting them in biblical categories: the Old Testament suggesting the dialogics of difference in its diversity of discourse, and the New Testament, in its unifying language of spirit, suggesting the dialectics of identity.

10. In the essay "Transcending the 'Loophole of Retreat': Paule Marshall's Placing of Female Generations," *Callaloo* 10.1 (1987): 79–90, Sabine Brock uses the image created by Harriet Jacobs when referring to her garret hiding place, the "loophole of retreat," to describe the ways in which Marshall "places" women characters and thereby reveals "obsessive, aggressive, and extensive efforts to create a space for women to move and thereby trespass not only the limits of Anglo-American discourse but those of closely circumscribed lives as well."

11. Marshall's novels deal with, respectively, childhood/youth; middle age; and maturity. For a reading of all three novels that describes the cumulative quest of black women, through different ages and in different contexts, see Missy Dehn Kubitschek's essay "Paule Marshall's

Women on Quest," *Black American Literature Forum* 21.1–2 (1987): 43–60.

12. Velma Pollard points out also that the appearance of a person already dead is expressed in the Anglophone Caribbean by the verb *dream* used actively with the dead person as subject. "Her great-aunt dream her" roughly translates the experience, and implicit in such an event is a dream message. See her "Cultural Connections in Paule Marshall's *Praisesong for the Widow*," *World Literature Written in English* 25.2 (1985): 285–98.

13. For this section Ebele E. Eko suggests that in historical terms readers consider as a parallel to Avey's purge the angry sixties in the United States and the overthrow of colonialism in most African countries at the same time, where many blacks expressed deep racial pride and rejected white values and aesthetics.

14. For a historical analog to this final section, Eko suggests that it represents the physical and psychological move of black Americans toward their roots in Africa since the 1960s.

15. It is interesting to note that apart from ancestors, the figure who most influences Avey is her daughter Marion, whom she had tried unsuccessfully to miscarry. In a sense Marion is also one of the "living dead."

16. Susan Willis reads Marshall's project as an attempt to recover or salvage cultural components generated by urban life and combine them with folk traditions, to blend urban and agrarian aspects of black culture.

17. Shug, a main character in *The Color Purple*, is also the name for a character who appears throughout the first section of *Mules and Men* (41–42). Obviously understanding the sanctified quality of a graveyard, Walker has documented her visits to the graves of both Hurston and Bob Marley (the latter in "Journey to Nine Miles," in *Living by the Word*). For fuller documentation of Walker's feelings about Hurston, see her introduction to the collection of Hurston's writings she edited, *I Love Myself When I Am Laughing* (New York: Feminist Press, 1979), and the essay "Looking for Zora," in *In Search of Our Mothers' Gardens*. See also Alma S. Freeman's essay "Zora Neale Hurston and Alice Walker: A Spiritual Kinship," *Sage* 2.1 (1985): 37–40.

18. An interesting parallel to Walker's concept of conversion as it operates within a global vision is offered by David J. Krieger in his essay "Conversion: On the Possibility of Global Thinking in an Age of Particularism," *Journal of the American Academy of Religion* 58.2 (1990): 223–41. Here he proposes that a "middle way between the unfounded claim to universality characteristic of modernism and the postmodern celebration of pluralism is methodological conversion

carried out concretely as nonviolent praxis that establishes a cosmotheandric solidarity. Global communication is possible by means of a language that speaks out of a pragmatically established togetherness that encompasses not only the human species but also nature and the divine."

19. For a full discussion of the controversy surrounding both the book and the film of *The Color Purple,* in which Walker was accused of an unsparingly harsh and inaccurate portrayal of black men, see Jacqueline Bobo's article "Sifting through the Controversy: Reading *The Color Purple,*" *Callaloo* 12.2 (1989): 332–42. See also Deborah E. McDowell's essay "Reading Family Matters," in *Changing Our Own Words.* McDowell discusses the various subtexts surrounding the criticism of Walker and other black women writers and shows how Walker's response to criticism takes the form of a discussion of self-identity.

20. See Lucinda H. MacKethan's essay "From Fugitive Slave to Man of Letters: The Conversion of Frederick Douglass," cited above. Also, King-Kok Cheung, in "'Don't Tell': Imposed Silences in *The Color Purple* and *The Woman Warrior,*" *PMLA* 103.2 (1988): 165, notes that the word *spell* nicely connotes the almost magical healing effect of words.

21. For a reading of the novel within a romance paradigm, see Molly Hite's essay "Romance, Marginality, and Matrilineage: *The Color Purple* and *Their Eyes Were Watching God,*" in *Reading Black, Reading Feminist,* ed. Henry Louis Gates, Jr. (New York: New American Library, 1990). In the same volume, bell hooks, in the essay, "Writing the Subject: Reading *The Color Purple,*" makes connections with slave autobiographies but cautions against bringing any comparative critical or genre category to the novel.

22. Among Williams's writings are "Women's Oppression and Lifeline Politics in Black Women's Religious Narratives," *Journal of Feminist Studies in Religion* 1.3 (1985): 59–71; "Black Women's Literature and the Task of Feminist Theology," in *Immaculate and Powerful,* ed. Clarissa W. Atkinson, Constance H. Buchanan, and Margaret R. Miles (Boston: Beacon Press, 1985), 88–110; "Womanist Theology: Black Women's Voices," in *Weaving the Visions,* ed. Judith Plaskow and Carol Christ (New York: Harper and Row, 1989), 179–86; "Examining Two Shades of 'Purple,'" *Los Angeles Times,* 15 March 1986; and "What Was Missed: 'The Color Purple,'" *Christianity and Crisis,* 14 July 1986.

23. Other important corresponding episodes of naming are when Mary Agnes insists on her name being used; when Shug names a song for Celie; when Celie first signs her name to a letter; and when Celie finally refers to Mister as Albert.

Bibliography

Abbott, H. Porter. "Organic Form in the Autobiography of a Convert: The Example of Malcolm X." *CLA Journal* 23.2 (1979): 125–46.

Abel, Elizabeth, ed. *Writing and Sexual Difference*. Chicago: Univ. of Chicago Press, 1982.

Abel, Elizabeth, Marianne Hirsch, and Elizabeth Langland, eds. *The Voyage In: Fictions of Female Development*. Hanover, N.H.: Univ. Press of New England, 1983.

Anderson, Sharon. "Faces of Faith: Bernice Johnson Reagon." *The Other Side* 28.6 (1988): 11–15.

Andrews, William L. "The Novelization of Voice in Early African American Narrative." *PMLA* 105.1 (1990): 23–34.

———. *Sisters of the Spirit*. Bloomington: Indiana Univ. Press, 1986.

———. *To Tell a Free Story: The First Century of Afro-American Autobiography*. Urbana: Univ. of Illinois Press, 1986.

Atkinson, Clarissa W., Constance H. Buchanan, and Margaret R. Miles, eds. *Immaculate and Powerful: The Female in Sacred Image and Social Reality*. Boston: Beacon Press, 1985.

Awkward, Michael. *Inspiriting Influences: Tradition, Revision, and Afro-American Women's Novels*. New York: Columbia Univ. Press, 1989.

Baker, Houston A. *Blues, Ideology, and Afro-American Literature: A Vernacular Theory*. Chicago: Univ. of Chicago Press, 1984.

Baker, Houston A., and Patricia Redmond. *Afro-American Literary Study in the 1990s*. Chicago: Univ. of Chicago Press, 1989.

Bambara, Toni Cade. Some Foreward Remarks. *The Sanctified Church*. By Zora Neale Hurston. Berkeley: Turtle Island, 1983. 7–11.

Banyiwa-Horne, Naana. "The Scary Face of the Self: An Analysis of the Character of Sula in Toni Morrison's *Sula*." *Sage* 2.1 (1985): 28–31.

Barbour, John D. "Character and Characterization in Religious Autobiography." *Journal of the American Academy of Religion* 55.2 (1987): 307–27.

Barnhart, Joe Edward, and Mary Ann Barnhart. *The New Birth: A Naturalistic View of Religious Conversion.* Macon, Ga.: Mercer Univ. Press, 1981.

Beckford, James A. "Accounting for Conversion." *British Journal of Sociology* 29.2 (1978): 249–62.

Bell, Roseann P., Bettye J. Parker, and Beverly Guy-Sheftall, eds. *Sturdy Black Bridges: Visions of Black Women in Literature.* Garden City, N.Y.: Doubleday, 1979.

Benstock, Shari, ed. *Feminist Issues in Literary Scholarship.* Bloomington: Indiana Univ. Press, 1987.

———. *The Private Self: Theory and Practice of Women's Autobiographical Writings.* Chapel Hill: Univ. of North Carolina Press, 1988.

Benston, Kimberly W. "Facing Tradition: Revisionary Scenes in African American Literature." *PMLA* 105.1 (1990): 98–109.

Bethel, Lorraine. "'This Infinity of Conscious Pain': Zora Neale Hurston and the Black Female Literary Tradition." In *But Some of Us Are Brave.* Ed. Gloria T. Hull, Patricia Bell Scott, and Barbara Smith. Old Westbury, N.Y.: Feminist Press, 1982. 176–89.

Blake, Susan L. "Toni Morrison." In *Afro-American Fiction Writers after 1955. Dictionary of Literary Biography* 33. Ed. Thadious M. Davis and Trudier Harris. Detroit: Gale, 1984. 187–99.

Blassingame, John W. *The Slave Community: Plantation Life in the Antebellum South.* New York: Oxford Univ. Press, 1979.

Bloom, Harold, ed. *Zora Neale Hurston.* New York: Chelsea House, 1986.

Bone, Robert A. *The Negro Novel in America.* New Haven: Yale Univ. Press, 1958.

Bonetti, Kay. "Alice Walker Interview." *American Audio Prose Library,* 1981.

Bradley, David. "Telling the Black Woman's Story." *New York Times Magazine,* 8 Jan. 1984.

Brauer, Jerald C. "Conversion: From Puritanism to Revivalism." *Journal of Religion* 58 (1978): 227–43.

Braxton, Joanne M. "Harriet Jacobs' *Incidents in the Life of a Slave Girl:* The Re-definition of the Slave Narrative Genre." *Massachusetts Review* 27 (1986): 379–87.

Brent, Linda [Harriet Jacobs]. *Incidents in the Life of a Slave Girl: Written by Herself.* New York: Harcourt Brace Jovanovich, 1973.

Brereton, Virginia Lieson. *From Sin to Salvation: Stories of Women's Conversions, 1800 to the Present.* Bloomington: Indiana Univ. Press, 1991.

Britt, Donna. "Alice Walker and the Inner Mysteries Unraveled." *Washington Post,* 8 May 1989.

Brock, Sabine. "Talk as a Form of Action: An Interview with Paule Marshall, September 1982." In *History and Tradition in Afro-American Culture*. Ed. Gunter H. Lenz. New York: Campus Verlag. 194–206.

———. "Transcending the 'Loophole of Retreat': Paule Marshall's Placing of Female Generations." *Callaloo* 10.1 (1987): 79–90.

Brodzki, Bella, and Celeste Schenck, eds. *Life/Lines: Theorizing Women's Autobiography*. Ithaca, N.Y.: Cornell Univ. Press, 1988.

Brown, Lloyd W. "Zora Neale Hurston and the Nature of Female Perception." *Obsidian* 4.3 (1978): 39–45.

Bryant, Cedric Gael. "The Orderliness of Disorder: Madness and Evil in Toni Morrison's *Sula*." *Black American Literature Forum* 24.2 (1990): 731–45.

Buber, Martin. *I and Thou*. New York: Scribner's, 1958.

Burgher, Mary. "Images of Self and Race in the Autobiographies of Black Women." In *Sturdy Black Bridges*. Ed. Roseann P. Bell, Bettye J. Parker, and Beverly Guy-Sheftall. Garden City, N.Y.: Doubleday, 1979. 107–22.

Bush, Trudier Blouser. "Transforming Vision: Alice Walker and Zora Neale Hurston." *Christian Century* 105.34 (1988): 1036–38.

Busia, Abena P. A. "What Is Your Nation? Reconnecting Africa and Her Diaspora through Paule Marshall's *Praisesong for the Widow*." In *Changing Our Own Words*. Ed. Cheryl A. Wall. New Brunswick, N.J.: Rutgers Univ. Press, 1989. 196–40.

Butterfield, Stephen. *Black Autobiography in America*. Amherst: Univ. of Massachusetts Press, 1974.

Byerman, Keith E. *Fingering the Jagged Grain: Tradition and Form in Recent Black Fiction*. Athens: Univ. of Georgia Press, 1985.

Caldwell, Patricia. *The Puritan Conversion Narrative*. New York: Cambridge Univ. Press, 1983.

Callahan, John F. *In the African-American Grain: The Pursuit of Voice in Twentieth-Century Black Fiction*. Urbana: Univ. of Illinois Press, 1988.

Campbell, Jane. *Mythic Black Fiction: The Transformation of History*. Knoxville: Univ. of Tennessee Press, 1986.

Campbell, Karlyn Kohrs. "Style and Content in the Rhetoric of Early Afro-American Feminists." *Quarterly Journal of Speech* 72 (Nov.1986): 434–45.

Cannon, Katie G. *Black Womanist Ethics*. Atlanta: Scholars Press, 1988.

Caputi, Jane. "'Specifying' Fannie Hurst: Langston Hughes's 'Limitations of Life,' Zora Neale Hurston's *Their Eyes Were Watching God* and Toni Morrison's *The Bluest Eye* as 'Answers' to Hurst's *Imitation of Life*." *Black American Literature Forum* 24.4 (1990): 697–716.

Carby, Hazel V. *Reconstructing Womanhood: The Emergence of the Afro-American Woman Novelist*. New York: Oxford Univ. Press, 1987.

Carr, Glynis. "Storytelling as Bildung in Zora Neale Hurston's *Their Eyes Were Watching God.*" *CLA Journal* 31.2 (1987): 189–200.

Chambers, Kimberly R. "Right on Time: History and Religion in Alice Walker's *The Color Purple.*" *CLA Journal* 31.1 (1987): 44–62.

Cheung, King-Kok. "'Don't Tell': Imposed Silences in *The Color Purple* and *The Woman Warrior.*" *PMLA* 103.2 (1988): 162–74.

Christ, Carol P. *Diving Deep and Surfacing: Women Writers on Spiritual Quest.* Boston: Beacon Press, 1980.

———. "Feminist Studies in Religion and Literature: A Methodological Reflection." *Journal of the American Academy of Religion* 44.2 (1986): 317–25.

———. "Images of Spiritual Power in Women's Fiction." In *The Politics of Women's Spirituality.* Ed. Charlene Spretnek. New York: Anchor Press, 1982. 327–37.

Christ, Carol P., and Judith Plaskow, eds. *Womanspirit Rising: A Feminist Reader on Religion.* San Francisco: Harper and Row, 1979.

Christian, Barbara. "Alice Walker." In *Afro-American Fiction Writers after 1955. Dictionary of Literary Biography* 33. Ed. Thadious M. Davis and Trudier Harris. Detroit: Gale, 1984. 258–71.

———. *Black Feminist Criticism: Perspectives on Black Women Writers.* New York: Pergamon Press, 1985.

———. *Black Women Novelists: The Development of a Tradition, 1892–1976.* Westport, Conn.: Greenwood Press, 1980.

———. "Paule Marshall." In *Afro-American Fiction Writers after 1955. Dictionary of Literary Biography* 33. Ed. Thadious M. Davis and Trudier Harris. Detroit: Gale, 1984. 161–70.

Cohen, Charles Lloyd. *God's Caress: The Psychology of Puritan Religious Experience.* New York: Oxford Univ. Press, 1986.

Collier, Eugenia. "The Closing of the Circle: Movement from Division to Wholeness in Paule Marshall's Fiction." In *Black Women Writers, 1950–80.* Ed. Mari Evans. Garden City, N.Y.: Anchor Press, 1984. 295–315.

Collins, Daniel F. "Black Conversion to Catholicism: Its Implications for the Negro Church." *Journal for the Scientific Study of Religion* 10 (1971): 208–18.

Collins, Kathleen. "Shadow and Substance: Sojourner Truth." *History of Photography* 7.3 (1983): 183–205.

Collins, Sheila D. *A Different Heaven and Earth: A Feminist Perspective on Religion.* Valley Forge, Pa.: Judson Press, 1974.

Cone, James. *For My People: Black Theology and the Black Church.* Maryknoll, N.Y.: Orbis Books, 1984.

Conn, Walter. *Christian Conversion: Developmental Interpretation of Autonomy and Surrender.* New York: Paulist Press, 1986.

Cooke, Michael G. *Afro-American Literature in the Twentieth Century: The Achievement of Intimacy*. New Haven: Yale Univ. Press, 1984.

Cooper-Lewter, Nicholas C., and Henry H. Mitchell. *Soul Theology: The Heart of American Black Culture*. New York: Harper and Row, 1986.

Corn, Alfred, ed. *Incarnation: Contemporary Writers on the New Testament*. New York: Viking, 1990.

Costas, Orland E. "Conversion as a Complex Experience." *Gospel in Context* 1.3 (1978): 14–40.

Cott, Nancy F. *Root of Bitterness: Documents of the Social History of American Women*. New York: Dutton, 1972.

———. "Young Women in the Second Great Awakening in New England." *Feminist Studies* 3.1–2 (1975): 15–29.

Couser, Thomas G. *American Autobiography: The Prophetic Mode*. Amherst: Univ. of Massachusetts Press, 1979.

Crabtree, Claire. "The Confluence of Folklore, Feminism and Black Self-Determination in Zora Neale Hurston's *Their Eyes Were Watching God*." *Southern Literary Journal* 17.2 (1985): 54–66.

Crites, Stephen. "The Narrative Quality of Experience." *Journal of the American Academy of Religion* 39.3 (1971): 295–311.

Daly, Mary. "Be-Friending: Weaving Contexts, Creating Atmospheres." In *Weaving the Visions*. Ed. Judith Plaskow and Carol P. Christ. New York: Harper and Row, 1989. 199–207.

———. *Beyond God the Father: Toward a Philosophy of Women's Liberation*. Boston: Beacon Press, 1973.

Davis, Charles T. *Black Is the Color of the Cosmos: Essays on Afro-American Literature and Culture, 1942–1981*. New York: Garland, 1982.

Davis, Charles T., and Henry Louis Gates, Jr., eds. *The Slave's Narrative*. New York: Oxford Univ. Press, 1985.

Deck, Alice A. "Autoethnography: Zora Neale Hurston, Noni Jabavu, and Cross-Disciplinary Discourse." *Black American Literature Forum* 24.2 (1990): 237–56.

Denniston, Dorothy L. "Early Short Fiction by Paule Marshall." *Callaloo* 6.2 (1983): 31–46.

DeVeaux, Alexis. "Alice Walker." *Essence* (Sept. 1989).

Dixon, Melvin. *Ride Out the Wilderness: Geography and Identity in Afro-American Literature*. Urbana: Univ. of Illinois Press, 1987.

Doherty, Thomas. "Harriet Jacobs' Narrative Strategies: *Incidents in the Life of a Slave Girl*." *Southern Literary Journal* 19.1 (1986): 79–89.

Doriani, Beth Maclay. "Black Womanhood in Nineteenth-Century America: Subversion and Self-Construction in Two Women's Autobiographies." *American Quarterly* 43.2 (1991): 199–222.

Douglas, Ann. *The Feminization of American Culture*. New York: Knopf, 1977.

Dove, Rita. "The Epistle of Paul the Apostle to the Ephesians." In *Incarnation: Contemporary Writers on the New Testament*. Ed. Alfred Corn. New York: Viking, 1990. 162–74.

Duclos, Geraldine. "The Shaker Family of Philadelphia." *The Shaker Messenger* 13.3 (1991): 5–7.

Dumitriu, Petru. *To the Unknown God*. New York: Seabury, 1982.

Edwards, Lee. *Psyche as Hero: Female Heroism and Fictional Form*. Middletown, Conn.: Wesleyan Univ. Press, 1984.

Eko, Ebele O. "Oral Tradition: The Bridge to Africa in Paule Marshall's *Praisesong for the Widow*." *Western Journal of Black Studies* 10.3 (1986): 143–47.

Eliade, Mircea. *Rites and Symbols of Initiation*. New York: Harper and Row, 1965.

———. *The Sacred and the Profane*. New York: Harper and Row, 1961.

———. *The Two and the One*. Chicago: Univ. of Chicago Press, 1962.

Evans, F. W. *Shaker Communism*. New York: AMS Press, 1981.

Evans, James H., Jr. "African-American Christianity and the Postmodern Condition." *Journal of the American Academy of Religion* 58.2 (1990): 207–22.

———. *Spiritual Empowerment in Afro-American Literature*. Lewiston, N.Y.: Edwin Mellen Press, 1987.

Evans, Mari. *Black Women Writers, 1950–80*. Garden City, N.Y.: Anchor Press, 1984.

Falk, Nance, and Rita Gross. *Unspoken Worlds*. San Francisco: Harper and Row, 1980.

Faludi, Susan. *Backlash: The Undeclared War against American Women*. New York: Crown, 1991.

Fannin, Alice. "A Sense of Wonder: The Pattern for Psychic Survival in *Their Eyes Were Watching God* and *The Color Purple*." *Zora Neale Hurston Forum* 1.1 (1986): 1–11.

Fleischmann, Fritz, ed. *American Novelists Revisited*. Boston: G. K. Hall, 1982.

Foreman, P. Gabrielle. "Looking Back from Zora, or Talking Out of Both Sides of My Mouth for Those Who Have Two Ears." *Black American Literature Forum* 24.4 (1990): 649–66.

Foster, Frances Smith. *Witnessing Slavery: The Development of Antebellum Slave Narratives*. Westport, Conn.: Greenwood Press, 1979.

Fowler, James. *Stages of Faith: The Quest for Human Development and the Quest for Meaning*. San Francisco: Harper and Row, 1981.

Fox-Genovese, Elizabeth. "My Statue, My Self: Autobiographical Writings of Afro-American Women." In *The Private Self*. Ed. Shari Benstock. Chapel Hill: Univ. of North Carolina Press, 1988. 63–89.

———. "Myth and History: Discourse of Origins in Zora Neale Hurston and Maya Angelou." *Black American Literature Forum* 24.2 (1990): 221–35.

———. "To Write Myself: The Autobiographies of Afro-American Women." In *Feminist Issues in Critical Scholarship*. Ed. Shari Benstock. Bloomington: Univ. of Indiana Press, 1987. 161–80.

———. "To Write the Wrongs of Slavery." *Gettysburg Review* 2.1 (1989): 63–76.

———. *Within the Plantation Household: Black and White Women of the Old South*. Chapel Hill: Univ. of North Carolina Press, 1988.

Fox-Genovese, Elizabeth, and Eugene D. Genovese. "The Divine Sanction of Social Order: Religious Foundations of the Southern Slaveholder's World View." *Journal of the American Academy of Religion* 55.2 (1987): 211–33.

Frazier, E. Franklin. *The Negro Church in America*. New York: Schocken Books, 1964.

Freeman, Alma S. "Zora Neale Hurston and Alice Walker: A Spiritual Kinship." *Sage* 2.1 (1985): 37–40.

Freud, Sigmund. *The Future of an Illusion*. New York: Norton, 1961.

Friedman, Susan Stanford. "Women's Autobiographical Selves: Theory and Practice." In *The Private Self: Theory and Practice of Women's Autobiographical Writings*. Ed. Shari Benstock. Chapel Hill: Univ. of North Carolina Press, 1988. 34–61.

Fulkerson, Mary McClintock. "Sexism as Original Sin: Developing a Theacentric Discourse." *Journal of the American Academy of Religion* 59.4 (1991): 643–52.

Galvin, Corrine B. "Sojourner Truth, Libyan Sybil." *New York Folklore Quarterly* 1.1 (1950): 5–21.

Gardiner, Judith Kegan. "On Female Identity and Writing by Women." In *Writing and Sexual Difference*. Ed. Elizabeth Abel. Chicago: Univ. of Chicago Press, 1982. 186–98.

Gates, Henry Louis, Jr. Afterword. "Zora Neale Hurston: 'A Negro Way of Saying.'" *Their Eyes Were Watching God*. By Zora Neale Hurston. New York: Harper and Row, 1990.

———. *Figures in Black*. New York: Oxford Univ. Press, 1987.

———. *The Signifying Monkey*. New York: Oxford Univ. Press, 1988.

———. *Six Women's Slave Narratives*. New York: Oxford Univ. Press, 1988.

———. *Spiritual Narratives*. New York: Oxford Univ. Press, 1988.

———. *Thinking Black, Thinking Feminist: A Critical Anthology*. New York: New American Library, 1990.

———, ed. *Black Literature and Literary Theory*. New York: Methuen, 1984.

Gelpi, Donald L., S.J. *Experiencing God: A Theology of Human Experience*. New York: Paulist Press, 1978.

Genovese, Eugene D. *Roll Jordan Roll: The World the Slaves Made.* New York: Random House, 1972.

Gilkes, Cheryl Townsend. "'Together and in Harness': Women's Traditions in the Sanctified Church." *Signs* 10.4 (1985): 678–99.

Gillespi, V. Bailey. *Religious Conversion and Personal Identity: How and Why People Change.* Birmingham: Religious Education Press, 1979.

Gillespie, Diane, and Missy Dehn Kubitschek. "Who Cares? Women-Centered Psychology in *Sula.*" *Black American Literature Forum* 24.1 (1990): 31–48.

Gilligan, Carol. *In a Different Voice: Psychological Theory and Women's Development.* Cambridge: Harvard Univ. Press, 1982.

Grant, Jacquelyn. "Black Women and the Church." In *But Some of Us Are Brave.* Ed. Gloria T. Hull, Patricia Bell Scott, and Barbara Smith. Old Westbury, N.Y.: Feminist Press, 1982. 141–56.

Grant, Robert. "Absence Into Presence: The Thematics of Memory and 'Missing' Subjects in Toni Morrison's *Sula.*" In *Critical Essays on Toni Morrision.* Ed. Nellie Y. McKay. Boston: G. K. Hall, 1988. 90–104.

Griffin, Emilie. *Turning: Reflections on the Experience of Conversion.* New York: Doubleday, 1980.

Guerrero, Edward. "Tracking 'The Look' in the Novels of Toni Morrison." *Black American Literature Forum* 24.4 (1990): 761–73.

Gunn, Janet Varner. *Autobiography: Towards a Poetics of Experience.* Philadelphia: Univ. of Pennsylvania Press, 1982.

Harris, Trudier. "Folklore in the Fiction of Alice Walker: A Depiction of Historical and Literary Traditions." *Black American Literature Forum* 11.2 (1977): 3–8.

Hartfield, Ronne. "Gifts of Power: The Writings of Rebecca Jackson, Black Visionary, Shaker Eldress." *Journal of Religion* 65 (1985): 282–84.

Helsa, David H. "Religion and Literature: The Second Stage." *Journal of the American Academy of Religion* 46.2 (1978): 181–92.

Hemenway, Robert E. *Zora Neale Hurston: A Literary Biography.* Urbana: Univ. of Illinois Press, 1977.

Henderson, Mae G. "*The Color Purple:* Revisions and Redefinitions." *Sage* 2.1 (1985): 14–18.

———. "Speaking in Tongues: Dialogics, Dialectics, and the Black Woman Writer's Literary Tradition." In *Changing Our Own Words.* Ed. Cheryl A. Wall. New Brunswick, N.J.: Rutgers Univ. Press, 1989. 16–37.

———. "(W)riting *The Work* and Working the Rites." *Black American Literature Forum* 23.4 (1989): 631–60.

Higginbotham, Elizabeth, and Sarah Watts. "The New Scholarship on Afro-American Women." *Women's Studies Quarterly* 1&2 (1988): 13–21.

Holloway, Karla F. C. *The Character of the Word: The Texts of Zora Neale Hurston.* Westport, Conn.: Greenwood Press, 1987.

————. "Revision and (Re)membrance: A Theory of Literary Structures in Literature by African-American Women Writers." *Black American Literature Forum* 24.2 (1990): 617–31.

Holloway, Karla F. C., and Stephanie A. Demetrakopoulos. *New Dimensions of Spirituality: A Biracial and Bicultural Reading of the Novels of Toni Morrison.* Westport, Conn.: Greenwood Press, 1987.

hooks, bell, and Cornel West. *Breaking Bread: Insurgent Black Intellectual Life.* Boston: South End Press, 1991.

Houchins, Sue E. Introduction. *Spiritual Narratives.* The Schomburg Library of Nineteenth-Century Black Women Writers. Ed. Henry Louis Gates, Jr. New York: Oxford Univ. Press, 1988. xxix–xliv.

Huber, Elaine C. *Women and the Authority of Inspiration.* Lanham, Md.: Univ. Press of America, 1985.

Hull, Gloria T., Patricia Bell Scott, and Barbara Smith, eds. *But Some of Us Are Brave.* Old Westbury, N.Y.: Feminist Press, 1982.

Humez, Jean McMahon, ed. *Gifts of Power: The Writings of Rebecca Jackson, Black Visionary, Shaker Eldress.* Amherst: Univ. of Massachusetts Press, 1981.

Hunter-Gault, Charlayne. "Illuminating the Color Purple." *MacNeil/ Lehrer News Hour,* 25 March 1987 (transcript), 11–14.

Hurston, Zora Neale. *Dust Tracks on a Road.* Urbana: Univ. of Illinois Press, 1984.

————. *I Love Myself When I Am Laughing . . . And Then Again When I Am Looking Mean and Impressive: A Zora Neale Hurston Reader.* Ed. Alice Walker. New York: Feminist Press, 1979.

————. *Mules and Men.* Bloomington: Indiana Univ. Press, 1978.

————. *The Sanctified Church.* Berkeley: Turtle Island, 1983.

————. *Tell My Horse.* Philadelphia: Lippincott, 1938.

————. *Their Eyes Were Watching God.* Urbana: Univ. of Illinois Press, 1978.

Jacobs, Donald R. "Culture and the Phenomena of Conversion." *Gospel in Context* 1.3 (1978): 4–14.

James, William. *The Varieties of Religious Experience.* New York: Collier Macmillan, 1961.

Jelinek, Estelle C., ed. *Women's Autobiography.* Bloomington: Indiana Univ. Press, 1980.

Johnson, Abbey Arthur, and Ronald Mayberry Johnson. *Propaganda and Aesthetics: The Literary Politics of Afro-American Magazines in the Twentieth Century.* Amherst: Univ. of Massachusetts Press, 1979.

Johnson, Cedric B. "The Process of Change: Sacred and Secular." *Journal of Psychology and Theology* 5 (1977): 103–9.

Johnson, Clifton H., ed. *God Struck Me Dead: Religious Conversion Experiences and Autobiographies of Ex-Slaves.* Philadelphia: Pilgrim Press, 1969.

Johnson, Diane. *Terrorists and Novelists.* New York: Knopf, 1982.

Jones, Bessie W., and Audrey L. Vinson. *The World of Toni Morrison: Explorations in Literary Criticism*. Dubuque, Iowa: Kendall/Hunt, 1985.

Jones, Major J. *Black Awareness: A Theology of Hope*. Nashville: Abingdon Press, 1971.

Jordan, June. *Civil Wars*. Boston: Beacon Press, 1981.

Kessler-Harris, Alice, and William McBrien, eds. *Faith of a (Woman) Writer*. Westport, Conn.: Greenwood Press, 1988.

Killinger, John. *The Fragile Presence: Transcendence in Modern Literature*. Philadelphia: Fortress Press, 1973.

Kilson, Marion. "The Transformation of Eatonville's Ethnographer." *Phylon* 33.2 (1972): 112–19.

King, Sigrid. "Naming and Power in Zora Neale Hurston's *Their Eyes Were Watching God*." *Black American Literature Forum* 24.4 (1990): 683–96.

Krailsheimer, A. J. *Conversion*. London: SCM Press, 1980.

Krasner, James. "The Life of Women: Zora Neale Hurston and Female Autobiography." *Black American Literature Forum* 23.1 (1989): 113–25.

Kubitschek, Missy Dehn. *Claiming the Heritage: African-American Women Novelists and History*. Jackson: Univ. Press of Mississippi, 1991.

———. "Paule Marshall's Women on Quest." *Black American Literature Forum* 21.1–2 (1987): 43–60.

———. "'Tuh de Horizon and Back': The Female Quest in *Their Eyes Were Watching God*." *Black American Literature Forum* 17 (1983): 109–15.

Lee, A. Robert, ed. *Black Fiction: New Studies in the Afro-American Novel since 1945*. New York: Barnes and Noble, 1980.

Lenz, Gunter H., ed. *History and Tradition in Afro-American Culture*. New York: Campus Verlag, 1984.

Lerner, Gerda. *Black Women in White America*. New York: Random House, 1973.

Lester, Julius. *To Be a Slave*. New York: Dial Press, 1968.

Levine, Lawrence W. *Black Culture and Black Consciousness: Afro-American Folk Thought from Slavery to Freedom*. New York: Oxford Univ. Press, 1978.

Levy, Andrew. "Dialect and Convention: Harriet A. Jacobs's *Incidents in the Life of a Slave Girl*." *Nineteenth-Century Literature* 45 (1990): 206–19.

Lincoln, C. Eric, ed. *The Black Experience in Religion*. New York: Doubleday, 1974.

Lionnet, Françoise. *Autobiographical Voices*. Ithaca, N.Y.: Cornell Univ. Press, 1989.

Long, Charles H. *Significations: Signs, Symbols, and Images in the Interpretation of Religion*. Philadelphia: Fortress Press, 1986.

Lounsberry, Barbara, and Grace Ann Hovet. "Principles of Perception in

Toni Morrison's *Sula.*" *Black American Literature Forum* 13.4 (1979): 126–29.

Love, Theresa R. "Zora Neale Hurston's America." *Papers on Language and Literature* 12.4 (1976): 422–37.

Lowe, Bernice. "Michigan Days of Sojourner Truth." *New York Folklore Quarterly* 12.2 (1976): 127–35.

Lowenberg, Bert James, and Ruth Bogin, eds. *Black Women in Nineteenth-Century American Life.* University Park: Pennsylvania State Univ. Press, 1976.

Lupton, Mary Jane. "Zora Neale Hurston and the Survival of the Female." *Southern Literary Journal* 15.1 (1982): 45–54.

Mabee, Carleton. "Sojourner Truth, Bold Prophet: Why Did She Never Learn to Read?" *New York History,* Jan. 1988, 55–77.

McCredie, Wendy. "Authority and Authorization in *Their Eyes Were Watching God.*" *Black American Literature Forum* 16.1 (1982): 25–28.

McDowell, Deborah E. "'The Changing Same': Generational Connections and Black Women Novelists." *New Literary History* 18.2 (1987): 281–302.

———. "New Directions for Black Feminist Criticism." *Black American Literature Forum* 14.4 (1980): 153–59.

———. "Reading Family Matters." In *Changing Our Own Words.* Ed. Cheryl A. Wall. New Brunswick, N.J.: Rutgers Univ. Press, 1989. 75–97.

———. "'The Self and the Other': Reading Toni Morrison's *Sula* and the Black Female Text." In *Critical Essays on Toni Morrison.* Ed. Nellie Y. McKay. Boston: G. K. Hall, 1988. 77–89.

McDowell, Deborah E., and Arnold Rampersad, eds. *Slavery and the Literary Imagination.* Baltimore: Johns Hopkins Univ. Press, 1989.

McFague, Sallie. *Speaking in Parables: A Study in Metaphor and Theology.* Philadelphia: Fortress Press, 1982.

McKay, Nellie. "Nineteenth-Century Black Women's Spiritual Autobiographies: Religious Faith and Self-Empowerment." In *Interpreting Women's Lives: Feminist Theory and Personal Narratives.* Ed. Personal Narratives Group. Bloomington: Indiana Univ. Press, 1989. 139–54.

———. "Race, Gender, and Cultural Context in Zora Neale Hurston's *Dust Tracks on a Road.*" In *Life/Lines: Theorizing Women's Autobiographies.* Ed. Bella Brodzki and Celeste Schenck. Ithaca, N.Y.: Cornell Univ. Press, 1988. 175–88.

McKay, Nellie, ed. *Critical Essays on Toni Morrison.* Boston: G. K. Hall, 1988.

MacKethan, Lucinda H. *Daughters of Time: Creating Woman's Voice in Southern Story.* Athens: Univ. of Georgia Press, 1990.

———. "From Fugitive Slave to Man of Letters: The Conversion of Frederick Douglass." *Journal of Narrative Technique* 16.1 (1986): 55–71.

McLaurin, Melton A. *Celia, a Slave*. Athens: Univ. of Georgia Press, 1991.

McLoughlin, William G. *Revivals, Awakenings, and Reform*. Chicago: Univ. of Chicago Press, 1978.

Marshall, Paule. "From the Poets in the Kitchen." *Callaloo* 6.2 (1983): 23–30.

———. "The Negro Woman in Literature." *Freedomways* 6 (1966): 21–25.

———. *Praisesong for the Widow*. New York: Dutton, 1983.

———. "Shaping the World of My Art." *New Letters* 40 (1973): 97–112.

Maslow, Abraham. *Religions, Values, and Peak Experiences*. New York: Penguin Books, 1970.

Mays, Benjamin E. *The Negro's God as Reflected in His Literature*. Boston: Chapman and Grimes, 1938.

Mbiti, James. *African Religions and Philosophies*. New York: Doubleday, 1970.

Meese, Elizabeth A. *Crossing the Double-Cross: The Practice of Feminist Criticism*. Chapel Hill: Univ. of North Carolina Press, 1986.

Middleton, Victoria. "*Sula:* An Experimental Life." *CLA Journal* 28.4 (1985): 367–81.

Midgley, Mary, and Judith Hughes. *Women's Choices: Philosophical Problems Facing Feminism*. New York: St. Martin's Press, 1983.

Mikell-Remy, Gwendolyn. "When Horses Talk: Reflections on Zora Neale Hurston's Haitian Anthropology." *Phylon* 43.3 (1982): 218–30.

Mintz, Sidney. *Slavery, Colonialism, and Racism*. New York: Norton, 1974.

Mol, Hans. *Identity and the Sacred*. Oxford: Basil Blackwell, 1976.

Montgomery, Janey Weinhold. *A Comparative Analysis of the Rhetoric of Two Negro Women Orators: Sojourner Truth and Frances E. W. Harper*. Ft. Hays Studies, n.s., 6. 1968.

Montgomery, Maxine Lavon. "A Pilgrimage to the Origins: The Apocalypse as Structure and Theme in Toni Morrison's *Sula*." *Black American Literature Forum* 23.1 (1989): 121–37.

Moody, Joycelyn K. "Ripping Away the Veil of Slavery: Literacy, Communal Love, and Self-Esteem in Three Slave Women's Narratives." *Black American Literature Forum* 24.4 (1990): 633–48.

Moraga, Cherrie, and Gloria Anzaldua, eds. *This Bridge Called My Back: Writings by Radical Women of Color*. Watertown, Mass.: Persephone Press, 1981.

Morey, Ann-Janine. "Toni Morrison and the Color of Life." *Christian Century* 105.34 (1988): 1039–42.

Morrison, Toni. "Behind the Making of the Black Book." *Black World* 23 (1974): 86–90.

———. "Memory, Creation, and Writing." *Thought* 59.235 (1984): 385–90.

———. "Rootedness: Ancestor as Foundation." In *Black Women Writers, 1950–1980*. Ed. Mari Evans. Garden City, N.Y.: Anchor Press, 1984. 339–45.

———. "The Site of Memory." In *Inventing the Truth: The Art and Craft of Memoir*. Ed. William Zissner. Boston: Houghton Mifflin, 1987. 103–24.

———. *Sula*. New York: New American Library, 1973.

———. "What the Black Woman Thinks about Women's Lib." *New York Times Magazine*, 22 Aug. 1971, 14–15, 63–64, 66.

The Mud Flower Collective. *God's Fierce Whimsy: Christian Feminism and Theological Education*. New York: Pilgrim Press, 1985.

Munro, C. Lynn. "The Tattooed Heart and the Serpentine Eye: Morrison's Choice of an Epigraph for *Sula*." *Black American Literature Forum* 18.4 (1984): 150–54.

Naylor, Gloria, and Toni Morrison. "A Conversation." *The Southern Review* 21.3 (1985): 567–93.

Neal, Larry. "A Profile: Zora Neale Hurston." *Southern Exposure* 1.3&4 (1984): 160–68.

Nock, A. D. *Conversion*. London: Oxford Univ. Press, 1933.

Oates, Wayne D. *The Psychology of Religion*. Waco, Texas: Word Books, 1973.

O'Brien, John. *Interviews with Black Writers*. New York: Liveright, 1973.

O'Connor, Lillian. *Pioneer Women Orators*. New York: Columbia Univ. Press, 1954.

Ogunyemi, Chikwenye Okonjo. "Womanism: The Dynamics of the Contemporary Black Female Novel in English." *Signs* 11.1 (1985): 63–80.

Olney, James, ed. *Autobiography: Essays Theoretical and Critical*. Princeton: Princeton Univ. Press, 1980.

Painter, Nell Irvin. "Sojourner Truth in Life and Memory: Writing the Biography of an American Exotic." *Gender and History* 2.1 (1990): 3–16.

Pannill, Linda. "From the 'Wordshop': The Fiction of Paule Marshall." *Melus* 12.2 (1985): 63–73.

Payne, Rodger. "'When the Times of Refreshing Shall Come': Interpreting American Protestant Conversion Narratives, 1630–1830." Ph.D. diss., Univ. of Virginia, 1988.

Peel, J. D. Y. "Syncretism and Religious Change." *Comparative Studies in Society and History* 10 (1968): 121–41.

Perry, Ruth, ed. *Mothering the Mind: Twelve Studies of Writers and Their Silent Partners*. New York: Holmes, 1984.

The Personal Narratives Group. *Interpreting Women's Lives: Feminist Theory and Personal Narratives*. Bloomington: Indiana Univ. Press, 1989.

Plaskow, Judith. *Sex, Sin, and Grace: Women's Experience and the Theologies of Reinhold Niebuhr and Paul Tillich*. Lanham, Md.: Univ. Press of America, 1980.

Plaskow, Judith, and Carol P. Christ, eds. *Weaving the Visions: New Patterns in Feminist Spirituality*. New York: Harper and Row, 1989.

Pollard, Velma. "Cultural Connections in Paule Marshall's *Praise Song for the Widow*." *World Literature Written in English* 25.2 (1985): 285–98.

Porterfield, Amanda. *Feminine Spirituality in America: From Sarah Edwards to Martha Graham*. Philadelphia: Temple Univ. Press, 1980.

Pratt, James Bissett. *The Religious Consciousness: A Psychological Study*. New York: Macmillan, 1926.

Procter-Smith, Marjorie. *Women in Shaker Community and Worship: A Feminist Analysis of the Uses of Religious Symbolism*. Lewiston, N.Y.: Edwin Mellen Press, 1985.

Pryse, Marjorie, and Hortense J. Spillers, eds. *Conjuring: Black Women, Fiction, and Literary Tradition*. Bloomington: Indiana Univ. Press, 1985.

Raboteau, Albert J. *Slave Religion: The "Invisible Institution" in the Antebellum South*. New York: Oxford Univ. Press, 1970.

Rainwater, Catherine, and William J. Scheick, eds. *Contemporary American Women Writers: Narrative Strategies*. Lexington: Univ. Press of Kentucky, 1985.

Rambo, Lewis R. "Conversion." *Encyclopedia of Religion*. Vol. 4. Ed. Mircea Eliade. New York: Macmillan, 1987, 73–79.

Rayson, Ann L. "The Novels of Zora Neale Hurston." *Studies in Black Literature* 5.3 (1974): 1–9.

Reagon, Bernice Johnson. "My Black Mothers and Sisters, or on Beginning a Cultural Autobiography." *Feminist Studies* 8.1 (1982): 81–96.

Redford, Dorothy Spruill, with Michael D'Orso. *Somerset Homecoming: Recovering a Lost Heritage*. New York: Doubleday, 1988.

Reuther, Rosemary. *Womanguides: Readings toward a Feminist Theology*. Boston: Beacon Press, 1985.

Reuther, Rosemary, and Rosemary Skinner Keller, eds. *Women and Religion in America*. Vol. 1. New York: Harper and Row, 1982.

Richardson, James T. "Conversion Careers." *Society* 17.125 (1980): 47–50.

Rigney, Barbara Hill. *Lilith's Daughters: Women and Religion in Contemporary Fiction*. Madison: Univ. of Wisconsin Press, 1982.

Robey, Judith. "Generic Strategies in Zora Neale Hurston's *Dust Tracks on a Road*." *Black American Literature Forum* 24.4 (1990): 667–82.

Rowell, Charles H. "'The Unravelling of the Egg': An Interview with Jay Wright." *Callaloo* 6.3 (1983): 3–15.

Royster, Philip M. "In Search of Our Father's Arms: Alice Walker's Persona of Alienated Darling." *Black American Literature Forum* 20.4 (1986): 347–70.

————. "A Priest and a Witch against Spiders and Snakes: Scapegoating in Toni Morrison's *Sula*." *Umoja* 2 (1978): 149–68.

Saiving, Valerie. "The Human Situation: A Feminine View." In *Womanspirit Rising: A Feminist Reader in Religion*. Ed. Carol P. Christ and Judith Plaskow. New York: Harper and Row, 1979. 25–42.

Samuels, Wilfred D., and Clenora Hudson-Weems. *Toni Morrison*. Boston: G. K. Hall, 1990.

Sandiford, Keith A. "Paule Marshall's *Praisesong for the Widow:* The Reluctant Heiress, or Whose Life Is It Anyway." *Black American Literature Forum* 20.4 (1986): 371–92.

Sargent, Robert. "A Way of Ordering Experience: A Study of Toni Morrison's *The Bluest Eye* and *Sula*." In *Faith of a (Woman) Writer*. Ed. Alice Kessler-Harris and William McBrien. Westport, Conn.: Greenwood Press, 1988. 229–36.

Sasson, Diane. *The Shaker Spiritual Narrative*. Knoxville: Univ. of Tennessee Press, 1983.

Schwalenberg, Peter. "Time as Point of View in Zora Neale Hurston's *Their Eyes Were Watching God*." *Negro American Literature Forum* 10.3 (1975): 104–8.

Seggar, John, and Philip Kunz. "Conversion: Evaluation of a Step-Like Process for Problem Solving." *Review of Religious Research* 13.3 (1972): 178–84.

Shea, Daniel, Jr. *Spiritual Autobiography in Early America*. Princeton: Princeton Univ. Press, 1968.

Sheffey, Ruthe T., ed. *Rainbow Round Her Shoulder: The Zora Neale Hurston Symposium Papers*. Baltimore: Morgan State Univ. Press, 1983.

Shelton, Frank W. "Alienation and Integration in Alice Walker's *The Color Purple*." *CLA Journal* 28.4 (1985): 382–92.

Shockely, Ann Allen. *Afro-American Women Writers 1746–1933: An Anthology and Critical Guide*. Boston: G. K. Hall, 1988.

Smith, Sidonie. *A Poetics of Women's Autobiography: Marginality and the Fictions of Self-Representation*. Bloomington: Indiana Univ. Press, 1987.

————. *Where I'm Bound: Patterns of Slavery and Freedom in Black American Autobiography*. Westport, Conn.: Greenwood Press, 1974.

Smith, Valerie. Introduction. *Incidents in the Life of a Slave Girl*. By Harriet Jacobs. The Schomburg Library of Nineteenth-Century Black Women Writers. Ed. Henry Louis Gates, Jr. New York: Oxford Univ. Press, 1988, xxvii–xl.

————. "The Quest for and Discovery of Identity in Toni Morrison's *Song of Solomon*." *Southern Review* 21.3 (1985): 721–32.

————. *Self-Discovery and Authority in Afro-American Narrative*. Cambridge: Harvard Univ. Press, 1987.

Smith-Rosenberg, Carroll. "The Female World of Love and Ritual: Relations between Women in Nineteenth-Century America." *Signs* 1 (1975): 1–29.

Smyth, William D. "O Death, Where Is Thy Sting? Reverend Francis J. Grimke's Eulogy for Harriet A. Jacobs." *Journal of Negro History* 70.1–2 (1985): 35–39.

Sobel, Mechal. *Trabelin' On: The Slave Journey to an Afro-Baptist Faith*. Westport, Conn.: Greenwood Press, 1979.

Sojourner, Sabrina. "From the House of Yemanja: The Goddess Heritage of Black Women." In *The Politics of Women's Spirituality*. Ed. Charlene Spretnak. New York: Anchor Press, 1982. 57–63.

Southerland, Ellease. "The Influence of Voodoo on the Fiction of Zora Neale Hurston." In *Sturdy Black Bridges*. Ed. Roseann P. Bell, Bettye J. Parker, and Beverly Guy-Sheftall. Garden City, N.Y.: Doubleday, 1979. 171–83.

Spacks, Patricia Meyer. *The Female Imagination*. New York: Knopf, 1975.

Spretnak, Charlene, ed. *The Politics of Women's Spirituality*. New York: Anchor Press, 1982.

Stanton, Domna C., ed. *The Female Autograph: Theory and Practice of Autobiography from the Tenth to the Twentieth Century*. Chicago: Univ. of Chicago Press, 1984.

Starbuck, Edwin Diller. *The Psychology of Religion: An Empirical Study of the Growth of Religious Consciousness*. London: Walter Scott, 1906.

Stein, Karen F. "Toni Morrison's *Sula*: A Black Woman's Epic." *Black American Literature Forum* 18.4 (1984): 146–49.

Stepto, Robert. *From Behind the Veil: A Study of Afro-American Narrative*. Urbana: Univ. of Illinois Press, 1979.

————. "'Intimate Things in Place': A Conversation with Toni Morrison." *Massachusetts Review* 18 (Autumn 1977): 473–89.

Sterling, Dorothy, ed. *We Are Your Sisters*. New York: Norton, 1984.

Stone, Albert E. *Autobiographical Occasions and Original Acts: Versions of American Identity from Henry Adams to Nate Shaw*. Philadelphia: Univ. of Pennsylvania Press, 1982.

————. "Identity and Art in Frederick Douglass' *Narrative*." *CLA Journal* 17 (1983): 192–213.

Stone, Olive M. "Cultural Uses of Religious Visions: A Case Study." *Ethnology* 1 (1962): 329–48.

Straus, Roger A. "Religious Conversion as a Personal and Collective Accomplishment." *Sociological Analysis* 40.2 (1979): 158–65.

Tanner, Laura E. "Self-Conscious Representation in the Slave Narrative." *Black American Literature Forum* 21.4 (1987): 415–24.

Tate, Claudia. *Black Women Writers at Work*. New York: Continuum, 1984.

Taves, Ann. "Spiritual Purity and Sexual Shame: Religious Themes in the Writings of Harriet Jacobs." *Church History* 56 (1987): 59–72.

Taylor, Brian. "Recollection and Membership: Converts' Talk and the Ratiocination of Commonality." *Sociology* 12 (1978): 316–24.

Terry, Esther. "Sojourner Truth: The Person behind Libyan Sybil." *Massachusetts Review* 26 (Summer/Autumn 1985): 425–44.

Thompson, Robert Ferris. *Flash of the Spirit: African and Afro-American Art and Philosophy*. New York: Vintage, 1983.

Tipson, Baird. "How Can the Religious Experience of the Past Be Recovered? The Examples of Puritanism and Pictism." *Journal of the American Academy of Religion* 43 (1975): 695–707.

Truth, Sojourner. *The Narrative of Sojourner Truth*. 1878. Rpt. New York: Arno Press, 1968.

Tucker, Lindsey. "Alice Walker's *The Color Purple:* Emergent Woman, Emergent Text." *Black American Literature Forum* 22.1 (1988): 81–95.

Turner, Darwin T. *In a Minor Chord*. Carbondale: Southern Illinois Univ. Press, 1971.

Turner, Paul R. "Religious Conversion and Community Development." *Journal for the Scientific Study of Religion* 18.3 (1979): 252–60.

Turner, Victor. *Dramas, Fields, and Metaphors: Symbolic Action in Human Society*. Ithaca, N.Y.: Cornell Univ. Press, 1974.

Wach, Joachim. *The Comparative Study of Religions*. New York: Columbia Univ. Press, 1958.

Wade-Gayles, Gloria. "The Truths of Our Mothers' Lives: Mother-Daughter Relationships in Black Women's Fiction." *Sage* 1.2 (1984): 8–12.

Walker, Alice. *The Color Purple*. New York: Washington Square Press, 1982.

————. *In Search of Our Mothers' Gardens*. New York: Harcourt Brace Jovanovich, 1983.

————. *Living by the Word*. New York: Harcourt Brace Jovanovich, 1988.

————. "On Refusing to Be Humbled by Second Place in a Contest You Did Not Design: A Tradition by Now." In *I Love Myself When I Am Laughing*. By Zora Neale Hurston. Ed. Alice Walker. New York: Feminist Press, 1979. 1–5.

————. Preface. *The Color Purple*. New York: Harcourt Brace Jovanovich, 1992. xi–xii.

Walker, Nancy A. *Feminist Alternatives: Irony and Fantasy in the Contemporary Novel by Women*. Jackson: Univ. Press of Mississippi, 1990.

Walker, S. Jay. "Zora Neale Hurston's *Their Eyes Were Watching God:* Black Novel of Sexism." *Modern Fiction Studies* 20.4 (1974–1975): 519–27.

Wall, Cheryl, ed. *Changing Our Own Words: Essays in Criticism, Theory, and Writing by Black Women.* New Brunswick, N.J.: Rutgers Univ. Press, 1989.

———. *"Mules and Men* and Women: Zora Neale Hurston's Strategies of Narration and Visions of Female Empowerment." *Black American Literature Forum* 23.4 (1989): 661–80.

———. "Zora Neale Hurston: Changing Her Own Words." In *American Novelists Revisited.* Ed. Fritz Fleishman. Boston: G. K. Hall, 1982. 371–93.

Wallace, Anthony F. C. "Revitalization Movements." *American Anthropologist* 58 (1956): 264–81.

Washington, Mary Helen. Foreword. *Their Eyes Were Watching God.* By Zora Neale Hurston. Ed. Henry Louis Gates, Jr. New York: Harper and Row, 1990. vii–xiv.

———. "'I Sign My Mother's Name': Alice Walker, Dorothy West, Paule Marshall." In *Mothering the Mind: Twelve Studies of Writers and Their Silent Partners.* Ed. Ruth Perry. New York: Holmes, 1984. 142–63.

———. "Zora Neale Hurston: The Black Woman's Search for Identity." *Black World* 21 (Aug. 1973): 68–75.

———. *Invented Lives: Narratives of Black Women, 1860–1960.* Garden City, N.Y.: Doubleday, 1987.

Welch, Sharon D. *Communities of Resistance and Solidarity: A Feminist Theology of Liberation.* Maryknoll, N.Y.: Orbis Books, 1985.

———. *A Feminist Ethic of Risk.* Minneapolis: Fortress Press, 1990.

Wessling, Joseph H. "Narcissism in Toni Morrison's *Sula.*" *CLA Journal* 31.3 (1988): 281–98.

West, Cornel. "The Loss of Hope." *Utne Reader* (Sept./Oct. 1991): 54–55.

White, Deborah Gray. *Ar'n't I a Woman? Female Slaves in the Plantation South.* New York: Norton, 1985.

Wideman, John. "Frame and Dialect: The Evolution of the Black Voice in American Literature." *American Poetry Review* (Sept./Oct. 1976): 34–37.

Williams, Delores S. "Women's Oppression and Lifeline Politics in Black Women's Religious Narratives." *Journal of Feminist Studies in Religion* 1.3 (1985): 59–71.

Williams, John, trans. "Return of a Native Daughter: An Interview with Paule Marshall and Maryse Condé." *Sage* 3.2 (1986): 52–53.

Williams, Richard E. *Called and Chosen: The Story of Mother Rebecca Jackson and the Philadelphia Shakers.* Ed. Cheryl Dorschner. Metuchen, N.J.: Scarecrow Press, 1981.

Willis, Susan. "Eruptions of Funk: Historicizing Toni Morrison." In *Black*

Literature and Literary Theory. Ed. Henry Louis Gates, Jr. New York: Methuen, 1984. 263–84.

———. *Specifying.* Madison: Univ. of Wisconsin Press, 1987.

Wimberly, Edward P., and Anne Streaty Wimberly. *Liberation and Human Wholeness: The Conversion Experiences of Black People in Slavery and Freedom.* Nashville: Abingdon Press, 1986.

Wolff, Maria Tai. "Listening and Living: Reading and Experience in *Their Eyes Were Watching God.*" *Black American Literature Forum* 16.1 (1982): 29–33.

Wright, Jay. *Selected Poems of Jay Wright.* Princeton: Princeton Univ. Press, 1987.

Yates, Gayle Graham. "Spirituality and the American Feminist Experience." *Signs* 9.11 (1983): 59–72.

Yellin, Jean Fagan. *The Intricate Knot: Black Figures in American Literature.* New York: New York Univ. Press, 1972.

———. Introduction. *Incidents in the Life of a Slave Girl.* By Harriet Jacobs. Cambridge: Harvard Univ. Press, 1987. xiii–xxxiv.

———. "Written by Herself: Harriet Jacobs' Slave Narrative." *American Literature* 53.3 (1981): 480–85.

Young, Josiah U. *Black and African Theologies: Siblings or Distant Cousins?* Maryknoll, N.Y.: Orbis Books, 1986.

Zinsser, William. *Inventing the Truth: The Art and Craft of Memoir.* Boston: Houghton Mifflin, 1987.

Index

Abbott, H. Porter, 283n23

Abel, Elizabeth, 171–72

Africa, 16, 19, 213–14, 215, 216–17, 218–19, 224, 230, 231, 232, 236, 255–56, 257, 268, 269; diaspora, 16, 126–31, 212, 213, 219, 227, 230, 233, 234, 235, 263; retentions, 11, 18, 24, 62, 68, 123, 125–27, 129, 173, 221, 222–23, 226, 232, 233, 235, 236, 237, 256, 272, 289n12

African-American culture, 4, 5, 6, 7, 11, 17, 19, 26, 27, 29, 38–39, 40, 46–47, 110–13, 115–17, 119, 132, 145, 149, 159, 164, 175, 178–80, 183, 185, 199, 215, 229, 234, 236, 239, 243, 256, 265, 289n13, 289n14, 289n16

African-American religion, 3, 11, 12–13, 15–26, 27, 31, 34, 35, 41–42, 43, 52, 62, 83, 87, 111, 117–24, 129–30, 132–33, 139, 147, 152, 156, 159, 161, 167–68, 173, 176, 186, 220, 226, 230–31, 261, 269, 273, 275n1, 277n9, 277n10, 279n25, 279n1, 280n6

Allen, Richard, 95

Ancestors, 6, 7, 24, 25, 42, 61, 152, 177–78, 179, 201, 211, 213, 216, 218, 222, 227, 229, 231, 232, 233, 237, 242, 245, 256, 267, 270, 274, 289n15

Andrews, William L., 10, 44, 46–47, 48, 81, 85, 89, 280n2, 281n9

Autobiographical theory, 106, 133–38, 140–41, 143, 166, 170–71, 235, 280n4, 283n23, 285n2, 285n10, 287n1

Awkward, Michael, 175, 180, 238, 258

Baker, Houston A., 50, 66–67, 152

Baldwin, James, 238

Bambara, Toni Cade, 43, 111

Banyiwa-Horne, Naana, 208, 288n8

Baraka, Amiri, 213

Barbour, John D., 137–38, 280n4

Beckford, James A., 278n18

Bednarowski, Mary Farrell, 99

Benstock, Shari, 133, 135

Bethel, Lorraine, 156, 162

Bible, 16, 19, 20, 45, 50, 59–60, 70, 83, 85–87, 94, 96, 98, 101, 102, 105, 108, 118, 141, 175, 181, 202, 235, 242, 251, 253, 259, 262, 263, 264, 267, 269, 283n21, 284n28, 285n5, 288n9

Biggs, Phyllis, 110, 157, 180, 233

Bildungsroman, 171–72, 216